Inside Subculture

Dress, Body, Culture

Series Editor **Joanne B. Eicher,** *Regents' Professor, University of Minnesota*

Advisory Board:

Ruth Barnes, *Ashmolean Museum, University of Oxford*
Helen Callaway, *CCCRW, University of Oxford*
James Hall, *University of Illinois at Chicago*
Beatrice Medicine, *California State University, Northridge*
Ted Polhemus, *Curator, "Street Style" Exhibition, Victoria & Albert Museum*
Griselda Pollock, *University of Leeds*
Valerie Steele, *The Museum at the Fashion Institute of Technology*
Lou Taylor, *University of Brighton*
John Wright, *University of Minnesota*

Books in this provocative series seek to articulate the connections between culture and dress which is defined here in its broadest possible sense as any modification or supplement to the body. Interdisciplinary in approach, the series highlights the dialogue between identity and dress, cosmetics, coiffure, and body alterations as manifested in practices as varied as plastic surgery, tattooing, and ritual scarification. The series aims, in particular, to analyze the meaning of dress in relation to popular culture and gender issues and will include works grounded in anthropology, sociology, history, art history, literature, and folklore.

ISSN: 1360-466X

Previously published titles in the Series

Helen Bradley Foster, *"New Raiments of Self": African American Clothing in the Antebellum South*
Claudine Griggs, *S/he: Changing Sex and Changing Clothes*
Michaele Thurgood Haynes, *Dressing Up Debutantes: Pageantry and Glitz in Texas*
Anne Brydon and Sandra Niesson, *Consuming Fashion: Adorning the Transnational Body*
Dani Cavallaro and Alexandra Warwick, *Fashioning the Frame: Boundaries, Dress and the Body*
Judith Perani and Norma H. Wolff, *Cloth, Dress and Art Patronage in Africa*
Linda B. Arthur, *Religion, Dress and the Body*
Paul Jobling, *Fashion Spreads: Word and Image in Fashion Photography*
Fadwa El-Guindi, *Veil: Modesty, Privacy and Resistance*
Thomas S. Abler, *Hinterland Warriors and Military Dress: European Empires and Exotic Uniforms*
Linda Welters, *Folk Dress in Europe and Anatolia: Beliefs about Protection and Fertility*
Kim K.P. Johnson and Sharron J. Lennon, *Appearance and Power*
Barbara Burman, *The Culture of Sewing*
Annette Lynch, *Dress, Gender and Cultural Change*
Antonia Young, *Women Who Become Men*

DRESS, BODY, CULTURE

Inside Subculture

The Postmodern Meaning of Style

David Muggleton

Oxford • New York

First published in 2000 by
Berg
Editorial offices:
150 Cowley Road, Oxford, OX4 1JJ, UK
175 Fifth Avenue, New York, NY 10010, USA

Paperback edition reprinted in 2002, 2004

Berg is an imprint of Oxford International Publishers Ltd.

Library of Congress Cataloging-in-Publication Data
A catalogue record for this book is available from the Library of Congress.

British Library Cataloguing-in-Publication Data
A catalogue record for this book is available from the British Library.

ISBN 978-1-85973-352-3

Typeset by JS Typesetting, Wellingborough, Northants.
Printed in the United Kingdom by Biddles Ltd, Guildford and King's Lynn.

Contents

Acknowledgements

During the past several years, I have become indebted to many people for their part in helping to make *Inside Subculture* possible. I would therefore like to acknowledge them here, and begin with the Economic and Social Research Council for the three-year Research Studentship award (R00429234234) that enabled me to undertake the original Ph.D. research on which the book is based. The transition from thesis to book would not have happened without the interest shown by Kathryn Earle of Berg publishers. The writing of the book was made possible by the generous sabbatical provided to me by University College Chichester. Thanks also to Professor Nick Abercrombie for his invaluable advice and skilful guidance on the original thesis. I could not have been more fortunate in my allocation of a supervisor. Grateful thanks also to my best friend Edwina for putting me up during my fieldwork sessions in Brighton, and for putting up with me more generally. I must also extend my appreciation to Pennie Drinkall, Julia Harrison and Maggy Taylor, who between them skilfully transcribed the vast majority of the taped interviews; and to Bob Jessop and Chris Quinn in the Sociology Department at Lancaster University, and Graham Stodd and Chris Laws at University College Chichester for making available important resources.

I would also like to mention Berg's anonymous reviewer for their very detailed and constructive comments on the original thesis, David Phelps for his skilful copy-editing of the typescript, and everyone else who sent letters, e-mails, articles, papers and theses, etc., made helpful remarks and suggestions, or in any way contributed to the finished product; they are in alphabetical order: Jeffrey Arnett, Gord Barensten, Shane Blackmon, Colin Campbell, Cathie Dingwall, Kathy Fox, Simon Gottschalk, Scott Lash, Ben Malbon, Cressida Miles, Justin O'Connor, Ted Polhemus, Steve Redhead, Balihar Sanghera, Dan Shapiro, David Sleightholme, Geoff Stahl, Sarah Thornton and Jeff Webb.

The biggest debt, however, is that I owe to all my interviewees. Without the willingness of subjects to put their trust in virtual strangers and talk about themselves at great length, such a book as this would remain an impossible undertaking. For their permission to allow my photographs of them to appear in this book, a particular thank you to Duncan, Robin, Jim, Jane, Sean and

Peter. I would also like to acknowledge the following for permission to reproduce flyers: Dave Nimmo (Backstreet Boogaloo!); Jimmy Tonik (Smashed Blocked); Ian Mackenzie (Immediate Clothing). An earlier version of Chapter 3 of this book appeared as 'The Post-subculturalist' in *The Clubcultures Reader* (edited by Steve Redhead *et al.*) 1997; and I would like to thank Blackwell publishers for their permission to re-use some of this material. Grateful acknowledgements also to Littlebrown for their permission to reproduce the cover of *Wigan Pier Revisited*.

David Muggleton
Chichester

Back to Reality? My Experience with Cultural Studies[1]

Despite Hebdige's own gloomy prognostication about the inevitable gulf that separates the intellectual from the practical semiotician, *Subculture* was reviewed in publications outside the academic circuit, and has become part of the 'currency' which circulates in and amongst those proclaiming some form of subcultural identity.

> Ann Beezer: 'Dick Hebdige, *Subculture: The Meaning of Style*'
> (1992: 115)

So what do you do about style? Sociology, yeah? Yeah, I did that stuff at college. Hebdige and them lot. It's all bollocks, isn't it?

> (Fieldwork 'currency exchange': A 'practical semiotician'
> on the 1994 crisis in the pound.)

According to Max Weber (1864–1920), all sociology is necessarily 'value-relevant' (Weber 1949) in that the selection of a research topic, the decision to investigate particular aspects over others, and the logic and method of enquiry employed are all inevitably grounded in the subjective values of the researcher. A useful way of introducing this book might therefore be to 'come clean' about my own personal reasons for writing it. From late 1976 onwards, I became increasingly involved in the emerging provincial punk rock scene. I took on certain aspects of the subculture's dress codes, jettisoning my flares for 'straights', platforms for trainers, and my bright orange, wing-collared shirt and fat knot tie for a white button-down bri-nylon museum piece worn with a stripy school tie left hanging at half-mast. I even amateurishly chopped my Ron Wood style feather-cut into a spiky crop *à la* Richard Hell. I listened less and less to Pink Floyd, Jefferson Airplane and The Byrds and more to The Ramones, Blondie and The Sex Pistols. I experienced the culture shock of progressing (regressing?) in a matter of months from the relative mellowness of an Eric Clapton concert (where we all sat on the floor) to the manic ferocity of a Stranglers gig (where, as in a crowded kop end at football, my feet didn't always touch the floor). I even 'played' the bass guitar in a punk rock band.

Yet this was never a sudden or complete transformation. It occurred gradually and sequentially. I cropped my hair in stages. I never sported safety pins through my lip, nor stopped wearing my beloved denim jacket. *Complete Control* was one of the most electrifying records I'd ever heard; yet so, too, was *Heartbreak Hotel*. But even then Rock 'n' Roll and the Beatles meant more to me than the Clash or the Damned – they still do. I hadn't heard of punk until 'after the subculture had surfaced and been publicized'.[2] I wasn't aware of Britain's economic decline or the fracturing of the political consensus, nor was I angry about unemployment (even when I was unemployed). On the other hand, personal freedom and the search for experience were (still are) very important to me. Had I been born several years earlier I might have been a hippy; a decade before, I would undoubtedly have become a mod. If I had been a 1950s teenager, I might even have taken on some form of teddy boy identity (after my punk haircut grew out, I wore it greased back in a rocker style). To those who will say that I can't have been a real or true punk, let me reply in the words of Geoff, one of my own informants, that 'there is no such thing as punk' (just as there is no such thing as hippy, mod and teddy boy), and therefore no basis for the distinction between real and pretend. Punk is what you make it. Paradoxically, this is the essence of punk, and only 'true' punks realize this.

This was, to use Frank Cartledge's phrase, 'how I lived punk' (Cartledge 1999: 143). And like Cartledge, I can argue that 'this experience stands apart from the historical and cultural theories I have read' (ibid.). Some years after the demise of punk (my version of punk, that is), I was browsing in a Leicester bookshop when my eye caught the lurid cover of Dick Hebdige's book *Subculture: The Meaning of Style* (1979). Both the cover image and the title prompted me to buy, hoping perhaps that it might help me to recapture the feeling and spirit of those heady times. I took it home, began to read, and could hardly understand a word of it. I fought my way through until the bitter end, and was left feeling that it had absolutely nothing to say about my life as I had once experienced it (thus confirming Hebdige's own concluding remarks on 'the distance between the reader and the text'). Years later still, having taken a Sociology A-level at night school, I entered University as a mature student, where I gained a degree in Sociology and Cultural Studies. I re-read Hebdige's book, now understood exactly what he meant, and *still* found that it had very little to say about my life! My earlier feeling was vindicated. The 'problem' lay not in myself and my failure to recognize what had ostensibly been the reality of my situation, but in the way the book appropriated its subject-matter.[3]

It is not that *Subculture: The Meaning of Style* is without its virtues. It's exceptionally well crafted and highly inventive (but clearly too inventive), and nowadays I thoroughly enjoy reading it, despite (or perhaps because of) not being able to take seriously such phrases as 'chain of conspicuous absences' and 'expressed itself through rupture'.[4] Nor is there any reason why Hebdige should be singled out for criticism. Although *Subculture* was the first academic text on this subject that I encountered, it was the last of four seminal works on subcultural theory to be published during the 1970s, the others being Stuart Hall and Tony Jefferson's *Resistance Through Rituals* (1976 – but initially published a year before as *Working Papers in Cultural Studies nos 7/8*); Geoff Mungham and Geoff Pearson's *Working-Class Youth Culture* (1976); and Paul Willis's *Profane Culture* (1978). All four were associated in some way with the Centre for Contemporary Cultural Studies at the University of Birmingham. Hebdige, Willis and Jefferson, along with John Clarke, another contributor, had been postgraduate students at the Centre; Hall was its director. As Waters then commented, 'the four books . . . taken together, manage to convey many of the concepts that have been important in this new approach to working class youth culture' (1981: 24). But in my view, this means they also display many of the same methodological and theoretical inadequacies. The most serious, with the qualified exception of Willis's ethnographic study, is their failure to take seriously enough the subjective viewpoints of the youth subculturalists themselves.[5] Throughout this book I will refer to this corpus of work as 'the CCCS approach'.

What lies behind this neglect of indigenous meanings? Caroline Evans has made the pertinent comment that 'subcultures, in all their complexity, are generally not studied in any serious, empirical way within cultural studies because of the state of British academic life. It is cheaper to do theory than ethnography, at least in the field of popular culture' (1997: 185). This is no doubt true; but as I argue in this book, not everything can be explained by reference to economic factors alone. We should instead look within the enterprise of cultural studies itself, and to its theoretical agenda for the study of (sub)culture. Sabin has stated that 'until recently . . . a form of determinism has held sway. Too often "big theories" have been relied upon (Marxism, the sociology of deviance, semiotics, etc.), which picture those involved in subcultures as passive pawns of history, their lives shaped by grand narratives beyond their control' (1999a: 5). And while this has now given way to what Sabin terms 'a more subjective approach' (ibid.), theory still retains its privileged position over ethnography; for in cultural studies ethnographic evidence on the lives of young people is treated less as a representation of their subjective experiences than as an expression of their 'subjectivities' – the texts, discourses, frameworks and social positions *through which* their lived reality is 'spoken' (see McRobbie 1994: Ch. 10). Not a great deal seems to have changed. As Sherwood *et al.* have remarked on the cultural studies agenda for the 1990s:

> The narratives that the latter-day CCCSers employ are as abstract as their theory. The brand of cultural studies they purvey remains confined within these abstracted political narratives, rather than engaging the stories by which social actors navigate their reality . . . exegesis replaces interpretation, for the object of analysis is not meaning but objective reality itself. Agents and hegemons inhabit this world; selves and others, as real subjects, are shoved out of the empirical frame (Sherwood *et al.* 1993: 373).

Hilary Pilkington not so long ago remarked how 'it is currently fashionable to criticise' the CCCS work on subcultures (1997: 25). Although this is a situation I welcome, it is surely less to do with fashion than with changes in the balance of power in the academic community (Featherstone 1992). Lovatt and Purkis have observed how much research in the sociology of popular culture is being undertaken by relatively young academics, 'many of whom are already immersed in their chosen culture prior to intellectual engagement with it' (1996: 250). This situation is producing a new cohort of academic taste-makers for whom the deficiencies of established theories are likely to be thrown into sharp relief by their own personal experiences as, say, punks or clubbers. If it is not stretching the point too far, perhaps their subsequent critiques can be understood as a need to satisfy what Andy Medhurst has referred to as 'the urge to shout – no, I know more about it than you, because I was there' (1999: 219). Pilkington also warned of the 'danger' in representing the CCCS as the 'mainstream' against which contemporary research on youth culture can be defined. This 'danger' is somewhat unavoidable if one wishes to write about youth *sub*culture, for the CCCS approach has attained the status of an orthodoxy. At the beginning of this decade, Anne Beezer (1992: 115) could confidently assert that critiques had so far failed to challenge its intellectual hegemony. Several years and a succession of innovative qualitative and ethnographic studies of subcultures later, this is no longer quite so convincing a claim.[6] Even so, the CCCS approach continues to provide the benchmark against which contemporary developments are measured, particularly assessments of the extent to which subcultures have become 'postmodern'.

Unfortunately, sociological analyses of postmodernism continue to be plagued by some of the most serious faults of the CCCS work, especially their use of grand theory, 'a model which can be articulated in, and be descriptive of, a whole series of cultural phenomena' (Stephanson 1987: 29). At their worst, such accounts appear to aspire to the status of a postmodern sociology, 'abandoning popular culture analysis altogether in favour of grandiose totalizing metaphors (Black holes, implosion, excremental culture etc.)' (Kellner 1992: 148).[7] Even those analyses that can be located within the more sober, rationalist tradition of modern sociology are still flawed by a tendency to provide theoretically overdetermined interpretations of events. To quote another understandably frustrated researcher, 'all too often this boils down to providing yet another paraphrase of Barthes, Baudrillard or Bourdieu, or giving yet another whiff of the latest hallucinogen drifting out of the second *arrondissement*, rather than as the cue for detailed research' (Moorhouse 1991: 223). Nor, of course, are we told how social actors themselves perceive postmodern phenomena. Strinati sums up the situation when he writes: 'there has, in fact, been a tendency to assume that post-modernism has become widespread in modern societies. However, less attention has been devoted to demonstrating that this is the case' (1995: 223).

My own position, however, is not one of assuming, but of demonstrating. The purpose of the interviews extracts presented in this book is to show how members of youth subcultures interpret and make sense of the post-modern characteristics imputed to them by social theorists.[8] In contrast to the neo-Marxist theory of the CCCS and the analyses of postmodern commentators, my own approach is one that I have termed neo-Weberian, for it is located within the tradition of conventional qualitative sociology that derives from Weber's insistence upon the need for sociological explan-ations to recognize the subjective goals, values and motivations of social actors. It also displays a number of more specific features taken from Weber's methodological writings, and draws upon the work of those who interpreted Weber or who work within this paradigm. The aims of this book are, therefore, twofold. First, to uncover the subjective meanings, values and motives of those involved in style subcultures such as punk, goth, skinhead, hippy, etc. Second, to examine empirically certain contemporary claims about the implications of the 'postmodern' for such subcultures. These two aims are related, in that I wish to discover if subcultural stylists have what, in another context, Seago (1995) has termed a 'postmodern sensibility'; in other words, are their subjective meanings and cultural practices consonant with, even celebratory of, contemporary developments that have been termed postmodern?

I associate the 'modern' with rational-Puritanism, and the 'Enlightenment' characteristics of stasis, homogeneity and demarcation. The 'postmodern', I argue, is an intensification of aesthetic-Romantic cultural traits always implicated in the development of modernity, which find their expression in flux, plurality and heterogeneity. Although both sets of traits can be found in the CCCS approach, it is the modern that predominates. I conclude that the members of my contemporary sample can be characterized as postmodern in that they display an individualistic, fragmented and diffuse sensibility. A postmodern celebration of style and image was not evident, however. Instead, informants expressed attitudes consistent with a modern 'depth' model. Their mixed class base and 'anti-structure' sentiments suggest that the distinction between collectivist working-class subcultures and individualistic middle-class countercultures is overemphasized. I argue that contemporary subcultural styles can be understood as a symptom of postmodern hyperindividualism, and that this process can be traced back at least to the 1960s. However, any assessment of the extent to which subcultures have become detached from collectivist working-class group formations must remain conjectural given the paucity of comparative historical data.

The content of particular chapters is as follows. After this introduction I set out in Chapter 2 my Weberian approach to the study of youth subcultures and attempt to convince you, the reader, that my methodological and theoretical recommendations and procedures avoid some of the main problems associated with the CCCS approach. In Chapter 3 I examine contemporary claims concerning the implications of the postmodern for fashion and subcultural style, and trace certain characteristics of postmodern style to their origins in aesthetic modernity. The remaining four chapters until the conclusion present an analysis of the empirical data. Chapter 4 examines the individualistic basis of subcultural affiliation, while Chapter 5 looks at stylistic mobility and how this might be reconciled with a commitment to subcultural membership. The topic of Chapter 6 is long-term subcultural change and whether this precludes the marking of subcultural boundaries through oppositions with other groups. Chapter 7 looks at media and commercial incorporation along with political values, and considers how subcultures can be regarded as a form of resistance. Chapter 8, my conclusion, proposes some theoretical explanations for my empirical findings. In particular, I argue that Romantic, liminal tendencies have permeated working-class culture.

The academic reader might claim that I have, amongst other things, neglected the importance of gender, ignored a major component of post-modernism, paid insufficient attention to material factors; but they are urged to consider that I am not attempting to provide anything more than a necessarily one-sided and partial understanding of subcultural phenomena. As I began by saying, my logic of inclusion and inquiry inevitably reflect my own values and interests (a point that is equally applicable to all authors and critics). 'Whatever event or situation we may investigate, its infinity ensures that we must always ignore certain of its features as not pertinent to the values in question' (Hindess 1977: 32). As to whether 'the members of any of the subcultures described in this book would recognize themselves reflected here',[9] I would *hope* this isn't unlikely. My aim, after all, is to privilege their subjective meanings. But this is a work of sociology; it appropriates such meanings, necessarily subjects them to a (more or less) complex process of analysis and overlays them with what Marsh *et al.* (1978) call 'an interpretative gloss'.[10] To take seriously the words of respondents is therefore no guarantee that your analysis or explanations of their accounts will not ultimately prove impenetrable to them.[11] Hence, there is always a danger in pointing an accusing finger, as I did earlier towards Hebdige, for by so doing it is possible to leave yourself open to much the same criticism. Perhaps, in the circumstances, the best I can hope for is to demonstrate that we are not always condemned to speak *quite* so excessively about reality.

Notes

1. See McRobbie (1997).

2. Hebdige (1979: 122).

3. Gottdiener also comments that Hebdige 'fails in explaining the meaning of punk' (1995: 249).

4. Hebdige (1979: 120, 122). As Tanner had already caustically commented on the CCCS, 'it is a very thin line that divides "insight" from pretension, and some of the accounts given in these works fall into the latter category' (1978: 367).

5. There is a section in *Resistance through Rituals* entitled 'ethnography', but we have to interpret this term somewhat loosely. As Blackman puts it, '"literary ethnography" on the three subcultures analysed, is substituted for direct empirical observation as a means of obtaining evidence for their theory' (1995: 4).

6. I am thinking here in particular of Moore (1994), Widdicombe and Wooffitt (1995), Thornton (1995), Blackman (1995), Arnett (1996), and Malbon (1999).

7. For a particularly good example, see the entry on fashion in Kroker *et al.* (1989). This is also cited, in part, in Muggleton (1997). On the distinction between a sociology of postmodernism and a postmodern sociology, see Featherstone (1992).

8. Details of the fieldwork and a copy of the interview schedule appear in the appendix.

9. Hebdige (1979: 39). Would informants, anyway, wish to recognize themselves in academic accounts? Evans (1997) has argued that, by seeking to explain the nature of subcultures, texts such as this are engaged in exactly that process of definition from which the members of subcultures are attempting to escape.

10. I would not dispute that 'individuals' accounts of their experience pose the same interpretative problems that any text or object does' (Nehring 1996: 338). This does not, however, entail the relativism of all such accounts. Nehring's own attempt to theorize subcultures though an analysis of literary and cultural texts raises the whole problem of how far such an enterprise imposes a spurious interpretation

upon the phenomenon in question, particularly when, as in Nehring's case, the project has an explicitly political agenda, 'to help shape cultural dissidence' (ibid.: 1).

11. For what I consider to be a prime example of this point, see Widdicombe and Wooffitt's discourse analysis of their interviews with subculturalists (Widdicombe 1993; Widdicombe and Wooffitt 1990, 1995).

2

A Neo-Weberian Approach to the Study of Subcultural Style

The analysis which I offer here is intended as an exercise in interpretative sociology . . . Like Max Weber, I am inclined to consider ideas, norms and values as powerful patterns which may facilitate, deflect, transmute and perhaps even preclude the development of possibilities which lie in the structural arrangements of societies.

> Bernice Martin: *A Sociology of Contemporary*
> *Cultural Change* (1985: 1)

Sociology (in the sense in which this highly ambiguous word is used here) is a science concerning itself with the interpretative understanding of social action and thereby with a causal explanation of its course and consequences.

> Max Weber: *Economy and Society – An Outline of*
> *Interpretative Sociology* (1968: 4)

Privileging Subjective Meanings

At one point in *Defending Ski-Jumpers: A Critique of Theories of Youth Sub-Cultures*, Gary Clarke makes the suggestion that the CCCS fail to provide us with a certain type of evidence because to have done so would have been considered a 'Weberian deviation' (G. Clarke 1982: 8). The whole of this book can on this basis safely be regarded as a Weberian deviation, but one that at least attempts to put subjective meaning back into the 'empirical frame' (Sherwood *et al.* 1993: 373). In this chapter, I want to sketch out what I regard as the main features of a neo-Weberian approach to subcultures. I argue that if we are to provide a sociological account that has the virtue of being grounded in the subjective reality of those under study, we must: (1) privilege the subjective meanings of subculturalists rather than deriving these from a pre-given totalizing theory; (2) take a 'nominalist' rather than 'realist' position on social reality – for example, proceed on the phenomenal level rather than viewing this as an expression of an underlying structure; and (3) recognize the independent explanatory role of cultural values rather than theorizing these as necessarily related to economic and social factors.

As the opening quotations of this chapter suggest, a Weberian study of subcultures must be based upon an interpretation of the subjectively held meanings, values and beliefs of the subculturalists themselves. This is the premise upon which Weber's *verstehen* methodology is founded, the literal translation of the term *verstehen* being 'human understanding'. Put simply, humans (social actors) possess 'inner states' by which they understand, interpret and evaluate the courses of action open to them. We must therefore take seriously the subjective meanings of subculturalists, for these provide the motivation for their conduct. This makes the subjective dimension a central component in any explanation of social phenomena.

This point can be seen in Weber's insistence that all explanations must establish 'adequacy on the level of meaning' (Weber 1968: 12). If, for example, we observe a regular sequence of actions but fail to gain an understanding of how the relevant actors subjectively interpret this situation, we are left with no more than 'an incomprehensible statistical probability' (ibid.). On the other hand, having ascertained a subjective motivation for an action, we must also demonstrate 'causal significance' by showing that it is likely to recur in the same way. In placing emphasis on both meaning and probability, Weber was acknowledging that individual actions are tempered by social and cultural constraints. A Weberian explanation of subcultures must therefore be adequate on the levels of both meaning and causality: it should begin with an empirical investigation of the subjective values of individual subculturalists, but go beyond the level of actors' meanings 'to the collective forces that impel the actor' (Ritzer 1981: 80), to identify the belief systems that have played a part in the emergence of subcultural phenomena.

In carrying out such an analysis, we need to guard against imposing our own conceptual reality upon that of our informants. Here, my procedure closely follows that of Alfred Schutz (1963, 1980) who, in reworking Weber's ideas on social action, posed the question: how is an objective social science of subjective meanings possible? (Ritzer 1981). Schutz's solution was to advocate the construction of scientific typifications of actors' subjective typifications, thus:

> The thought objects constructed by the social scientist, in order to grasp this social reality, have to be founded upon the thought objects constructed by the common-sense thinking of men, living their daily life within their social world. Thus, the constructs of the social sciences are, so to speak, constructs of the second degree, that is, constructs of the constructs made by the social actors on the social scene,

whose behaviour the social scientist has to observe and explain in acc
with the procedural rules of his science (Schutz 1963: 242).

One example of empirical research that appears to follow this method of
concept formation is the study on football hooliganism, *The Rules of Disorder*
(Marsh *et al.* 1978). Here, Marsh and his co-authors talk of the 'interpretive
gloss' of the social scientist, which is derived *from* and 'overlaid' upon the
common-sense 'insider' accounts given by the fans themselves (1978: 118–
20). We are warned that, 'if one was to listen carefully to the fans and on the
basis of this build up an account of the insider reality but then found that
this reality was unrecognisable when offered back to fans, one would have
to admit one had got it wrong' (ibid.: 95).

Yet this relationship between first- and second-degree constructs is fraught
with problems for the social scientist. Marsh's own criterion of validity seems
to be premised upon what is arguably a common misunderstanding of Schutz's
'postulate of adequacy'[1] (Schutz 1963: 247). Here, Schutz does not state
that social scientific models are required to be recognizable *as* common sense
by social actors; rather, they 'must refer *to*' the subjective constructs of such
actors (ibid.: 245). This is hardly the same thing. As I suggested in my opening
chapter, sociology has its own conceptual vocabulary, which can be far
removed from the everyday language and modes of thought that provide its
subject-matter. What Schutz does stipulate is that the relationship between
'the thought objects constructed by the social scientist' and 'the constructs
of everyday life' is one of 'compatibility' (ibid.: 247–8). On this basis, I want
to propose a criterion of validity that is based, not on recognition, but on
compatibility – the degree of 'fit' between the social scientific constructs and
the common-sense reality of social actors. This, in my opinion, is still a
stringent criterion, and one that I do not think the CCCS satisfy.

It is not always fully recognized that the CCCS also aimed to provide an
understanding of subcultures at the level of the individual consciousness of
the participants. Phil Cohen (1984: 83), for instance, suggested that a
comprehensive analysis of subculture should take place at three levels, the
historical (the specific conditions facing the working class as a whole), the
structural or semiotic (the articulation of subcultures as a response to these
conditions), and the phenomenological (how the subculture is 'lived out' by
its members). J. Clarke *et al.* (1986: 57) similarly proposed that an analysis
at the levels of structure, culture and biography would demonstrate how
individual pathways are carved out within common cultural responses to
shared structural conditions. Yet, despite such recommendations, 'these
writers were noticeably silent about the subjective experience of everyday
life as a member of one of these subcultures' (Moore 1994: 1). As Clarke

s readily admitted in *Resistance Through Rituals*, 'we
e, to deal at all adequately with the level of biography'
7). I would, however, argue that this is not an oversight
f the employment of an *a priori* theoretical framework
ciples determined in advance) that has resulted in a
ermination of subjective meanings.

ve in the CCCS approach to youth subcultures what Saunders
has elsewhere identified as 'two central principles' of Marx's own method –
materialism and totality (1989: 16). Materialism is the principle that material
reality exists independently of our consciousness of it, that economic resources
are the ultimate basis of power and conflict, and that material interests are
the driving force of history. The emphasis on social totality emerges from
Marx's dialectical analysis – the principle of the unity of opposites. This
stresses that any specific element of society must be analysed in terms of the
whole social relations of which it forms a part, 'as a rich totality of many
determinations and relations' (Marx 1973: 100). Clarke and Jefferson, for
example, stipulate that 'the analysis must relate the specific phenomenon in
question [youth subculture] to the social totality (1978: 157). The problem
with this approach is that it imposes a holistic framework upon the phenomenon with the 'answer' known in advance – some subcultures have a
largely working-class membership, therefore they are solutions to economic
contradictions. As Woods points out, 'theory is not "generated" here, but is
rather *related* to whatever aspects of the empirical scene seem relevant' (1977:
75. Original emphasis). Moreover, although the CCCS authors foreground
particular subcultural groups, this logic of procedure does not investigate
the subjective meanings of the members; rather, it retrospectively identifies
the 'historical problematic' faced by the class as a whole (and to which the
subculture is an attempted 'solution'), and semiotically decodes the political
and ideological meanings of the subcultural response (see, for a discussion
of this methodological orientation, Jefferson 1973; Murdock and McCron
1978, 1986; G. Clarke 1982).

While this procedure implicitly informs the CCCS project as a whole, it is
most apparent in Phil Cohen's (1984) seminal paper 'Subcultural conflict
and working-class community', which examines how the economic and social
changes acting upon London's East End during the late 1950s and early 1960s
effectively forced a remaking of the working class in a 'bourgeois' image. At
the 'historical level' of subcultural analysis, Cohen charts how economic
restructuring and post-war redevelopment schemes combined to dismantle
the traditional supports of a working-class culture.[2] The communal neigh-
bourhood and extended kinship system were eroded as families moved away
to the new 'privatized' housing estates located on the outskirts of London,

while the local family businesses and craft-based economy were undermined by large-scale concerns operating outside the immediate district. This process of restructuring was to 'polarize' the indigenous working class: some of its members were presented with a vision of upwards social mobility into the working-class elite, while others faced the threat of downwards mobility into the 'rough'.

At the structural and semiotic level of analysis, Cohen's thesis is that the original mod and skinhead subcultures can be understood as attempted solutions by working-class youth to these problems facing the parent culture, but expressed symbolically through *bricolage*, the appropriation and recontextualization of cultural items to communicate new meanings. In this way, the mod style can be interpreted (or decoded) as an exploration of the 'upwardly mobile option': they 'attempt to realize, *but in an imaginary relation*, the conditions of existence of the socially mobile white collar worker … their dress and image reflected the hedonistic image of the affluent consumer' (ibid.: 83; original emphasis). Conversely, the skinhead lifestyle and appearance can be regarded as an exploration of the 'downwards option': 'a reaction against the contamination of the parent culture by middle-class values and a reassertion of the integral values of working-class culture through its most recessive traits – its puritanism and chauvinism' (ibid.: 84).

There is, however, no phenomenological level of analysis in Cohen's paper. It does not attempt a reconstruction of the subjective motives and meanings of the mods and skinheads, but presents a semiotic interpretation of subcultural solutions. Subcultures 'carry "secret" meanings : meanings which express, in code, a form of resistance to the order which guarantees their subordination' (Hebdige 1979: 17–18). Style is read as text, and only the semiotician is entrusted to crack the code. There is, in other words, an academic 'elitism' implicit in this method (Turner 1992: 131). Moreover, as Stanley Cohen has famously remarked in his classic critique of the CCCS, 'this is, to be sure, an imaginative way of reading the style; but how can we be sure that it is not also imaginary?' (S. Cohen 1980: xv). He goes on to say:

> In one way or another, most of the problems in the 'resistance through rituals' framework are to be found at the theory's third level: how the subculture is actually lived out by its bearers. The nagging sense here is that these lives, selves and identities do not always coincide with what they are supposed to stand for (1980: xviii).

While according to Dorn and South:

> The acknowledgement of important changes in the structure of the local economy and the family was obtained at the expense of an empathy with the experiences of

those facing structural changes. There was seldom, in the Birmingham Centre's work, much sense of the authenticity of the individual account, or of social psychology. Male youth cultures were interpreted as systems of resistance to dominant ideologies without much regard to the question of the relation between the meaning of youth cultures for participants and that for sociologists (Dorn and South 1982: 15–16).

Here, I would invoke my criterion of validity, that social scientific explanations should at least 'fit' the subjective reality of the subjects of the study. Trowler and Riley point out that 'if this is not the case the sociologist is merely imposing a set of meanings on the participants' (1985: 162). Clearly, the combination of a Marxist theory and semiotic analysis has led to such an imposition, and I would not hesitate to follow Trowler and Riley (ibid.: 163) in suggesting 'that the CCCS "got it wrong" for this very reason'. The source of the problem is the claim of an *a priori* theoretical knowledge of the social totality that has already provided the CCCS with the economic and social factors (the historical problematic) that are most relevant to subcultural analysis and in terms of which the structural/semiotic and phenomenological levels are interpreted. Phil Cohen claims that 'no real analysis of subculture is complete without all those levels being in place' (1984: 83). Yet, as we shall see, it is not possible to have this exhaustive knowledge of social reality, nor of pre-given theoretical principles; our comprehension of the world can only ever be empirical, partial and one-sided.

A Nominalist Approach to Concept Formation

According to Weber, reality is given to us in appearances. A Weberian approach to youth subcultures therefore takes place only at the level of observable phenomena. Yet Weber also took the neo-Kantian view that reality is composed of a limitless number of individual entities and events, each one capable of being described in an infinite number of ways. As the world cannot therefore be known in its entirety we must necessarily impose a conceptual 'ordering framework' upon it (Sayer 1984: 49) by which we can define, select and abstract those aspects that are relevant to our own interests and concerns. Here is the rationale behind Weber's methodological concept of the 'ideal-type' – a 'one-sided accentuation' of what we regard as the particularly 'significant' characteristics of a phenomenon (Weber 1949: 90). The identification of 'significant' features is undeniably an expression of value; but the infinite complexity of the social world means that value-free, objective accounts of phenomena are impossible. Different researchers may therefore choose to select different aspects of the same phenomenon for study or regard certain features as inherently more important than others; but *all* such choices are necessarily grounded in the values and interests of the academics concerned – *all* concepts are ideal-typical in character.

Jenks has stated of the ideal-type that it 'has remained elusive and confounding to generations of students of socio-cultural life' (1993: 51). The concept, however, loses some of its mystery when we recognize that we all use ideal-types even though we may be unaware of it. 'Student' is itself an ideal-type. In using the term we are simply classifying certain individuals together on the basis of one general shared attribute (that they are taking a course of, usually post-compulsory, education) while ignoring all the other innumerable differences or similarities between them. 'The ideal type is the pure case, never actualised, uncluttered by extraneous attributes and ambiguities' (MacRae 1982: 66). Exactly this same logic applies to 'subculture'. It is therefore inevitable that:

> The subculture concept involves abstract construction. A subculture is typological in the sense that it involves selection and abstraction of cultural aspects of socio-cultural systems. Only some of a great range of cultural features are selected, such selection normally being made according to what the researcher sees as the main distinguishing features of the subculture. Insofar as the selected and frequently accentuated (abstract) features are woven into a patterned construct, 'subculture' may be regarded as an 'ideal type' . . . The criteria enabling such a boundary to be drawn around what is and what is not subculture, are of a more abstract conceptual order than those usually used in the selection of sample populations (Pearson 1979: 15).

Ideal types do not and cannot faithfully represent reality in all its confusion and complexity, but abstract from reality in a consistent manner those features most relevant to our interests. They are heuristic devices to aid empirical research, and we construct them wholly with this purpose in mind. As we will see in the next chapter, this study utilizes two subcultural ideal types; one emphasizes those traits typical of a modern subculture, the other selects typical postmodern features. By comparing these ideal types with the actual sensibilities of a sample of contemporary subculturalists, explanations can be proposed for the observed similarities and discrepancies. It is important to stress that these modern and postmodern characteristics cannot be found in their pure form in any one individual subculturalist. In Chapters 4 to 8 I therefore select and present through interview extracts those features and sensibilities that characterize the 'typical' contemporary subculturalist.

How does this method of concept formation differ from that used by the CCCS? From our discussion of the ideal type it should be clear that, for Weber, it is not possible to identify the essential features of reality. 'Social reality does not possess a real essence because it is always capable of being constructed in various different ways' (Parkin 1982: 28). On this point Weber clearly differs from Marx, for whom there is a true essence of reality that exists objectively and independently of how it appears to us in phenomenal forms. As Morrison puts it, 'reality presents itself in a distorted way and appears to be other than it actually is' (1998: 47). In Marxist terminology, the relationship of our 'lived reality' to this 'true reality' is an 'ideological' one.[3] While ideology constitutes reality for individuals, it nonetheless involves them in a 'common misrecognition of the real mechanisms which have distributed them to their respective positions' (Robins and Cohen 1978: 113) – we may, in other words, hold erroneous (ideological) conceptions of our (real) identities and interests. We can identify this approach quite clearly in *Resistance Through Rituals*. Its project is to penetrate the ideological discourses of the time (affluence and classlessness) and the cultural and phenomenal forms through which they are lived and understood (the teenage youth culture), in order to give causal priority to 'real', essential (i.e. Marxist class) relations.

The language of classical Marxism used in *Resistance Through Rituals* is indicative of such a project. 'This exercise of penetrating beneath a popular construction' (J. Clarke *et al.* 1986: 9); 'the "phenomenal form" – Youth Culture provides a point of departure, only, for such an analysis' (ibid.: 10); 'to move from the most phenomenal aspect of youth subcultures to the deeper meanings' (ibid.: 17). The influence of Althusserian Marxism is also apparent here: 'the ideology of affluence constructed the "real relations" of post-war British society into an "imaginary relation"' (ibid.: 37). In identifying these 'real relations' as class relations of production, the authors also make the traditional Marxist claim that 'conflicts of interest arise, fundamentally, from the difference in the structural position of classes in the productive realm, but they "have their effect" in social and political life' (ibid.: 38). These essential class relations are not ideal-typical constructs, such as we find in Weberian sociology, but structural relationships of exploitation that have a real existence not given to us in direct experience. As Clarke and his colleagues argue 'class conflict never disappears . . . it cannot "disappear" – contrary to the ideology of affluence – until the productive relations which produce and sustain it disappear' (ibid.: 41).

The CCCS approach therefore situates youth subcultures within a theoretical framework of class oppression, conflict and exploitation. Thus, while youth subcultures are seen to 'win space' in the battle against the hegemonic incorporation of the subordinate class into bourgeois culture, they are merely symbolic responses, 'imaginary', 'magical' or 'ideological' solutions, for they fail to perceive and, hence, mount a challenge to, the real relations of society underlying phenomenal forms.[4] 'No amount of stylistic incantation can alter the oppressive mode in which the commodities used in subculture have been produced' (Hebdige 1979: 130). Marshall's less charitable interpretation of this approach is that 'youth subcultures must be read . . . as a form of resistance to bourgeois ideological domination – despite the fact that the subjects of the research cannot and do not recognise themselves in such an account' (1990: 173). But this transcendence of the limits of subjective experience could be regarded as the very strength of the method. Indeed, it is precisely because of its claimed ability to penetrate our common-sense categories of thought that many of its adherents champion Marxism as a scientific analysis of society, while continuing to regard as ideological all other perspectives (including Weberian sociology) that remain at the level of phenomenal appearances.

This claim to scientific superiority raises what Saunders calls 'the obvious question': namely, how 'Marx's method of dialectical materialism can analyse the totality and come to discover its essential features when all other methods are doomed to remain partial in their scope and superficial in their insight' (1989: 18). According to Derek Sayer (1979), Marx uses a logic of hypothesis formation called 'retroduction', which is a method of reasoning from appearances to the mechanisms that could have caused those phenomena. 'Marx has no mysteriously privileged starting point'. Like everyone else he has access only to 'the phenomenal forms of our everyday experience' (Sayer 1979: 102). Of course, for Marx, such phenomenal forms are ideological and misleading. He therefore moves retroductively from observable phenomena to postulate the existence of essential relations that could account for those appearances. There are, of course, limits on what constitutes a reasonable hypothesis, since it must be able to explain the original observations; yet Sayer regards this as 'evidently a weak form of inference' (ibid.: 135), since for any observed effect there may be a number of possible causes. How then can we ever know, asks Saunders, 'that the essential relations posited by the theory are the correct ones since there is always the possibility that other essences could be put forward which could explain phenomenal forms equally as well?' (1989: 20–1). It is here that we begin to encounter problems in the verification of 'realist' explanations in social science.[5]

I have already outlined Weber's method of concept formation, the ideal-type, the selection and abstraction of elements from empirical reality. In this sense, Weber can be identified as taking a 'nominalist' approach. A nominalist approach regards the empirical as all that can be known about reality. Its concepts are empirical constructs that do not add to our knowledge of reality, but classify, divide and organize observable events and appearances (Burrows 1989: 48). By contrast, a realist approach considers empirical reality to be only the surface level of reality, generated by the structures and mechanisms of the underlying level. Realist concepts are theoretical constructs that identify these real, underlying (but unobservable) mechanisms and thus add to our knowledge of reality. Given Marx's own distinction between the appearance of reality (phenomenal forms) and the essence of reality (class relations of production), his approach can be clearly identified as realist (Benton 1977; Keat and Urry 1982). Although Marx's definition of class includes an empirical component (the identification of a class that own the means of production, and a class that own only their labour power), there is a deeper level (the real but 'hidden' extraction of surplus value that is the basis of conflict and exploitation) at which these essential relations can be known only theoretically.

Realism also operates with a different conception of causation to nominalism. Whereas nominalism is concerned to establish an empirical sequence of cause and effect, such that event A helps to create B (as we will see in our discussion of Weber's Protestant ethic thesis), realism seeks to identify the underlying structural mechanisms that generate particular social phenomena. Andrew Sayer (1984) conceptualizes these mechanisms as 'causal powers' and 'liabilities', inherent properties of an object that necessarily produce a tendency to behave in a particular way. These tendencies continue to operate even though their empirical manifestation depends upon their coming into contact with a variety of contingent conditions. To draw upon Saunders's discussion of Sayer's own example from the natural sciences (Saunders 1989: 207), we may observe that copper wire has a tendency to conduct electricity. The mechanism that has generated this tendency is inherent to copper (viz. its ionic structure). Some pieces of copper wire will, however, fail to act as conductors because certain contingent factors, such as dampness, have intervened to prevent the tendency from being realized. The presence of counteracting contingent factors does not, of course, mean that the necessary tendencies do not exist. Copper still has an inherent capacity to act as a conductor of electricity despite, in this case, the absence of any empirical evidence for this assertion.

Now, clearly, in the natural sciences such contingent factors can be controlled and manipulated in experimental conditions (what Andrew Sayer (1984) calls 'closed' systems), enabling us to assess the validity of our hypothesized causal mechanisms. But in the 'open' systems of the social sciences, where it is impossible to control or even identify all the variables, and there are obvious ethical and practical obstacles to the setting up of experiments, the problems of confirming and falsifying realist causes become insurmountable (Saunders 1989: 358). A relevant example is Marx's own assertion that in capitalist societies there is a necessary tendency for the rate of profit to fall. As Derek Sayer (1979) points out, Marx also identified six 'counteracting tendencies' that make it impossible to verify this claim. Indeed, the tendency of the rate of profit to fall is an example of a so-called 'law' of social science that, on these grounds, can never be falsified despite its failure to operate empirically as a law, for empirical 'events reflect contingent conditions while theory is concerned with necessary conditions which exist irrespective of whether they become manifest' (Saunders 1989: 356–7).

Proponents of realism, such as Andrew Sayer, argue that the construction of a nominalist concept proceeds without reference to the real structure of the world, 'and hence is unable to recognize that some selections are better than others according to their relationship to this structure' (A. Sayer 1984: 216). Yet how can we know that realist concepts have mapped 'real' structures? From what we have seen of Marx's method, it can be regarded as scientific only in so far as it produces plausible or conjectural claims about unobservable essential relations. But the existence of these relations and the truth or falsity of the propositions derived from Marxist theory can never be conclusively demonstrated. We can never therefore be certain that the world does have the 'real' structure that Sayer attributes to it. This is not, however, to credit Weberian sociology with the scientific superiority that we deny to Marxism. Weber fully realized that *all* social explanations can never be more than partial and one-sided; that 'every "ism" which claims complete validity, is in part a reflection of the point of view of the social scientist' (Lee and Newby 1985: 171). This does, however, ensure that there can be no basis for the claim that Marxism (or, indeed, any theory) produces scientific knowledge whereas all other approaches merely reproduce ideological categories of thought. As Hirst argues, there is no 'general criterion of validity' (1979: 21) by which different social theories can be rated and a science–ideology distinction asserted. All perspectives have a purchase on plausibility, and must be judged according to their own procedures and principles.

Authenticity, Mobility and Change

From the arguments so far presented it should be clear that there are no reasons why we must necessarily accept a Marxist theory of youth subcultures over a Weberian approach. Equally, however, this does not in itself justify a rejection of the CCCS work. It is insufficient to dismiss a position merely because it can provide no 'final guarantee' of validity. It must instead be evaluated 'by a concrete analysis of the substance of its arguments' (Larrain 1984: 211). What I therefore want to demonstrate is that the employment of a Marxist theory has led to three major problems in youth subcultural analysis that a Weberian approach is able to avoid. These are the problems of: (a) authenticity and origins; (b) mobility and change; and (c) realist ethnography.

Authenticity and Origins

The problem of authenticity is really the issue as to what constitutes 'proper' or 'genuine' membership. Yet before we can address such a question we must first establish the 'real' purpose or reason for subcultural affiliation, for without this knowledge we cannot decide who is, or is not, authentic. It seems logical to argue that if we want to discover the 'real point' of being a mod or punk or whatever, then we must ask the individuals concerned to provide their subjective motives and reasonings. In other words, the question of authenticity can only properly be addressed by having recourse to the views of individual members themselves (see Widdicombe and Wooffitt 1995). In this way, the relationship of authenticity to such issues as class membership, how the style was constructed, or the point in time at which one joined the subculture, would be established empirically. The alternative method would involve imposing external criteria of authenticity derived from *a priori* theory, thereby presenting the problem of how to accommodate theoretically those members who do not conform to such definitions. But this is exactly what the CCCS do. 'Genuine' membership is located in an original moment of collective working-class stylistic innovation. It is by reference to this theoretical standard that 'subcultural practices could then be construed as active, innately (and authentically) oppositional and resistant' (Stahl 1998: 16).

Class, in the CCCS approach, is a structure with the causal power to *generate* subcultures as counter-hegemonic responses to specific historical contradictions. The task is therefore one of explaining the emergence or genesis of subcultures in their first 'authentic' moment of resistance. As such, the prime focus is on stylistic innovation through *bricolage*, the creative construction of an ensemble to carry new meanings. Now, it is true that the CCCS approach also examines how the world of commerce eventually takes these innovative styles and transmits them to a wider public, producing a fashion statement that effectively negates the radical action of the original *bricoleurs*. Yet this process of 'diffusion and defusion', as it is called, is given only a very brief and schematic treatment in the CCCS literature.[6] As the CCCS authors themselves readily admit, it is of secondary importance compared to the main project of theorizing the 'authentic' point of subcultural inception: 'This is not to deny the role of commercial interests in the perpetuation, modification and eventual incorporation of youth styles, but it is to assert a "moment" of originality in the formation of such a style. And it is this formative "moment" we are most interested in' (J. Clarke and Jefferson 1978: 148).

In contrast, then, to the 'moment' of originality, 'the moment of incorporation itself remains untheorized' (Cagle 1995: 40). This effectively produces an abrupt theoretical dichotomy between the authentic subcultural members, and the incorporated followers of commodified subcultural fashions. Here is the theoretical justification for Hebdige's infamous 'distinction between originals and hangers-on' (1979: 122). As it is phrased with regard to punk, 'the style no doubt made sense for the first wave of self-conscious innovators at a level which remained inaccessible to those who became punks after the subculture had surfaced and been publicized' (ibid.). Here, I concur with Gary Clarke in finding this theoretical demarcation 'particularly problematic' (G. Clarke 1982: 14). I, too, 'would like to ask for whom this distinction is significant?' (ibid.).

A focus on authentic origins also produces a particular conception of subcultures as internally homogeneous and externally demarcated. Clarke describes them as 'the abstract essences of subcultures . . . non-contradictory and "pure"' (1982: 8). Waters talks of 'a closed anthropological entity . . . a static category . . . frozen in time' (1981: 29, 30). This problem is compounded by the too tight fit drawn between subculture and class, leading to caricatures based on pre-given assumptions about the form an authentic working-class response should take; for example (the emphasis in all cases is my own), 'the *shared* social experiences of adolescents in *particular class locations* are *collectively* expressed and negotiated through the construction of *distinct* leisure styles' (Murdock and McCron 1986: 203); 'so *highly structured*, visible and *tightly-bounded* a response' (J. Clarke et al.1986: 33); 'the *collectivity* of their being-as-a-group . . . a *collective response* to the material and situated experience of their class' (ibid.: 47); 'an *organised group-identity* in the form and shape of a *coherent and distinctive* way of "being-in-the-world"' (ibid.: 54); 'clearly articulated, *collective structures* – often, "near-" or "quasi-gangs"' (ibid.: 60); and finally, 'a *tightly bound* entity . . . sets the group off, distinctively, from other similar and dissimilar groups . . . the symbolic use of things to express *an internal coherence*' (ibid.: 56).[7]

This strong emphasis on class-based forms carries with it the 'dangerous assumption', as Gary Clarke calls it, 'that all members of a subculture are in the same class location' (1982: 9). Empirically, this assumption is easily contradicted. Murdock and McCron (1986: 205) mention the problem of the 'class defectors' found in studies by Willmott (1969) and Buff (1970), the working-class youths who favoured the bohemian style and ideas of the middle-class 'hippy'. While it therefore becomes important for Murdock and McCron 'to explain why adolescents sharing the same class location should be attracted to styles developed by other class fractions' (1986: 205), we should note how this remark still assumes that there is a pure class origin to styles, and that members of other class fractions are only subsequently attracted. This line of reasoning could easily lead to empirical evidence of mixed-class subcultural membership being explained away by reference to Hebdige's distinction between the 'originals and hangers-on' (1979: 122). As Roberts puts it, 'successful fads need only time to spread beyond their origins and straddle class boundaries (1985: 119). Here, the class defectors become in realist terms the 'contingent events' that can be distinguished from, and hence said not to negate, the 'necessary' point of origin, the initial emergence of authentic members from a specific class fraction.

We might think that styles that travel beyond their origins would, in the process, undergo transformation and modification. Cagle, for example, assumes that subcultural style is open to 'multiple interpretations' in the market-place (1995: 40). But, as we have already seen, the moment of transformation is also the point of incorporation, after which the wearers of the style are no longer resolving contradictions but merely following fashion, and therefore of no real concern to the CCCS. Hence, Gary Clarke can refer to 'an uncomfortable absence in the literature of any discussion as to how and with what consequences the pure subcultures are sustained, transformed, appropriated, disfigured or destroyed' (1982: 8). What is therefore missing from this analysis is a whole dimension of change.

Mobility and Change

The issue here, as raised by Kenneth Roberts, is: 'do most young people move through a succession of rebellious youth styles?' (1985: 129). Such a question is all the more important because of its obvious links to the problem of how subcultures are modified and transformed. Fine and Kleinman have proposed that subcultures are kept in a constant 'state of flux' because of the actions and interactions of individuals transmitting 'cultural elements' between groups (1979: 6). Yet such a level of analysis is often overlooked, and subculture portrayed 'as a homogeneous and static system' (ibid.: 5), because of the tendency of academics to reify the concept of subculture – to treat the concept as a real, material thing with its own properties that stand apart from the complex lived reality of individual members.

Now Weber fully realized that sociologists cannot avoid the use of collective concepts such as 'the state' or 'the working class' (or, in our case, 'subculture'). Yet he insisted that they should be regarded as nothing more than shorthand terms for aggregates of individuals. This methodological individualism, as it is called, can be seen in Weber's use of the ideal-type. As we have already seen, 'subculture' is merely a nominalist abstraction, a purely arbitrary way of grouping together a number of individuals on the basis of certain selected features that we choose to highlight for the purpose at hand. From this perspective there are no real boundaries within which members of subcultures are 'contained', nor can there be, for as Hughes *et al.* put it, 'there is no dividing line built into reality' (1996: 109) according to which such boundaries can be identified. Or, to put the same point in a different way, there are no collective realities in the world to which such concepts can directly refer (we cannot see 'a subculture', only individual members). The notion of a collective concept that 'acts' is therefore a sociological fiction; only individuals have this ability. 'Collectivities must be treated as *solely* the resultants and modes of organization of the particular acts of individual persons, since these alone can be treated as agents in the course of subjectively understandable action' (Weber 1968: 13).

Weber's method is therefore expressly designed to clarify the actions and meanings of individuals. By contrast, the CCCS framework is not equipped to provide an analysis at the individual level. Evans has recently remarked how 'the way in which individuals negotiate and move through subcultures is something very different from, even contradictory to, the way in which writing on subculture tends to "fix" such identities' (1997: 179). It is not that the CCCS failed to recognize the potential for subcultural mobility. As Clarke *et al.* state in the opening pages of *Resistance Through Rituals*, 'individuals may, in their personal life-careers, move in and out of one, or indeed several, such sub-cultures' (J. Clarke *et al.* 1986: 16). The problem is that, despite the lip service paid to 'biographies', such pathways are seen *only* 'in terms of' structures and cultures (ibid.: 57). Thus, we hear much about collective concepts, 'youth', 'subcultures', 'the young'; but there is no theoretical space for individuals in this analysis. The CCCS concept of subculture is a realist structure that exists independently of individual members and draws real boundaries around them.[8] As Phil Cohen puts it, using the language of Marxist class analysis, 'subcultures are symbolic structures and must not be confused with the actual kids who is its bearers and supports' (1984: 83). It is the subculture that is the unit of analysis here, not the individual subculturalists.

The CCCS approach, in other words, falls into the trap of reifying the concept of subculture. It is treated, in effect, as a real, material entity that 'acts'. As such, the concept stands in for the individual members. Individuals appear in the analysis only as epiphenomena of essences, structures and totalizing theories. The lack of concern shown by the CCCS in the individual actor and the absence of any consideration of change are not merely regrettable oversights, but direct consequences of their theoretical and methodological approach.

We are left with many questions that cannot be satisfactorily answered within the CCCS framework. How do we identify the point at which innovative style becomes incorporated fashion? On what criteria can particular subculturalists be regarded as authentic or inauthentic? Where can we draw the line that separates the originals from the followers? To go back to the question raised by Gary Clarke: for whom (and how) are these distinctions significant? The CCCS regard them as significant, for they are predicated upon their own political project of attributing authenticity according to pre-given criteria of resistance. But Clarke's question demands an empirical investigation that considers the actions and meanings of individual subculturalists. It cannot be answered by the imposition of a totalizing framework into which the distinction is already built. Real individuals pay no heed to theoretical injunctions.

Realist Ethnography

I have so far talked of 'the CCCS approach' as if it were a unified body of theory. But Blundell *et al.* have insisted that the internal 'diversity' of the 'subculture group' must be respected (1993: 43). I indicated in the opening chapter that the work of Paul Willis provides a qualified exception to the criticism that the CCCS failed to consider the lived reality of those under study. McGuigan identifies these methodological differences more precisely:

> The broadly 'culturalist' and 'structuralist' strands in Birmingham subcultural analysis are best exemplified by the work of Paul Willis and Dick Hebdige respectively. There was considerable interaction and overlap between these two strands. However, the alternative methodological strategies of ethnographic field work, on one hand, and the reading of subculture as 'text', on the other, call into question accounts which oversimplify the unity of the Birmingham School's perspective (McGuigan 1992: 97–8).

While not wishing to deny the basic premise of this argument, I want to demonstrate that Willis's ethnographic observations were, to employ an Althusserian term, 'overdetermined' by his *a priori* commitment to the same structuralist principles of Marxism and homological analysis that we find elsewhere in the CCCS. In this sense, Willis's position can be seen as realist, 'concerned with the clarification of structures and their associated generative mechanisms, which have been contingently capable of producing the observed phenomena' (Tsoukas 1989: 556).

Willis opens *Profane Culture* with a testimony of his commitment to field work that immediately serves to distance him from textual analysis. As he famously argues: 'the sheer surprise of a living culture is a slap to reverie. Real, bustling, startling cultures move. They exist. They are something in the world. They suddenly leave behind – empty, exposed, ugly – *ideas* of poverty, deprivation, existence and culture. Real events can save us much philosophy' (Willis 1978: 1). For Willis, therefore, the potential of participant observation is that it enables us to 'be surprised', allowing us the 'profoundly important methodological possibility . . . of reaching knowledge not pre-figured in one's starting paradigm' (Willis 1984: 90). But exactly *how much* philosophy does this 'save us'? Willis also states that 'the researcher should be as flexible as possible, and suspend so far as possible specific theories – while admitting his general theoretical orientation – for the explanation of what he expects to encounter' (1978: 195), and it is clear that *Profane Culture* operates within a general Marxist framework.

First there is the emphasis on the dialectic. 'The essential theme of the book is that oppressed, subordinate or minority groups can have a hand in the construction of their own vibrant cultures' (1978: 1), cultures that are 'not free-floating', but situated within 'social locations and determinations' that are not of the respondents' own making (ibid.: 170). Secondly, this is a class-based, materialist analysis. By 'taking what is radical' from their parent culture, working-class bikers and middle-class hippies have responded to 'massive contradictions' generated at the socioeconomic level (ibid.: 171). Thirdly, there is the theoretical reading of subcultures as 'magical' solutions (although Willis does not use this term), in that their cultural response 'never worked back single-mindedly to the causes of the suffering, oppression and exclusion of their members' (ibid.: 176). This pre-given framework inevitably impinges upon the project as a whole. Dworkin has stated that Willis 'was certainly aware that youth subcultures had failed to challenge the dominant order, but he had no theoretical means of grasping the nature of the process' (1997: 157). Yet the language of Marxism is stamped on virtually every page of the introduction to *Profane Culture*. As Marcus has commented on Willis's ethnographic method: 'The Marxist system is *there*, so to speak, to be invoked. A commitment to it by the ethnographer makes it available as an image of a system to be worked into the ethnography' (1986: 173; original emphasis).

If this is Willis's 'general theoretical orientation', then his lower-level theory also shares much with that found elsewhere in the CCCS. Willis does not provide a detailed semiotic reading of the 'meaning' of subcultural style as we find in J. Clarke (1986), P. Cohen (1984) and Hebdige (1979), but he was the first of the CCCS authors to analyse the homologies existing between a group's self- consciousness and their use of such symbolic objects as style. As Willis tells us, a homological analysis 'is concerned with how far, in their structure and content, particular items parallel and reflect the structure, style, typical concerns, attitudes and feelings of the social group' (1978: 191).

But, of course, this logic of inquiry inevitably produces what Downes and Rock have called 'a considerable symmetry' in the internal relations of a subculture (1988: 161). It constructs an altogether too *coherent* portrayal. And in so far as we compare subcultures to each other, as Willis does here with the bikers and hippies, then we invariably create homological oppositions between groups. There are, I think, three issues here.

First, Willis's observations appear as a manifestation of the structuralist framework within which homological analysis is conducted. Elements cannot exist in isolation, but only in relationships of association. This reproduces at the empirical level 'a framework of meanings that is both coherent and meaningful . . . style as a signifier of a unified subcultural practice, rather than as a series of distinct subcultural expressions' (Muncie 1984: 102). As I argue in Chapter 4, it is not that homologies may not be present, but that Willis's employment of a particular theoretical framework enabled him to discover exactly that for which he was already looking. Subcultures are far more 'fluid and amorphous formations' (Osgerby 1998: 24) than Willis conveys here.

Second, this analysis takes place at the group level, and thus begins with the assumption that individuals are tied to group homologies: 'my study was of the larger social and cultural whole and not of a specific group or of specific individuals except in so far as they embodied central meanings and values' (Willis 1978: 12). Yet to have begun with individual members might have problematized the whole concept of a coherent subculture, for individuals can be 'significantly related' (ibid.: 192) to a range of cultural forms (music, styles, ideas and values) that complicate or even contradict the homologies identified at the group level.

Thirdly, this ensures that the question of change is again undertheorized. Reading *Profane Culture*, it seems beyond the bounds of possibility that some bikers may have become suedeheads, or that certain hippies could have transformed themselves into glam rockers or punks, so imprisoned are individuals by group homologies. Willis's analysis does allow for the different interpretations that the same 'cultural item' can offer to different groups, or to the same group over time, 'so that what was once accepted is rejected' (ibid.: 192–3). But if, as I have argued, individuals can embrace a range of complex cultural forms, these can open up for them a variety of subcultural trajectories.

Despite his testimony to ethnographic field work, Willis's study of subcultures is therefore beset by the same two methodological problems that can be found elsewhere in the CCCS work. One: it utilizes a totalizing framework that obscures the inevitable partiality of its analysis. Fornäs has, for example, argued that 'no identities can be reduced only to homologies – they always include heterologies . . . an internal differentiation and diversity . . . that make the homologies only relational and partial' (Fornäs 1995: 114). Two: it demonstrates an *a priori* commitment to inviolable Marxist principles in terms of which the empirical data are interpreted. The effect is to relegate ethnography to the role of providing the descriptive richness to the 'pure' conceptual categories (internally cohesive, externally demarcated) found elsewhere in the CCCS literature. This is not, of course, to suggest that an alternative approach can dispense with theoretical starting-points. My discussion of the ideal-type has remarked on the *inevitability* of a conceptual and theoretical ordering framework. Yet, as we have also seen, a Weberian approach does recognize the partiality of any analysis, and will derive its concepts empirically rather than from *a priori* theory, and amend its constructions and propositions on the basis of empirical evidence.

The Independent Role of Beliefs and Values

A Weberian approach must take seriously the independent role of cultural factors in any explanation of subcultural phenomena. Cultural values, in other words, 'cannot be reduced to economic, material, political, or other factors . . . [They] are a determining factor in their own right' (Himmelfarb 1995: 257). Weber's clearest demonstration of this position can be found in *The Protestant Ethic and the Spirit of Capitalism* (Weber 1976). As the title might partly suggest, Weber's intention was to examine how a particular set of religious beliefs could have helped to foster the attitudes necessary to the growth of modern rational capitalism. Simplistic readings of this work are largely responsible for the impression (quite mistaken, as we shall see) that Weber takes an 'idealist' stance (defined here as being concerned only with the causal role of ideas in effecting social change), in direct contrast to Marx's status as a 'materialist' (emphasizing the causal role of material or economic factors).

This is undeniably a crude caricature of Weber's position, for nowhere did he posit a simplistic one-way causal interpretation of history or claim that religious ideas directly 'caused' the emergence of capitalism. In his 'Protestant ethic' study, Weber placed as much importance on material pre-conditions as he did on the role of ideas, demonstrating that even in cases where 'the capitalist spirit is alive and flourishing, but lacks the proper institutional supports', capitalism as an economic system could not develop (Parkin 1982: 42). As Weber was at pains to point out, 'it is not our aim to substitute for a one-sided materialistic interpretation an equally one-sided spiritualistic causal interpretation of culture and of history' (1968: 91). Any suggestion that historical change can be explained by one primary set of causal relations, either material or cultural, would also have run directly contrary to Weber's pronouncements on the infinite complexity of social reality, where a multiplicity of factors operate independently in any given context. Ironically, it is this very position that may have helped form Weber's reputation as an idealist, for the complexity of the social world ensures that analysts must select and abstract those factors relevant to their own investigation. Weber also makes this point quite clear when he writes: 'There is no absolutely "objective" scientific analysis of culture or . . . of "social phenomena" independent of special and "one-sided" viewpoints according to which – expressly or tacitly, consciously or unconsciously – they are selected, analysed and organized for expository purposes' (Weber 1949: 72).

From this perspective, a focus on a particular set of factors is a self-conscious attempt to present a necessarily one-sided view of social change. Weber's emphasis on the role of religious beliefs is therefore 'merely intended to provide a corrective to any unbalanced emphasis on economic ones . . . to make up for the fact that they had been unduly played down in other places, and not because he considered these the single most significant factors in history' (Hughes *et al.* 1996: 99).

My argument here takes a similar form. I am not disputing that material factors (for example, a growth in the purchasing power of youth) and changes in the class structure (see Chapter 3) are implicated in the development of subcultures. I want, however, to demonstrate that subcultures can also be explained by reference to changes in cultural belief systems that have an autonomous, although interactive, relationship to socioeconomic factors. Let us conclude this chapter by illustrating this point. To do so we must return again to Weber's 'Protestant ethic' thesis. Put simply, Weber's argument is that modern capitalism required a set of attitudes conducive to rational entrepreneurial activity – a capitalist 'spirit', which emphasized the moral imperative of hard work, discipline, and the rational accumulation of profit. This spirit was itself stimulated by an earlier set of religious beliefs that interpreted business activity as a duty towards God – an ethic of ascetic Protestantism (or as it is commonly known, a puritan ethic) that stressed the importance of worldly success through the values of thrift, frugality and self-denial. In a complementary thesis, Colin Campbell (1987) has logically argued: if there is a cultural imperative behind the development of modern production, then why not also behind modern consumption? Campbell goes on to demonstrate his case convincingly – that a pleasure-seeking ethic of Romanticism (or as it is sometimes referred to, a permissive or expressive ethic), itself derived from a religious ethic of pietistic Protestantism, lies behind the restless and hedonistic search for novelty that characterizes modern consumer behaviour.

We have here what, on the face of it, appear to be two opposing ethical guides for conduct – restraint/licence; renunciation/pleasure; control/ expression. The original carriers of both ethics were the upper-middle classes, and the central values of those (now fully secularized) belief systems remain fundamental to the world-view of that class. The CCCS were certainly correct to regard the 1960s counterculture as a 'crisis *within* the dominant culture' (J. Clarke *et al.* 1986: 65). It was a conflict between the puritan work ethic of the respectable, bourgeois middle classes, and the expressive Romanticism of the youth of that same class.[9] But, of course, variants of those values can be found in different social groups. Bernice Martin (1985) has illustrated how the respectable fractions of both the manual and non-manual classes were traditionally puritanical 'cultures of control', concerned with order, self-discipline and, above all, the maintenance of boundaries and categories (a time and place for everything and everything to be kept in its place). Why, then, should we not also find Romantic-expressive values in the working class that promote *cultures of freedom* from order, control and the rigidity of convention? There is a hint of this in Phil Cohen's (1984) discussion of the origin of the mods and skinheads. Here, we find that the problems produced by the so-called *embourgeoisement* of the working-class are overlaid by contradictions at the ideological level, 'between traditional working-class puritanism and the new hedonism of consumption' (ibid.). The subcultural solution is designed to address these ideological tensions, so that, according to Roberts's commentary, 'rockers and skinheads revive puritan masculinity, while mods accentuate consumption-oriented values' (Roberts 1978: 75).

That the skinheads were reviving the more 'recessive' working-class elements of the puritan work ethic is readily understandable. So were the mods expressing some variant of a consumption-related permissive 'play' ethic? And how, then, could we place them in relation to the middle-class hippies of the 1960s counterculture? According to Martin (1985), the mods and the hippies both display certain characteristics of Romanticism (but the hippies to a far greater extent), in that both are concerned with the exploration of 'liminoid' moments of spontaneity, anti-structure and individual expression. There is here, in other words, an explanation framed in terms of cultural conflict, a conflict between 'the values of change, diversity, individuality and imagination [and] those of uniformitarianism, universalism and rationalism'

(C. Campbell 1987: 181), and between the groups who embody these values. Again, this does not mean that socioeconomic changes are unrelated to the development of subcultures; rather, that cultural change has its own independence from economic factors. This is not, of course, the view of the CCCS, who explain the mod subculture an attempt to cover the gap between the 'largely mythical' promise of affluence and the 'mundane reality' of their economic circumstances (J. Clarke and Jefferson 1978: 150, 153). But if we view subcultures as an expression of cultural values rather than as a 'solution' to class-based contradictions we are liberated from all the theoretical problems we have seen to arise from defining subcultural authenticity according to economic criteria.

The relationship between subculture and class is therefore one that is contingent, and in so far as subcultures establish a form of cultural 'sensibility' through attitudes and values, consumption practices and various leisure activities, they can more accurately be conceptualized as 'lifestyle' groupings. The concept of lifestyle (Bocock 1992; Veal 1993; Reimer 1995; Chaney 1996) arguably has its basis in Weber's distinction between class, defined in terms of the 'production and acquisition of goods', and status, concerned with the '*consumption* of goods as represented by special "styles of life"' (Weber 1970: 193; original emphasis). For Weber, class and status represented autonomous spheres of power and influence. While these two dimensions may empirically coincide, status cannot simply be reduced to class. Culture or consumption (values, ideas, lifestyles) cannot be considered a mere reflection, or epiphenomenon of, class position (Scheys 1987). In the CCCS approach, however, despite Hebdige's description of subcultures as 'cultures of conspicuous consumption' (1979: 103), the connection between class and culture is always a theoretically necessary one. Hetherington has commented that Hebdige's position 'is one that is not particularly interested in the connotations within a style but what that style denotes in terms of broader issues of class and class politics' (1998: 55).

Hence the CCCS view is of working-class subcultures resisting the hegemonic culture. But who exactly is doing the resisting? In noting the tendency for the CCCS to 'present punk, skinhead and teddy boy styles as examples of *working-class* youth subcultures', Roberts has asked: 'Is the label justified?' (1985: 128). There are two points to raise briefly here. First, as Roberts (ibid.) has noted, too little attention is given to the different class fractions from which subcultures originate. Martin, for example, describes the mods as the progeny of 'the "privatized", consumer-oriented new working class, the "middle class from the flats not the 'ouses" so resented by the skinheads a few years earlier' (Martin 1985: 146).[10] Martin's argument (as I read it) is that in both outlook and structural location, the mods were the embodiment of *embourgeoisement*, and were culturally as close, if not closer, to the middle-class hippies as they were to the lumpen, lower-working class teds, rockers and skins. Second, we have already remarked on the 'class defectors' of the 1960s. We have no reliable evidence as to the extent of these 'defections', but we know that nearly a third of Brake's sample of fifty hippies from the 1970s were from manual backgrounds (see Brake 1977). Moreover, remarks on the undeniably mixed class membership of the punk subculture of that decade (Frith 1978, 1983; Muncie 1982) suggest the difficulty of establishing whether it is by now the middle or the working classes who should be regarded as the defectors. What this indicates is the possibility of a value convergence across social classes; that youths from different class backgrounds can hold similar values that find their expression in shared membership of a particular subculture. The extent and implications of this are something that we will consider in our concluding chapter.

In this chapter I have sketched out the general features of the neo-Weberian approach that, throughout the book, will continue to inform our analysis of the more specific issues raised in this chapter – authenticity, change, mobility, fashion, collectivism and individualism, control and freedom. In introducing such issues we have anticipated some of the debates about the characteristics of a postmodern society. I indicated in the last chapter that postmodern analyses, like those of the CCCS, typically fail to consider the relationship between the theoretical assumptions they make and the lived reality of social actors. In order to re-establish this connection we must first discover the implications of the postmodern for subcultural styles. It is to an examination of this issue that we now turn.

Notes

1. I am grateful to Dan Shapiro for this observation.
2. The classic study of how these social changes impacted upon the 1950s East End community is by Young and Willmott (1980).
3. For a discussion of the use of the concept of ideology in the CCCS, see D. Clarke (1980), Hall (1981, 1984), Turner (1992) and Blundell *et al.* (1993).
4. This description of the subcultural response as both counter-hegemonic strategy and imaginary solution bears testimony to the influence of Gramsci (1971) and Althusser (1971) upon the CCCS.
5. For a discussion of realism, see Bhaskar (1978), Keat and Urry (1982), A. Sayer (1984), Outhwaite (1987) and Burrows (1989). Saunders (1989) provides a first-rate critique.
6. A mere four and a quarter pages are devoted to it by J. Clarke (1986: 185–9), and just seven and a half by Hebdige (1979: 92–9).

7. It is worth contrasting this with the description of middle-class countercultures as 'diffuse, less group-centred, more individualised' (J. Clarke *et al.* 1986: 60).

8. There is a further assumption here, reinforced by the emphasis on a *collective* response, that the members of a subculture must see themselves in group terms (e.g. I'm a mod; I'm a skinhead). On this point, see Widdicombe and Wooffitt (1995).

9. On the close relationship between dominant middle-class values and those of the counterculture, see Levin and Spates (1970), Mills (1973), C. Campbell (1980, 1987) and Heelas (1996).

10. Tanner (1978: 364) also provides a comparison between the class origins of mods and skinheads. The classic study of the affluent (privatized) worker is by Goldthorpe *et al.* (1969). See also Lockwood (1966).

3

Postmodern Subcultures and
Aesthetic Modernity[1]

The cultural logic of modernity is not merely that of rationality as expressed in the activities of calculation and experiment; it is also that of passion, and the creative dreaming born of longing.

> Colin Campbell: *The Romantic Ethic and the Spirit of*
> *Modern Consumerism* (1987: 227)

There are in fact only 'traits' of modernity which, at one level, tend to a particular homogeneity in great contrast to the immense diversity of traditional cultures. Yet modernity implies change, and constant changefulness, in contrast to the stability of other cultures.

> Mike Gane: *Baudrillard's Bestiary* (1991: 92)

The Postmodern: A Periodizing Concept?

As Featherstone tells us, 'there is, as yet, no agreed meaning to the term "postmodern" – its derivatives, the family of terms which include post-modernity, *postmodernité*, postmodernization and postmodernism are often used in confusing and interchangeable ways' (1992: 11). Hebdige has likewise remarked on 'the degree of semantic complexity surrounding the term' (1992: 331–2), while Lyon has asked: 'is postmodernity an idea, a cultural experience, a social condition, or perhaps a combination of all three?' (1999: 6). Some of this confusion has undoubtedly been accentuated by our different concept-ualizations of 'the modern' – the benchmark against which postmodern developments are usually measured. Following Featherstone's own example (1992: Ch. 1), I would therefore like to clarify the meaning of two sets of terms that will commonly appear in this chapter – modernity/postmodernity and modernism/postmodernism. The first pair are used in an epochal sense, with postmodernity conveying the idea of a shift from, or transformation of, modernity, such that we have made, or are in the process of making, a move to a new historical period or form of society. The latter set more specifically refer to the cultural aspects of a particular society or epoch, with, for example, postmodernism emerging as the culture of postmodernity.[2]

This historical focus should be kept in mind throughout this chapter, for my aim is to examine what implications there might be for subcultures if we are, indeed, moving towards a postmodern society. I intend to explore this theme, as it relates to both fashion in general and subcultural style more specifically, through examining the assertions of other writers and commentators on this topic. Lest I be misunderstood, let me make it clear that I am *not* in this chapter providing an opinion as to whether the changes to which I refer are actually taking place, nor am I claiming that subcultures necessarily have the characteristics that can be inferred from these changes. My point is to use this debate to construct two ideal-types, respectively representing what we might expect to be the logically purified characteristics and sensibilities of a modern and a postmodern subculture. These provide the necessary conceptual clarification to enable us to assess empirically the extent to which a sample of contemporary subculturalists display a postmodern sensibility.

A useful point of departure for our analysis is the work of those writers who have theorized postmodernity or postmodernism in broad transitional terms. One such opinion is that we are moving towards a postindustrial age, a theme found in the work of both Lyotard (1984) and Baudrillard (1983b). Lyotard talks of the production of new forms of computerized knowledge in an information society. Modern knowledge, Lyotard claims, was founded upon totalizing claims to legitimacy and rational progress – what he calls the 'grand narratives' of Marxism, Humanism, Science, Feminism, etc. In the face of contemporary scepticism towards these grand narratives, postmodern knowledge can no longer appeal to universal validity, but has atomized into a plurality of localized 'language games' (1984: 17). Certainty and absolutism must be replaced by indeterminacy and difference. Baudrillard (1983b) theorizes how 'information networks' and media proliferation have brought about a transition from an 'industrial order' of mass production to a society premised on the *re*production of signs and images (ibid.: 100). Whereas images once reflected and represented reality, or even produced an ideological mystification of reality (as in the Marxist sense), the image now serves to distract us from the fact that there is no reality to which it seems to refer. Indeed, Baudrillard goes so far as to claim that free-floating signs reach a stage in which they refer only to each other: the image 'bears no relation to any reality whatsoever: it is its own pure simulacrum' (ibid.: 11). This is the order of simulation, 'the generation by models of a real without origin or reality: a hyperreal' (ibid.: 2).

Other writers have seen the postmodern less in terms of a break with the existing mode of production than as a development within it. Jameson (1984, 1985, 1991), for example, theorizes postmodernism as the 'cultural dominant' of post-war, multinational/late/consumer capitalism. In citing as one defining feature of postmodernism the transformation of reality into images, and claiming that almost everything in the social becomes mediated by the cultural, Jameson breaks down the very distinction between the cultural and socioeconomic realms on which his model is based. Two distinguishing characteristics of this culture, as outlined by Jameson, are its 'schizophrenic' fragmentation of time, and its 'depthlessness', the foregrounding of 'spectacle' over narrative. Lash and Urry (1988) similarly propose an 'elective affinity' between postmodern culture and the post-war stage of disorganized capitalism. According to the authors, postmodern cultural forms foreground impact, pleasure and spectacle, signifying through the visual image and the electronic impulse (ibid.: 287). Through the media of television, advertising, video, and home computers postmodernism pervades both high and popular culture, instilling itself into the fabric of everyday life. By so doing it transgresses the 'modern' boundaries that once demarcated culture and society, image and reality, original and reproduction, art and everyday life.

These analyses provide a useful beginning for an understanding of the postmodern. In their different ways they tend to concur in their identification of a major postmodern impulse: that it collapses modern boundaries and hierarchies, both vertically and horizontally, producing as a consequence a culture that is both superficial and fragmented. Yet the above discussions are restricted in that they all effectively utilize periodizing conceptions of society: postindustrial follows industrial, or modernism is succeeded by postmodernism. This tends to obscure the differences within and the continuities across different historical periods. What I want to argue is that, far from there having been just one modern period, there have been two very different modernities, a modernity of 'order' and a modernity of 'disorder' (Rojek 1995), or what Lash and Friedman (1992) call 'high' (or Enlightenment) modernity and 'low' (or Aesthetic) modernity (see also Berman 1987; Lovatt and Purkis 1996; Hetherington 1998).

As Lash and Friedman outline the distinction, enlightenment modernity is premised on scientific reason and is characterized by '*stasis*', '*fixity*' and 'universality' (1992: 1; original emphasis). We think here of Weber's figure of the rationally motivated individual; also of Weber's warnings on the 'iron cage' of bureaucratic capitalism. Aesthetic modernity, on the other hand, is very much about expressivity and the experience of rapid social change – 'a matter of *movement*, of *flux*, of *change*, of *unpredictability*' (ibid.). Its origins lie in Baudelaire's Paris and Simmel's Berlin (see Frisby 1985a), with its 1980s embodiment in Berman's New York. My argument for invoking this distinction is that while the postmodern represents a break with many of the tendencies in enlightenment modernity, it expresses substantial continuities with aesthetic modernity, and could be regarded as an intensification of such features (Kellner 1992: 174).

The Paradoxes of Modernity: 'From Modern Styles to Postmodern Codes'

Although Daniel Bell (1976) has stressed the contradictory relationship that exists between a rational economy organized on the basis of efficiency and a hedonistic culture ruled by the principle of self-gratification, it is possible to posit rationalism and Romanticism as contrasting cultural traditions of modernity locked together into a symbiotic relationship (C. Campbell 1987). As we saw in the last chapter, the origins of modern production lie in ascetic puritanism, founded upon rationalization, utilitarianism and regulation, while the sphere of modern consumption obtains its dynamic from pietistic puritanism, Romanticism and an ethic of sensibility. The series of contrasts suggested here, between stasis and dynamism, rational and aesthetic, puritan and hedonist, are particularly pronounced within the paradoxical phenomenon of fashion. There is, as Flügel (1930) has noted, a central ambiguity in fashion between the desire for adornment and the puritan requirement for modesty. Wilson, likewise, sees enshrined within fashion the contradiction between the hedonism of a secular capitalism or modernity and the 'asceticism of Judaeo-Christian culture' with its emphasis on repression and conformity (1985: 9). For König, the central paradox of dress is that it clearly entails both 'a compulsion to change [and] a compulsion to adaptation . . . to the new kind of style' (1973: 54). Simmel clearly agrees, seeing fashion combining 'the attraction of differentiation and change with that of similarity and conformity' (quoted in Frisby 1985a: 98). Baudrillard, continuing in a similar vein, talks of the apparent contradiction in modernity between 'a linear time of technical progress . . . and . . . a cyclical time of fashion' (1993: 89).

From one perspective, the social upheavals and dislocations of the past two centuries, the sweeping away of traditional economic and cultural structures where 'all that is solid melts into air' (Marx and Engels 1979: 83; Berman 1987), have defined an insecure epoch of modernity in direct opposition to the stability, certitude and predictability of traditional society. As Wilson puts it: 'the colliding dynamism, the thirst for change and the heightened sensation that characterize city societies particularly of modern industrial capitalism go up to make this "modernity", and the hysteria and exaggeration of fashion well express it' (1985: 10). But if Wilson sees a congruence between this 'aesthetic modernity' and the phenomenon of fashion, there is the other modernity. This 'Enlightenment modernity' was the attempt to refound and stabilize the principles of truth, justice and beauty upon rational foundations opposing the pre-modern 'irrationalities of myth, religion, superstition' (Harvey 1991: 12). It is therefore a modernity of certainty, universalism and immutability, a legitimization of authority upon the bedrock principles of rationality, science and technological progress. It was this 'Enlightenment modernity' that was to provide our dominant conceptions of modern fashion from the late nineteenth century until the 1960s.

> Of course, the history of fashion does have a significant and well-attested modernist phase. The insistence on purity and function, along with the hatred of superfluous ornament, that are expressed in the work of architects like Miles van der Rohe, artists like Piet Mondrian and theorists like Alfred Loos, resulted in attempts to rationalize dress, and figures like Victor Tatlin, Kasmir Malevich, Sonia Delaunay, Walter Gropius and Jacobus Ord were all interested in extending the modernist revolution in the arts to matters of clothing. It is even possible to conceive of the invention of something like a 'modernist body', the slim and functional female figure of the 1920s, liberated from the corset and the paraphernalia of female ornament (Connor 1991: 190).

It is instructive to preface a discussion on modern fashion with Connor's quotation, because it places an emphasis on both the avant-garde culture of 1920s artistic modernism and its congruence with the broader 'rationalist' culture of modernity. Yet artistic modernism contained elements that were symptomatic of both the Enlightenment and the aesthetic dimensions to modernity. In making what is virtually this argument, Wollen draws on some telling and familiar contrasts:

> [the] antimony between the 'pictorial' and the 'decorative', like that between 'functional' and 'ornamental', is basic to the dominant modernist aesthetic. It is one of a whole series of similar antinomies which can be mapped on to each other: engineer/leisure class, production/consumption, active/passive, masculine/feminine, reality principle/pleasure principle, machine/body, west/east . . . Of course, these are not exactly homologous, but they form a cascade of oppositions, each of which suggests another, step by step (Wollen 1987: 7–8).

Connor also cites this article, drawing attention to Wollen's argument for 'an alternative history of dress design to be discerned in modernism, a history of a continuing infatuation with decorative excess and stylistic extravagance' (Connor 1991: 191). Modernity, in the epochal sense of the term, was also a witness to decorative trends in fashion not usually associated with 'high modernism', including that of women's dress in the Edwardian era: exactly that excess of ornament that the inter-war female figure was 'liberated from'. Indeed, we might go further and hypothesize that since both a rationalist-utilitarian and a romantic-aesthetic ethic are implicated in the development of modernity, fashions throughout this epoch would display both sets of characteristics, but in a cyclical pattern. Empirical evidence, although open to interpretation, does seem to bear witness to this hypothesis – see Holdsworth (1989), Tyrrell (1986), Wilson (1985, 1990), Lurie (1992).

The sociological variables of class and gender must, however, be considered in any such analysis. Fashion, in the sense of aesthetic display and rapid change, is a gendered term in the history of modern dress: women have 'fashion'; men, sober, sombre and static, have 'style'. This gender division, which is predicated upon the relationship of masculinity to a puritan business ethic (Flügel 1930; König 1973; Wilson 1990) and the linking of femininity through Romanticism to consumption (C. Campbell 1987), is also cross-cut by the cleavage of social class. Historical accounts (Steedman 1986; Holdsworth 1989) have shown how the dimensions of middle-class/working-class have tended to work themselves out along the axis of decoration-fashion/utility-necessity. Yet, despite this presence of a decorative-aesthetic element, it is the functional and utilitarian axis of modern dress codes that possesses a particular affinity with the rational precepts of Fordist mass production techniques. Utilizing Taylor's principles of 'scientific management', Fordism generated a standardized set of products tied to mass markets (J. Clarke 1991: Ch. 4; Harvey 1991: Ch. 8; Crook *et al.* 1992: Ch. 6). Hence the uniformity of 'looks' in an era of mass consumption; what, in an American context, Thomas Frank has described as 'a time of intolerance for difference, of look-alike commuters clad in grey flannel' (1998: 10).[3] So even through 'the clothing industry could never be as Fordist, as concentrated and as Taylorist as most other sectors because it entails a much higher turnover of styles' (Lash and Urry 1994: 176), the prevailing image of twentieth century fashion is one of uniformity, predictability and conformity, its form governed by the dictates of functional rationality (Negrin 1999).

It is exactly this dominant conception of Enlightenment modernity against which the postmodern is defined. In contrast to a modernism of purity, functionality and utilitarianism, to be fashionable in postmodernism is to involve oneself in aesthetic play, with the focus on hedonism, pleasure and spectacle, 'a return to ornament, decoration and stylistic eclecticism' (Connor 1991: 191). Wilson, in agreement, acknowledges how: 'fashion does appear to express such a fragmented sensibility particularly well – its obsession with surface, novelty and style for style's sake highly congruent with this sort of post-modernist aesthetic' (1985: 11). From this viewpoint, postmodernity is highly complicit with the aesthetic impulses of modern consumer capitalism.

> Fashion is what has become the propelling momentum, the dominant MODE of consumption itself . . . As both the organizational thematic and fluctuating dynamic of consumption, fashion is rapidly instituting itself as the universal code under which all other previous cultural codes are subsumed . . . Far from signalling the end of capitalism, postmodernity then can be seen as its purest stage, one in which fashion represents the dominant expression and widening extension of the logic of the commodity form (Faurschou 1990: 235).

In the era of postmodernity the development of flexible forms of technology and the shift from Fordist to post-Fordist production techniques (Murray 1989) have generated 'the capacity to produce an expandable range of highly specialized products to meet rapidly changing market demand' (Crook *et al.* 1992: 179). The acceleration in the emergence of new fashions has been matched by an accelerated turnover time in consumption. Connor talks of the 'furious rush of images which is the fashion industry itself' (1991: 193). Fashion and style have become correspondingly more heterogeneous (Kratz and Reimer 1998). This is, indeed, a time which comes 'after the masses' (Hebdige 1989). With the advent of 'specialized consumption' and 'market segmentation', 'lifestyle enclaves' are said to be losing their correspondence to, and indeed superseding as a basis for social stratification, modernist grids of class, gender, age and ethnicity (Evans and Thornton 1989; Mort 1989; Crook *et al.* 1992; Nixon 1992). 'Modernist styles', once firmly structured along these traditional lines of demarcation, become 'postmodernist codes' (Jameson 1991) available for the pleasure of the (apparently ironic, reflexive and knowing) postmodern consumers, who wish to construct their own identities through the wearing of 'stylistic masks' (Jameson 1985: 114). The prevailing mood of the times is best captured through the slogans of Ewen and Ewen: 'Today there is no fashion, only fashions.' 'No rules, only choices.' 'Everyone can be anyone' (1982: 249–51).[4]

In an attempt to chart these changes, Evans and Thornton note that 'since the decline in the 1960s of a seasonal "look" of which women could be sure, mainstream fashion has deliberately constructed itself as a variety of "looks". But in the 1980s the turnover of looks speeded up hysterically' (1989: 59). Connor also views the sixties as being something of a watershed, citing 'the abundant multiplicity of styles and accelerated rhythm of fashion from the prosperous years of the 1960s onwards' (1991: 191). Similarly, for Wilson, 'the "confusion" that so puzzled fashion writers in the 1970s, the apparent ending of the orderly evolution of one style out of another, is explicable once it is seen as part of postmodernism' (1990: 223). Postmodernism also begins in the 1970s for Wilson and Taylor (1989: 191), while Quentin Bell sees the middle of this decade as 'so heterogeneous that it does seem to me to be difficult to speak of a fashion for the year 1974' (1992: 175). Kaiser *et al.* (1991) claim that now even the last bastions of puritanism are susceptible to a decorative impulse:

> The tendency towards a breakdown of conventional rules may be found in a much more limited extent in the American business world . . . Even in some professional contexts, in a subtle manner within conventional bounds, men as well as women seem to have more freedom (if they are so inclined) to experiment with color and accessories (for example, braces or suspenders for men, brightly colored suits for women) (Kaiser *et al.* 1991: 183).

Elsewhere, in a comparison with the modern, Lash manages to capture together both sensibilities of postmodern dress – the fragmented and the aesthetic:

> Consider for example a photo of British (soccer) football supporters in the interwar period. The similarity and 'mass-ness' of their dress is striking to the contemporary observer. Compare this, then, with the very diversity of clothing styles and associated subcultures among British working-class youth in more recent times . . . the shift has not just been of one from mass-ness to specialization but also from a focus on function to a concern with style (Lash 1990: 39).

While Lash looks at soccer supporters,[5] my own example focuses on the outfits worn by the players. Whereas twenty years ago, British soccer club strips were relatively plain, unadorned and functional, today we find a strange combination of lurid colours (fluorescent salmon pinks and lime greens) arranged in intricate designs using a plethora of decoration (motifs, numbers in imitation 3-D, superimposed letters). We even have instances of 1920s pastiche with lace-up V-necks. Furthermore, whereas team designs used to remain comparatively stable over a number of seasons with only minimal changes, clubs today issue radically new versions of their kit at a much faster rate, with manufacturers and retailers only too eager to announce the arrival in the sportshops of this season's new Manchester United, Arsenal or Liverpool third-choice away strip.

Our views of modern mainstream fashion consumption are defined negatively against what is perceived to be the active postmodern consumer. Certainly, given the dominant conception of modern fashion as uniform, massified and predictable, it is easy to understand how it might be consumed 'passively', for outfits to be taken over 'wholesale' without the need for symbolic creativity by consumers.[6] We might think here of the mass-produced 'ready-to-wear' suit, or the costume with matching accessories. Modernist 'appearance management' would, in other words, tend towards the uncomplicated, the utilitarian and the functional. In semiotic terms the codes associated with particular forms of dress would be relatively unambiguous and tied unproblematically to particular contexts; in other words, the mode of signification would be realist. Postmodernism complicates this process. 'In postmodernity fashion is more ambiguous than in modernity' (Kratz and Reimer 1998: 208). Kaiser *et al.* observe how 'modernist American culture, based on puritanism, industrialism and utilitarianism, has traditionally demanded univocal, rather than ambiguous forms of discourse. The business suit is a prime example . . . this rational, technological ethos of univocality [is] a "flight from ambiguity". Postmodern capitalism, however, problematizes this flight' (1991: 171).

This problematization has at its root what might be termed the postmodern expansion of eclecticism: a greater variety of styles now travel at a faster rate than ever before, allowing consumers greater scope for their creative and aesthetic outlets. The result is an 'emphasis on individual diversity' (Tseëlon 1995: 127), 'a promotion of do-it-yourself style', where 'postmodern appearance management may be compared with the formal technique of collage' (Kaiser *et al.* 1991: 173–4). This trend towards the construction of complex appearances through the self-conscious act of stylistic *bricolage* is particularly notable in Willis's (1990) study of the 'grounded aesthetics' and 'symbolic creativity' of youth culture. As Willis discovered, 'young people don't just buy passively or uncritically. They always transform the meaning of bought goods, appropriating and recontextualizing mass-market styles . . . Most young people combine elements of clothing to create new meanings . . . and sometimes reject the normative definitions and categories of 'fashion' promoted by the clothing industry' (1990: 85).

While the decoding of modernist style was facilitated by its 'univocality' – a limited availability of signifiers and a stable anchorage in a particular space–time context – it was also assisted by the clear demarcation of specific social groups, each with its own style boundaries. Postmodernity, however, entails the fragmentation of mass identities (Lash and Urry 1988; Lyon 1999), even to the extent that the boundaries between established groups are breaking down. This is what Lash (1990) terms 'de-differentiation', a reversal of the modernist tendency towards the differentiation of cultural spheres. A surfeit of signs and a breaking down of boundaries might problematize the way in which social groups use style as a means of classification and demarcation (Featherstone 1992). As differentiated unities are replaced by a similarity of difference, 'appearance perception' becomes a hazardous undertaking, an ever-increasing number of interpretations being possible. If modern main-stream fashion was 'readerly', then Kaiser *et al.* would appear to see postmodernist style as analogous to Barthes's 'writerly' text (Barthes 1975), where 'signifiers, it seems, hold a certain privilege over what is signified' (Kaiser *et al.* 1991: 174).

Subcultural Style: From the Grand Narratives of Modernity to Hyperfragmentation in the Postmodern Global Village.

In the last chapter we examined the pioneering work on youth subcultural theory that emerged from the CCCS during the 1970s. We are now able to locate this neo-Marxist theory firmly within an Enlightenment conception of the world (Lovatt and Purkis 1996: 258). Its emancipatory meta-narrative, which claims to provide a 'scientific' analysis of society, its totalizing conception of the social formation within which the specific element under study must be reinstated, the sense of linear time along which these successive subcultures are seen to unfold, the portrayal of subcultures as externally differentiated, yet internally homogeneous groups, existing in clear opposition to each other and to conventional style: all these characteristics betray a high modernist ideal. Yet while this modernist paradigm is predicated upon a 'depth model' of the social formation from which a whole host of subcultural oppositions were derived – subcultural/conventional, essence/appearance, class/consumption, authentic/manufactured, style-as-resistance/style-as-fashion, and so on – postmodernity collapses these oppositions. In particular, it undercuts them by problematizing the distinction between representations and reality. For while Marxism was concerned to stress the misleading character of appearances, postmodernity 'takes pleasure in the play of surfaces and derides the search for depth as mere nostalgia' (Gitlin 1989: 52). One might begin here with Jameson's reference to 'a society of the image or the simulacrum' (1991: 48), and consider Lash's (1990) contention that postmodern communication represents a triumph of the figural over the discursive, before arriving our final destination, the wholly artificial, yet all-encompassing, hermetically sealed, computer-generated world of virtual reality, prophesied by Kroker and Cook (1991) as the logical conclusion to the encroachment of the visual into the province of the real.

The increasingly central role of the visual media as an image bank from which knowledge of fashion is derived has not gone unnoticed by sociologists and cultural commentators alike. McRobbie talks of 'the expansion of media goods and services which has come into being in the last ten years, producing more fashion magazines, more television from independent companies, more reviews about other media events, more media personalities, more media items about other media phenomena, and so on' (1989: 38–9). Savage heralds the rise of 'Culture as a Commodity, the biggest growth business of the lot: the proliferation of television, video (especially amongst lower income groups), computers and information' (1989: 171). Willis documents how the young people in his study 'use the media to understand and keep up with the latest fashions. They get ideas about clothes from sources such as television programmes, like The Clothes Show, fashion and music magazines, or from the personal dress styles of particular pop groups' (1990: 86). Television, particularly MTV, along with video, and the style magazines of the 1980s, *i-D*, *Blitz* and *The Face* – which are primarily visual rather than textual in their impact – are most usually quoted as the postmodern paradigm case.[7] As Evans and Thornton tellingly comment, 'at the heart of the new magazines was the idea that identity (*i-D*) is forged by appearance' (1989: 60).

Here, we might discern the homogenizing impulse of this scenario: the progressive obliteration of cultural difference following the weakening of local powers of resistance to the inexorable stylistic globalizing processes of the mediascape. Yet an aesthetic, fragmentary tendency is clearly detectable in Jameson, particularly his understanding of schizophrenia as a postmodern sensibility, 'a series of pure and unrelated presents in time' (1985: 27). Such an emphasis fits well, claims Harvey, with the 'ephemerality', 'instantaneity', 'disposability' and volatility that is said to typify postmodern 'fashions, products [and] production techniques' (1991: 285, 291). What faces us is not therefore necessarily the stifling of change by an all-encompassing 'astral empire of signs', but rather the paradox of a McLuhanian global village of ever-fragmenting fashions, 'an eclectic blend of cross-cultural commodities' (Kaiser 1990: 406), which forces into prominence the proclivities of consumers to become sartorial *bricoleurs* (Kratz and Reimer 1998: 208–9). As commodity production, exchange, and creative appropriation intensify, signs become free-floating, travelling towards the point at which they become irrevocably divorced from their original cultural contexts.

> Individuals obtaining ideas about what to wear may neither be aware of, nor necessarily care about the ideology to which styles have originally referred. Hence PLO headscarves become trendy on the streets of New York City, skulls and crossbones become insignia on children's clothing, and Rastafarian dreadlocks are preempted by runaway fashion models and rock (not necessarily reggae) musicians (Kaiser *et al.* 1991: 176).

Lipovetsky has remarked how 'our borrowings no longer have a fixed origin: they are taken from myriad sources' (1994: 233). So have social relations become saturated with an excess of information in the form of shifting cultural signs and simulations to the extent that the meaning of style is unable to stabilize (Craik 1994: 8) and we are faced with what Baudrillard (1983a) has called 'The End of the Social'? Perhaps, like their attitude towards God, Baudrillard's masses retain only the image of fashion, 'never the idea' (ibid.: 7). Similarly, Jameson's (1991) 'breakdown in the signifying chain', which leads to the destruction of narrative utterance and its replacement by the intensification of aesthetic 'affect', can be interpreted as having identical consequences for fashion. In both cases, meaning gives way to spectacle. Style is now worn for its look, not for any underlying message; or rather, the look is now the message.

Narrative meaning is intimately bound up with questions of temporality. Lyotard's *grands recits* are a testimony to the optimism of the Enlightenment project, with its progressive notion of history. At an individual and personal level, the deferment of gratification and the construction of lifelong narratives are equally symptomatic of this same modernist confidence, investment and faith in the future. With the postmodern fragmentation of these ongoing, linear narratives and the move from the rationality of 'clock time' to 'instantaneous time', a projection into the future appears neither possible nor desirable. Rather than wait for an empty promise, we are said to 'want the future now' (Lash and Urry 1994: Ch. 9). Hence that remarkable surge of contemporary fascination with nostalgia, its stylistic manifestation being an 'accelerating tendency in the 1980s to ransack history for key items of dress, in a seemingly eclectic and haphazard manner . . . This instant recall on history, fuelled by the superfluity of images thrown up by the media, has produced a non-stop fashion parade in which "different decades are placed together with no historical continuity"' (McRobbie 1989: 23, 40).

Here, we enter Jameson's world of pastiche, 'in which stylistic innovation is no longer possible, all that is left is to imitate dead styles, to speak through the masks and with the voices of the styles in the imaginary museum' (1985: 115). Faced with this postmodern predicament, subcultural styles have two options: they can feed off each other in a cannibalistic orgy of cross-fertilization, destroying their own internal boundaries in the process; or indulge in the stylistic revivalism that Johnston (1993) has derisively termed 'post-punk nostalgia'. The teddy boy, mod, skinhead and hippy subcultures have all made their reappearance since the end of 'linear' subcultural time in the late 1970s (Redhead 1990, 1993). We must also mention in this context the contemporary interest in second-hand dress or 'retro style' (Carter 1983; McRobbie 1989). And, as a virtual *bricolage*, a Burroughs cut-up, of previous subcultural styles, punk really does seem to have been the historical turning-point here. Punk style defies interpretation, 'refuses meaning' (Hebdige 1979), has heralded the subcultural break from modernity to postmodernity.

If post-punk stylistic revivals are examples of pastiche, then, as Jameson (1984) would have it, they can say nothing new, represent nothing more than our 'pop images' and 'cultural stereotypes' of the past, for the peculiarity of postmodern time has now and for evermore precluded any possibility of subcultural 'originality'. The concept of 'authenticity' must likewise be expunged from the postmodern vocabulary. The all-encompassing power of the contemporary mass media has ensured that there can no longer be a sanctuary for the original, 'pure', creative moment of subcultural innovation that preceded the onset of the contaminating processes of commercialization, commodification and diffusion. Redhead is a proponent of a 'weak' version of this thesis, where 'post-punk subcultures have been characterized by a speeding up of the time between points of "authenticity" and manufacture' (1991b: 94). McRobbie, however, proposes a stronger version whereby 'the "implosionary" effect of the mass media means that in the 1980s youth styles and fashions *are born into* the media. There is an "instantaneity" which replaces the old period of subcultural incubation' (1989: 39; my emphasis).

We can make two criticisms of this thesis that proclaims the postmodern death of subcultural originality and authenticity. The first reinstates authenticity by pointing to the increased potential for *bricolage* in postmodern appearance management (Kaiser 1990). Hence, the postmodern proliferation and fragmentation of style involves the reassembling, juxtapositioning and blending of elements, thus implying at least a minimum degree of creativity, originality and uniqueness in the resulting ensembles. As Barnard has argued, *bricolage*, unlike pastiche, does suggest 'the creation of new meanings' (1996: 167). The second criticism admits to subcultural inauthenticity, but refuses to see this as specifically postmodern. It argues that there never was a privileged moment of 'authentic' subcultural inception untainted by media, commercial and entrepreneurial influences in the manner that modernist theory suggested, for 'media representations provide the ideological framework within which subcultures can represent themselves, shaping as well as limiting what they can say ... Hebdige claims that the punks did not so much express the alienation they felt from mainstream society as dramatise contemporary media and political discourse about Britain's "decline"' (Beezer 1992: 109).

McRobbie's example is also punk, but again her point has a general applicability.

The very idea that style could be purchased over the counter went against the grain of those analyses which saw the adoption of punk style as an act of creative defiance far removed from the mundane act of buying. The role of McLaren and

Westwood was also downgraded for the similar reason that punk was seen as a kind of collective creative impulse. To focus on a designer and an art-school entrepreneur would have been to undermine the 'purity' or 'authenticity' of the subculture (McRobbie 1989: 25).

But to concur with these two criticisms does not necessarily weaken the postmodern claim. For whereas modernist subcultural 'originality' and 'authenticity' are defined in terms of an attempted solution to real social contradictions, postmodern theory denies that there exists any province of the social to which subcultural styles can be a cultural response. Hebdige is still intent on holding on to a modernist explanation of 'postmodern' post-punk subcultures – 'the revival of the mod subculture . . . cannot be interpreted as an arbitrary reworking of purely aesthetic codes. In its revived form, the style was being used to express, reflect and "magically" resolve a *specific* set of problems and contradictions' (1981: 93; original emphasis). Yet, in postmodern terms, subcultures *are* 'purely aesthetic codes', for styles have become subject to time–space compression (Harvey 1991), a dislocation from their original temporal–spatial origins. 'The firm and exclusive referents that once guided the teddy boys or the mods in their distinctive options in clothing or music are apparently no longer available' (Chambers 1990: 69). In the wake of the irrevocable loss of these referents we cannot experience the real but 'live everywhere already in an "aesthetic" hallucination of reality' (Baudrillard 1983b: 148). Following Baudrillard's logic (1983a) subcultural styles have become simulacra, copies with no originals. By inscribing visual signs upon their bodies, subculturalists revel in this simulation culture, refusing meaning in the name of the spectacle, becoming, in turn, mere models themselves and 'imploding' into the media. In this move from production to reproduction, subcultural simulacra become *hyperreal* as reality is eclipsed.

This might all sound somewhat abstruse, but one particularly good empirical example can help to illustrate a point far more clearly and immediately than long theoretical exposition. For that reason I will close this section by quoting at some length Kotarba's (1991) experience while conducting research on the US heavy metal rock scene. As he takes up the story, he was about to see a heavy metal Christian rock band. He continues:

When I entered the club just before opening and approached the stage, I was struck by a most unusual figure: a young man sporting a four-color mohawk haircut, facial make-up appropriate for warriors from some prehistoric tribe, all sorts of dagger and paperclip earrings, rusty chains around his neck, and just about every other indication that I was in the presence of an angry or anarchistic punk rocker. What could he possibly be doing here, looking to beat up some unsuspecting and well-scrubbed little Christian rocker? I approached him and found out that *he* was the little Christian rocker and, perhaps most surprisingly, that he was a Southern Baptist metal head! (Kotarba 1991: 46).

This leads Kotarba to remark on just how puzzling all this would be to the modernist theorists of the CCCS. What would be the underlying significance or structural meaning to this person's identity? What are the problems or contradictions being addressed? What, exactly, is being resisted? From a postmodernist viewpoint, however: 'the significance of styles need go no further than the immediate affective effects they elicit. Culture is merely cognitive and symbolic veneer. Postmodernism suggested to me that contradictions in cultural forms are to be expected and appreciated, not automatically and compulsively explained away' (ibid.).

The Post-Subculturalist?

If we do grant complete acceptance to the full implications of the postmodern, then it is probably apt to talk of postmodernity as the era of the post-subculturalist. Post-subculturalists no longer have any sense of subcultural 'authenticity' where inception is rooted in particular socio-temporal contexts and tied to underlying structural relations. In fact the post-subculturalist will experience all the signs of the subculture of their choosing time and time again through the media before inscribing these signifiers on their own bodies. Choosing is the operative word here, for post-subculturalists revel in the availability of subcultural choice. While, for example, modernist theory stressed a series of discrete subcultural styles unfolding in linear time up until the late 1970s, the postmodern 1980s and 1990s have been decades of subcultural fragmentation and proliferation, with a glut of revivals, hybrids and transformations, and the co-existence of myriad styles at any one point in time. This enables post-subculturalists to engage in 'Style Surfing' (Polhemus 1996), to move quickly and freely from one style to another as they wish; indeed, this high degree of sartorial mobility is the source of playfulness and pleasure. They do not have to worry about contradictions between their selected subcultural identities, for there are no rules, there is no authenticity, no ideological commitment, merely a stylistic game to be played.

If modern subcultures existed in a state of mutual opposition with members maintaining strong stylistic and ideological boundaries through expressed comparisons with other such groups, then in postmodernity the need for boundary maintenance becomes negligible as the lines of subcultural demarcation dissolve. We should as a result expect to discover that post-subculturalists, who exemplify ephemeral attachments to a variety of styles, find it problematic to make strong comparisons with out-groups. Following the logic of Kellner (1992) we can therefore understand postmodern subcultural identities to be multiple and fluid. Constituted through consumption, subcultural style is no longer articulated around the modernist structuring relations of class, gender or ethnicity. Instead, these modernist looks become recycled as free-floating signifiers, enabling subcultural identity to be constructed through the succession of styles that 'Style Surfers' try on and cast off. Chambers surveys the postmodern catwalk upon which the post-subculturalists play their game:

> Subcultures, and youth cultures in general, have gradually separated out their particular imagery from the world of daily labour and immediate social contexts. Allowed to float free of immediate referents the result has been a kaleidoscope of styles, and an increasingly sophisticated semiology of goods, that, drawn into an endless shopping list and an ever more rapid stylistic turnover, has spun right out of the orbit of a precise subcultural history. What it has left behind is a rich coffer for eventual retro fashions, ironic revisiting, suggestive appropriations and irreverent revivals (Chambers 1990: 68–9).

But perhaps the very concept of subculture is becoming less applicable in postmodernity, for the breakdown of mass society has ensured that there is no longer a coherent dominant culture against which a subculture can express its resistance (Evans 1997). If, moreover, it is 'the communication of significant *difference*' that is the point of spectacular subcultural style (Hebdige 1979: 102; original emphasis), then, as Connor realizes, 'such an analysis encounters difficulties when faced with the fact that this visibility of diverse and stylistically distinct groups is part of the official or dominant mode of advertising and the media in the West . . . Under these circumstances, visibility and self-proclamation may have become a market requirement rather than a mode of liberation' (1991: 195). And as Beezer concludes, 'without this surface difference, subcultures slip from view, to the point where their existence can be thrown into question' (1992: 113). And while this may eclipse subcultural visibility, is there still an analytical distinction to be drawn? It would appear not. For as we have seen, if modernist subcultures were defined in terms of a series of theoretical oppositions to non-subcultural style, then postmodernity dissolves such distinctions.

It remains to be seen what implications this has for subcultures as a struggle within ideology, a battle for possession of the sign. Crook *et al.* feel that 'the critical point is not that style cannot resist, clearly it can in many registers, but contests between resistance and conformity do not conform to a single line between the subordinate and the hegemonic' (1992: 72). But what, if anything, is being resisted? Gitlin (1989: 58) has argued that a postmodern politics embraces pluralist and libertarian concerns. Post-subcultural ideology will, in other words, value the individual over the collective, elevate difference and heterogeneity over collectivism and conformity, Or perhaps subcultures are just another form of de-politicized play in the postmodern pleasuredome, where emphasis is placed on the surface qualities of the spectacle at the expense of any underlying ideologies. For the post-subculturalists, the trappings of spectacular style are their right of admission to a costume party, a masquerade, a hedonistic escape into a Blitz Culture fantasy characterized by political indifference.

I would like to conclude by reiterating that the traits I have identified as postmodern are, by and large, not novel, but can be found in strains of aesthetic modernity. I suggested earlier in this chapter that the CCCS approach could be designated as 'modern' in an Enlightenment sense, for it postulates a succession of 'authentic', cohesive and discrete subcultures unfolding in linear time. There is, however, an undoubted conceptual ambiguity in the CCCS work. In Chapter 2, I remarked on the process of subcultural incorporation, of 'defusion and diffusion'. Upon closer examination, we find this process leading in contradictory directions: on the one hand, towards increasing uniformity; on the other, to dispersal and diversity. Hebdige (1979: 96), for example, talks of subcultural styles being commodified on a 'mass scale', only then to remark on the 'variations' (in this instance, of punk) thus produced. These two meanings emerge from an explicitly recognized contradiction 'between the demands of marketing – novelty, rapid turnover of fashion, trendiness and discontinuity – and the demands of production, for standardisation, the ease and economy of continuity and scale' (J. Clarke 1986: 185). The first set of terms have a distinct postmodern or post-Fordist feel, with the latter evoking Fordist precepts of modernity.

In line with the generally modernist project of the CCCS work, Clarke does suggest the latter movement to be dominant (ibid.: 187–8), a process particularly notable in the creation of a mass consumption style based on mod. We can, however, dispute this assumption. The submerged aesthetic dimension to this approach indicates that subcultural styles never were the pure, abstract and homogeneous entities that the CCCS made them out to be, and that the commercializing process did not lead only towards homogenization. Evans, for instance, argues that Hebdige's discussion of mod 'does not distinguish between mods who became skins, mods who became hippies, and mods who became jazz casuals' (Evans 1997: 179). There is, in other words, a hidden history to post-war subcultures, identified here by Osgerby:

Many accounts of post-war youth subcultures have also overlooked the dynamic quality to their styles. All too frequently subcultural forms are discussed as though they were immutably fixed phenomena, frozen statically at a particular point in history. In reality nothing could be further from the truth. Constant change and flux have been endemic to the universe of youth subcultures. Styles have continually developed over time making sense in different ways for different groups of youngsters at different historical moments (Osgerby 1998: 76).

My suggestion is that postmodernity entails an *intensification* of these aesthetic characteristics, which have *always* been present in the development of subcultures.

How might we account for this intensification? We have in this chapter established that Romanticism and the dynamic of consumer culture connect the experience of aesthetic modernity to features foregrounded in the postmodern. It is this which, according to Harvey, 'appears to be the most startling fact about postmodernism: its total acceptance of the ephemerality, fragmentation, discontinuity and the chaotic that formed the one [aesthetic] half of Baudelaire's conception of modernity' (1991: 44). That postmodernism is intimately related to changes in consumer culture is one of its most commonly recognized features (Featherstone 1992; Strinati 1995; Lury 1996). Waugh closes the circle by claiming that 'postmodernism as an aesthetic and body of thought can be seen as a late-flowering Romanticism' (1992: 3). What, though, is the precise nature of the relationship between Romanticism and the postmodern?

It is Colin Campbell (1987) who takes us a large part of the way in establishing this connection. In the last chapter we remarked upon his thesis that the attitudes necessary for the development of modern consumer culture have their origin in the sensibilities of the Romantic movement of the early nineteenth century. There is, as Campbell points out, a close correspondence (an 'elective affinity') between the Romantic's perennial quest to find emotional pleasure in all experiences, and modern consumers' ceaseless desire to satisfy imaginative longings (that dream car or holiday) that underpins their restless pursuit of novelty. The relationship outlined here is an ironic one, for the Romantics were concerned above all with the moral principle of self-renewal through art, and certainly did not condone either the selfish satisfaction of wants or the commercialization of pleasure (ibid.: 207). Yet, as Campbell argues, Romantic idealism can unintentionally generate periods of 'self-seeking hedonism' and vice versa (ibid.: 210). This intimate connection between 'the Romantic ethic and the spirit of modern consumerism' can be seen in the way that subsequent flowerings of countercultural activity, in the 1890s, 1920s and 1960s, are accompanied by a period of consumer boom.

It is easier to understand this relationship if we examine more closely the Romantic values of the 1960s 'hippy' counterculture.[8] The mistake we must avoid making is to regard Romanticism and its embodiment in the counter-culture as wholly antagonistic to capitalism and consumer culture, for it acted as both critique and catalyst. It is true that the hippy movement manifested itself as a withdrawal from the dominant achievement-oriented values of the puritan work ethic. This was, above all, an attack not only on the moral imperative of work as a desirable end in itself, but on the associated bourgeois values of regulation, self-discipline and restraint. Yet by continually breaking free from traditional and restrictive cultural codes, each generation of Romantic cultural innovators continues to provide modern consumerism with its dynamic. It is precisely through the desire to give free reign to creative self-expression and promote the values of play and pleasure that the counterculture is highly complicit with the central capitalist values of entrepreneurial individualism and consumer creativity (see Heelas 1996). As Clarke *et al.* have said of this relationship, the counterculture's 'hedonism, its narcissism, its permissiveness, its search for immediate gratification, its anti-authoritarianism, its moral pluralism, its materialism' were all '*pro-foundly adaptive* to the system's productive base' (1986: 65; original emphasis).

Yet Keniston (1971), Lipset (1971) and Mills (1973) have each stressed that the countercultural members of the 1960s were recruited from only a small section of upper-middle-class youth, mainly students and intellectuals in idealistic arts and social science disciplines. How, then, can the values and tastes of this small minority be involved in the emergence of a postmodern culture? The argument here is that the period since the Second World War has seen a rapid growth in certain middle-class occupations – what are variously termed the 'cultural industries' (media, advertising, fashion, design, marketing) and the 'expressive professions' (teaching and lecturing, therap-eutic and social work).[9] Those employed in these occupations emerged via a 1950s and 1960s cohort passing through an expanding higher education sector. These new middle classes are characterized by a 'postmodern' lifestyle orientation based on a pursuit of pleasure, creative self-expression and stylistic innovation. But as a rising class fraction they also act as middle-class missionaries, promoting and disseminating their ideologies and cultural tastes to a wider audience. In so doing they present a challenge the legitimacy of the values of the traditional bourgeoisie, who have always advocated adherence to the puritan work ethic and commitment to a culture of control, restraint and regulation.

The characteristics of postmodern culture and lifestyles can in this way be traced back, via new middle-class cultural intermediaries, to countercultural sensibilities and practices. Frank (1998), for example, has examined how a new breed of post-war advertising and marketing executive formed the vanguard of a 1960s revolution in American business culture. Frank describes this as a 'revolution against conformity' (ibid.: 118), for the new 'hip consumerism' it promoted was designed to appeal to the youthful counter-cultural values of stylistic subversion and individual innovation, defining itself against the stifling restrictions of a 1950s mass society. Gottdiener also writes that 'cultural differentiation has been common since at least the 1960s when the counter culture brought ideological and appearance diversity to school populations' (1995: 205).[10] Here, there is agreement with the claims made earlier in this chapter, that a postmodern 'individualistic' fashion pattern emerged around this time. It would seem, then, that countercultural sensibil-ities are implicated in this emergence. In Lipovetsky's reading of history, the uniformity that characterized the 'bureaucratic system' of modern fashion was disrupted by a hedonistic and narcissistic ethic that was particularly pronounced within the 1950s and 1960s youth culture, and that promoted 'the individualist assertion of personal autonomy' (1994: 149).

If these arguments are correct then contemporary subculturalists may be expected to display a number of 'postmodern' characteristics, some of which have an affinity with certain countercultural sensibilties.[11] To examine this proposition we can turn to our two sets of ideal-typical traits that have been constructed from the arguments presented in both this and the last chapter.

MODERN	POSTMODERN
Group identity	Fragmented identity
Stylistic homogeneity	Stylistic heterogeneity
Strong boundary maintenance	Boundary maintenance weak
Subcultural provides main identity	Multiple stylistic identities
High degree of commitment	Low degree of commitment
Membership perceived as permanent	Transient attachment expressed
Low rates of subcultural mobility	High rates of subcultural mobility
Stress on beliefs and values	Fascination with style and image
Political gesture of resistance	Apolitical sentiments
Anti-media sentiments	Positive attitude towards media
Self-perception as authentic	Celebration of the inauthentic

From these, we can derive a series of primary hypotheses about postmodern subcultures that can be subjected to empirical investigation in particular chapters:

- Group identifications will be problematized, and subculturalists will not regard themselves in collective terms (Chapter 4).
- A de-differentiation of the subcultural–conventional divide means that

subculturalists will be unable to maintain this boundary through comparisons with conventional style (Chapter 4).

- Subculturalists will display a superficial and transient attachment to any
  one style as they regularly transgress the conventional and subcultural
  boundaries (Chapter 5).
- Stylistic mobility relies upon weakened boundaries between different
  subcultures and precludes oppositional reactions to other groups (Chapter
  6).
- Subculturalists will exhibit a celebratory attitude towards style, fashion
  and the media rather than view their affiliation as a normative or political
  gesture of resistance (Chapter 7).

Each of these hypotheses will therefore develop a theme to be explored in
the next four chapters. Featherstone (1992) has made the point that theorizing
postmodernism as the outcome of a systems 'logic' obscures lower-level theory
in the form of the influence of particular social groups and also ignores how
supposed postmodern changes are perceived by social actors themselves. We
began this chapter by examining postmodernism as a broad and abstract set
of processes situated within periodizing conceptions of history. We then moved
to consider how more specific aspects of the postmodern could impact upon
subcultures via the intensification of features always present in aesthetic
modernity. Having traced the origins of the aesthetic to Romantic and
bohemian countercultures, we argued that new middle-class fractions were
instrumental in transmitting related postmodern sensibilities to a wider
audience. Out task is now to examine whether the sensibilities and practices
of a specific set of social actors do, in fact, display the kind of features which
have come to be defined as 'postmodern'.

Notes

1. This is a fully revised version of Muggleton (1997).
2. Modernism and postmodernism can also refer to more specific artistic,
intellectual and cultural movements, in which case modernism can be identified as
an artistic avant-garde that emerged in the middle to late nineteenth century as a
reaction to realism, while postmodernism emerged in the middle to late decades of
this century as a reaction to the institutionalization of modernism in the museum
and academy. For a sociological analysis of artistic and intellectual modernism and
postmodernism, see Back (1985), Huyssen (1986), Gitlin (1989), Lash (1990),
Abercrombie *et al.* (1992), Featherstone (1992: Ch. 1), Hebdige (1992), Walker
(1994), Seago (1995) and Rose (1996).

3. As Urry has said in the context of a sociology of tourism, 'central to modernism is the view of the public as a homogeneous mass' (1990: 87).

4. This is a typical example of postmodern overstatement. A more careful evaluation is provided by Tseëlon (1992a, 1995: 133–4), Lipovetsky (1994: 120), and Kratz and Reimer (1998: 208).

5. It is interesting to compare Lash's assessment with Mort's (1988) remarks on the stylistic individuality of contemporary soccer supporters.

6. Even so, the aesthetic impulse to modernity suggests that there has always existed some degree of latitude for consumers to engage in acts of *bricolage*, to rearrange and customize items of clothing, attaching their own meanings to the new constructs. For example, Partington (1992) suggests that British working-class women in the 1950s actively created their own 'hybrid' versions of Dior's 'New Look'. By selecting, mixing and matching items from both utility and glamour wear, they undermined the dominant expectations of designer dress codes.

7. See, for example, Hebdige's (1988) assessment of *The Face*. Also Frith *et al.* (1992) on music video.

8. Writings on the 1960s counterculture used in this section and not cited elsewhere in this book are Roszak (1970), Brown (1973), Leech (1973), Neville (1973), Hogan (1983) and Brake (1985).

9. See Bourdieu (1984), Martin (1985), Lash and Urry (1988), Featherstone (1992), Savage *et al.* (1992) and Lury (1996) on attempts to define and theorize these new middle classes.

10. Gottdiener continues by saying how 'the apparent eclecticism precedes the postmodern' (1995: 205). But, as we have seen, other writers make a strong case for the connection between postmodernist pluralism and the counterculture.

11. Keniston had, back in 1968, identified certain 'personality traits' of Romantic student radicals, including 'flux, fluidity, change, movement, self-transformation, expressiveness' – as exemplifying a 'post-modern' style (1968: 275–85).

4

Distinctive Individuality and Subcultural Affiliation

The idea seemed to me was never to fit in . . . and if you never fitted in, then there was never going to be any competition.

Malcolm McLaren on the Sex Pistols and Punk Rock: 'Mavericks',
(BBC Radio One, Feb. 1995)

Have no rules. If people start to build fences around you, break out and do something else. You should never, ever be understood completely . . . I just went my own way. All of my friends were people who went their own way. I don't have many friends, but the few I still have are worth keeping because of just that. Highly individualistic. Unable to fit cozily into systems.

John Lydon: *Rotten: No Irish, No Blacks, No Dogs* (1994: 4, 53)

Some Case Studies: Or How to be 'Widespread' and Yet Not 'Fit-in'

In the last chapter we noted that one characteristic of postmodernity was the 'dissolution of collective identity' (Lash and Urry 1988: 297). We then charted how the modern conformity to mass-produced fashion has apparently fragmented into a postmodern or post-Fordist stylistic pluralism, with a similar process of differentiation taking place within the sphere of subcultural style. On the basis that such changes are occurring we can put forward two hypotheses. First, that group identifications (such as, I'm a punk; I'm a mod) would be problematized, and that subculturalists would not regard themselves in such specific terms. Second, that the fragmentation of both conventional and subcultural style has led to a de-differentiation (Lash 1990) of the subcultural–conventional divide, meaning that subculturalists would be unable to maintain this boundary through comparisons with conventional style. Let us now have our first look at some interview extracts to see whether the data from these tend to support our hypotheses. Each extract is identified by a letter and the Christian name(s) of the interviewee(s) involved.

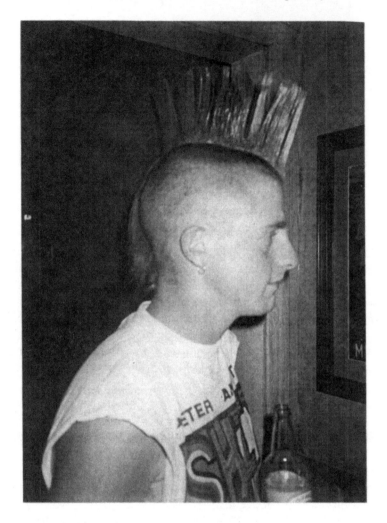

Figure 1. Duncan

(A)   DUNCAN

DM: *If I said 'What are you?' how would you describe yourself?*
D: *Punk.*
DM: *You're a punk, right. Definitely, yeah?*
D: *Through and fucking through.*
DM: *Yeah, right, good, OK.*
D: *Fourteen year . . . um, no, about twelve years.*
DM: *What's – OK, this is a big question, right – what's punk mean to you?*

D: *Punk is basically being yourself, freedom, doing what you wanna do, looking like you wanna, like, look like; and then if you look like a punk, well you don't even have to look like a punk, 'cos there's a lot that don't have mohicans or nothing.*

(B)   JIM, JANE AND SEAN

DM: *Do you see yourselves as some, belonging to some sort of group of people? That you could name?*

Jim: *Well, mods. I've always been a mod since I was twelve.*

S: *Psychedelic mods, really, I suppose. We've always been part of that scene, but we were always on the edge of it because we were a bit too psychedelic for it.*

DM: *Do you think you'll always be like this?*

Jim: *I used to say: mod till you die. That was when I was younger, but labels are terrible. Self-defeating, labels. Like it's a way of boxing*

Figure 2. Jim, Sean, Jane

people, isn't it? Unity is what you want. That's what we are trying to create with the club. Bit of unity. Anyone who's into anything and feels passionate about it.

Ja: *People section themselves off too much.*

Jim: *It's like the true mod's a loner, isn't he? But I don't know, you can't be like that, not nowadays, because there's not enough going on.*

Ja: *You can't.*

S: *It's more of a spirit of helping each other.*

Ja: *Of sticking together.*

Jim: *Er . . . group consciousness. Group consciousness. You do get that, yeah, you do notice it of people.*

DM: *Do you have it? Do you feel it?*

Jim: *No, we're not, we're not going to get caught in that trap, sort of thing. That's the thing, that's probably why we're not really . . . you can't really label us really as such because, you know, not really . . .*

Ja: *. . . one definite thing and nothing else.*

Jim: *Because that's really self-destructive. That's really bad, like that group consciousness, you see.*

Ja: *We're not narrow-minded like that, you know.*

(C)   SAUL

S: *I mean I've been typecast before as a gothic punk, and . . . urh . . . the band Bone Orchard were the first band to be described as jazzpunk. It's just people clawing for labels to try and sling you under. I think, you know, people should have credit for being a bit more widespread for their . . . what they're into, than just sort of pigeon-holed, you know.*

So how do we start to analyse an interview? What is it we look for? To begin with there are three things we might notice about extract (A). First, that Duncan undoubtedly sees himself in terms of a group identity (he describes himself as a 'punk' – a collective label), and does so very emphatically, leaving us in no doubt of his affiliation. This response seems typical of what the CCCS approach leads us to expect. The second point to observe is that, given his emphasis on a *group* identification, we might have expected the meaning of punk to be understood in group terms (e.g. collective values, shared style, group activities). But what we are offered is an *individualistic* definition: 'being yourself, freedom, doing what you wanna do', even to the point at which one does not even have to wear those central aspects of the style that mark one out as a contemporary punk. Thirdly, and following on from the previous claim, this is a definition of punk that places emphasis, not on the style or image, but on attitudes and values that underlie the purely visual. Drawing attention to meanings in this way tells us that there is far more to a subculture than what Hebdige calls 'the profoundly superficial level of appearances' (1979: 17).

We might be left with the thought that there is a contradiction in (A) between Duncan's unequivocal identification with a subcultural (i.e. group) identity and his ability to present the meaning of punk in individualistic (anti-group) terms. After all, allegiance to a group suggests conformity to its image, values and practices, while individual freedom implies a refusal to comply to group dictates. Yet for those with an insider knowledge of the punk subculture, this combination of communal activity and individualistic ideology comes as no surprise:

> To start with, I'll tell you what I think punk isn't – it isn't a fashion, a certain style of dress . . . it is an idea that guides and motivates your life. The punk community that exists, exists to support and realize that idea through music, art, fanzines and other expressions of personal creativity. And what is this idea? Think for yourself, be yourself, don't just take what society gives you, create your own rules, live your own life (Andersen 1985, cited in O'Hara 1995: 22).

My stance throughout this book, moreover, is that that the categories and definitions of sociologists must be derived from, rather than imposed upon, the sensibilities of the people under study. To claim, from the outside as it were, that people's indigenous meanings are contradictory is to ignore how such apparent contradictions can make perfect, logical sense to those involved given their own definitions of the situation.

To begin to see how such contradictions and tensions are resolvable in practice, let us therefore examine (B), which displays an explicit blend of pro and anti-group sensibilities. The three 'psychedelic mods' begin by stating their identification with this named subculture, but we can see how this is tentatively expressed (note the use of 'well' . . . 'really, I suppose') particularly when compared to Duncan's unequivocal declaration of allegiance to punk in (A). Undercutting or lessening the severity of the implications of a statement in this way is a form of mitigation (Widdicombe and Wooffitt 1995), further examples of which will be seen in following extracts. Why is it that a group identity is accepted, yet mitigated? Jim talks of a need for 'unity', yet makes clear how this unity stretches so far as to encompass 'anyone who is into anything'. This suggests that the aim of the club is to create, what we might usefully term, a *diverse unity*. Evidence for this appears further on in the extract. The meaning of mod is defined by Jim in individualistic, almost isolationist terms[1] ('the true mod's a loner') only for this to be rejected in favour of a 'spirit' of 'sticking together'. The assumption that this communal feeling is congruent with the earlier stress on a diverse unity is suggested by the almost immediate recognition of the negative, sectionalist implications involved in *too specific* a conception of the group.

For example, Jim then makes reference to 'group consciousness', but talks of this as something that can be observed only in others, and goes on to deny explicitly that it can be applied to himself or his two friends. We can infer that 'group consciousness' is equated with a specific identity that would reintroduce sharp lines of demarcation and cause internal compartmental-ization of the diverse unity. An occurrence of this kind would clearly be viewed negatively, for, as Jane complains, 'people section themselves off too much'. That named group identities, such as mod, do have this effect causes them to be derided as labels that are seen to be 'self-defeating', 'self-destructive' and suggestive of 'narrow-mindedness'. This dislike of the compartmentalizing implications of labelling ('boxing people' as Jim puts it) is reflected in the chosen subcultural identification, for, although this is a named group, it is a hybrid of two previous and distinct cultural forms and musical genres (psychedelia and mod), and breaks out of the more specific categorization imposed by a single subcultural identity such as we find expressed by Duncan in (A). As Jane is keen to stress, they are not 'one definite thing and nothing else'.[2]

Even so, their attempts at mitigation indicate that they are still not totally comfortable with the acceptance of even a hybrid label. Saul, in (C), is even more explicitly critical of the 'typecasting' and 'pigeon-holing' implied by the application of hybrid labels, and points, by contrast, to the virtue (i.e. deserving of 'credit') of having 'more widespread' tastes. As he makes clear, it is the element of *restriction* that is a prime reason for the dislike of labelling consistently expressed by subcultural interviewees. It is relevant that, earlier in the interview, Saul described himself as a 'nonconformist', a somewhat vague identification that could equally well be applied to any subcultural style. It does not make reference to specific forms of dress, values, or cultural tastes that are aligned to a particular group, and therefore satisfies Saul's own need for a 'more widespread', less restricted, form of identity.

We can now say that the apparent contradiction between individual freedom and group affiliation in extract (A) is resolvable in so far as subculturalists are attempting to re-characterize their social group as one of 'anti-structure' (Martin 1985) – a group, in other words, that is not tightly-bounded, sharply defined or composed of uniform practices. We might therefore suspect that Duncan holds a subjective conception of 'punk' that is diverse enough to accommodate individual variation. In most cases, however, giving a specific name (or label) to the group is likely to emphasize its collective aspects, and imply that it does possess these negative qualities. A consequence of this, a phenomenon we can term label-rejection, can be seen in both the next extracts. Neal, in (E), states his hatred of being labelled and refuses to accept either a hippy or a traveller identity. In (D), Beth also refuses the application of two different subcultural labels (gothic and heavy metal). She admits to 'being into' and liking heavy metal, so unlike my initial attempt at locating her within with the goth subculture, 'metaller' or some equivalent term would not necessarily be a wholly mismatched identity. Yet this does not prevent her from rejecting it for what amounts to virtually the opposite, a declaration of her *individuality* – she is her 'own person'.

(D)   TONY AND BETH

DM: *What I want to ask you is: do you think of yourself as belonging to a certain type of group of people?*

T: *Yeah.*

DM: *What is it?*

T: *Gothics.*

DM: *What, both of you?*

B: *For me that's a matter of the kind of person.*

DM: *So you don't think of yourself as being a . . .*

B: *No, no.*

T: *Beth's into the heavy sort of heavy metal.*

B: *Yeah.*

DM: *Do you think of yourself as a heavy metal person, do you think of yourself as a heavy metal-type person?*

B: *No. I am own person, not heavy metal. I like heavy metal, but I am own person.*

(E)   NEAL

DM: *Do you see yourself, because of the way you dress, belonging to a certain type of group that you could name or identify?*

N: *To name or identify it would be like labelling it, and I hate being labelled. But like I said before, I just wear what I feel comfortable in and other people form their own opinions. They can call you a hippy, they can call you a traveller, they can call you what they like. I don't really care.*

DM: *Do you compare yourself with people who dress what I call conventionally?*

N: *I think I'm very different from conventional-dressing people,*
     actually.

DM: *In what way? How do you view them as well?*

N: *Er, how do I view them? I see them I suppose a little as sheep,*
     people who've never really thought much about the randomness
     of life, and I think they take as said by other people as what is
     right, sort of thing, don't really make up their own minds them-
     selves. Erm . . . I like them. I like anyone who's friendly, basically.
     It's just a case of, I feel a little bit sorry for them because in a way
     I think they don't know anything else. To fit into their social circle
     or whatever it is – workplace or whatever – they have to dress in a
     certain way and they get used to it and like it, sort of thing, and
     that's fine, but I suppose they haven't really looked at many
     alternatives. But clothes does reflect lifestyle. I think that is what
     you're vaguely getting at.

It would be difficult to quantify my interview responses into either group acceptance or rejection, nor would this produce a valid figure, for affiliation is a subtle and complex procedure and there are many ways in which subculturalists can modify, mitigate and resist rather than simply endorse or oppose group labels. Suffice to say that an unequivocal acceptance of a single label, such as punk (extract A) or gothic (extract D) occurred only rarely in the interviews as a whole. Although this goes against what the CCCS approach has led us to think, a variety of contemporary sources (Andes 1998; Evans 1997; Polhemus 1996, 1997; Widdicombe and Wooffitt 1995) have confirmed that subculturalists do tend to resist rather than accept single group identifications – a point that also supports our first hypothesis.

Widdicombe and Wooffitt have argued that we define our identity as much by reference to what we 'are not' as to what 'we are' (1995: 180). We can see this in (E), where Neal attributes characteristics to a 'reference group' against which to define himself. Now, it can be argued that I invited this comparison and even named the reference group in question, but Neal does not contest the existence of such a comparison group, nor the legitimacy of the label 'conventional'. On the contrary, he explicitly makes clear his difference from conventionally dressing people.[3] Moreover, while my initial question refers only to conventional dress, Neal takes it upon himself to broaden this focus. This emphasis upon factors other than appearance was also found in (A). Duncan in that first extract was concerned to emphasize that his commitment to punk existed at more than just the stylistic level; Neal is making the same point here about his difference from conventional people. Initially, he discusses attitudes. He then suggests that the implications of dress for conventional people are felt both socially and in the 'workplace', thus encompassing both major spheres of their existence and making his difference from them all the more comprehensive. Finally, he states explicitly that that dress is a reflection of 'lifestyle'.

So what is it about conventional attitudes and lifestyle that make this such a useful reference group? Attributing certain qualities to the conventional reference group allows Neal to cast himself in terms that are very much the opposite, and are in keeping with the positive emphasis that subculturalists place upon individuality and anti-restriction. Comparing conventional people to 'sheep' carries all the negative connotations of group conformity resulting from an unquestioning following of a flock. This theme continues in the next lines, where conventional people are characterized not by independence of mind, but by an acceptance without much thought of what others say is socially acceptable. Claiming that 'they haven't really looked at many alternatives' or have not given much thought to 'the randomness of life' suggests, of course, that Neal has. The existential connotations of this term 'randomness' are not, I suggest, coincidental, for the suggestions of individual autonomy, unpredictability and refusal to be constrained by the determinist influences of social conventions are very much used to distance Neal from the conformity, predictability and regulation that is said to characterize the comparison group. If the social role of conventionals is to 'fit in', then clearly the subcultural motive (as the McLaren quote at the beginning of this chapter suggests) is *not* to 'fit in'.

Distinctive Individuality

Through the use of these five extracts we have seen a connection, in terms of dress, attitudes and lifestyle, between individuality and nonconformity. We can refer to this as 'distinctive individuality', the way that subculturalists highlight their individuality through a distinction from a collective reference group, in this case, conventionally dressing people. A clear independent example is given by Beattie. A woman on her way to the Manchester Hacienda is quoted as saying, 'We're the opposite of Townies, you know. We're into style, fashion, X-cess, with a capital "X". We're individualists – the opposite of Townies, who all buy the same old boring Blazer from Next' (1990: 45). Tomlinson has further observed, also in the context of dance culture, that where such individualistic comparisons are concerned 'the key word is *insiders*' (1998: 203; original emphasis). Invoking a reference group enables certain individuals to emphasize their 'insider' status as members of an esoteric, subterranean scene through self-exclusion from a larger category of uninitiated 'outsiders'.[4] All these sets of oppositions – the individual against the collective; the insider vs the outsider; the minority against the majority – can be found in Sarah Thornton's (1995) study *Club Cultures*.

Thornton's ethnography is indebted to the work of Pierre Bourdieu, particularly his concept of cultural capital (Bourdieu 1984). To possess such capital is to have acquired the kinds of knowledge, tastes and social competencies that provide a marker of social status. Different social groups are consequently engaged in struggles over cultural capital with a view to legitimating their own personal identities as *the* lifestyle, a process that involves making distinctions from other groups who are thought to possess poor taste, suspect tastes, or even no taste at all. A useful illustration of this type of distinction as it pertains to subculture is given by Moore, who observes how British-born Australian skinheads elevate their own status by regarding 'moidies' (their slang term for the stereotypical Australian male) as 'lacking style' (it is, Moore comments, 'just a different style') (1994: 121). These attempts to maintain subcultural status can be understood through Thornton's own concept of 'subcultural capital', where possession of the required taste denotes 'hipness' or 'being in the know' (1995: 11). Of course, subcultural tastes remain exclusive only for so long as they are unknown or inaccessible to the majority, and this suggests why Thornton's clubbers, and my own informants, emphasize their own diversity and difference by invoking the conventional (or 'mainstream') as the symbol of the mass 'Other'.

There is, however, a potential objection to be raised concerning the way in which subculturalists emphasize this distinctive individuality: that neither of the descriptions on which it relies – subcultural individuality on the one hand, conventional homogeneity on the other – are sociologically convincing. Thornton would appear to concur with this, for she spends much time deconstructing each part of this distinction. In line with the postmodern logic that 'the dominant culture, of which subculture is a sub-set, has lost its coherence' (Evans 1997: 171), Thornton argues that the 'homogeneous' mainstream is in fact composed of highly differentiated taste publics (1995: 97–8). She also investigates how 'heterogeneous' subcultures are themselves 'unified' by shared tastes. Factors such as 'self-selection', media communications, and 'door policies' ensure that clubcultures remain organized along specific lines of social identification (ibid.: 111–14). The views of her respondents are, in effect, regarded as false – merely 'ideologies' though which clubbers 'imagine' the composition of social groups (ibid.: 10) – and not to be confused with the way in which such groups are 'objectively organized' (ibid.: 96). Subculturalists, in other words, fail to perceive the bounded reality of their own situation and the equally real internal differentiation of the mainstream.

Yet, as we argued in Chapter 2, groups do not have objective characteristics and boundaries. We can, in fact, regard both Thornton and her informants as engaged in the process of describing the world through ideal-types, producing different abstractions of the same phenomenon. Ideal-types cannot be regarded as true or false, objective or subjective (for they are *all* necessarily value-relevant and partial in their selection of attributes), they can only be more or less useful for the purpose for which they are constructed. Clearly, the clubbers' typification of the mainstream is useful for their own purposes for, as we saw in extract (E), one way to emphasize one's own heterogeneity and internal differentiation is through a comparison with the most typical features of an outsider group. I also want to argue, however, that subculturalists are quite able take a different perspective and recognize differentiation within the mainstream as well as the socially shared dimension to their own individuality. Let us look first at the subcultural view of the mainstream.

Here, we need to draw upon the work of Schutz (1980), who theorized in detail how all social actors use ideal-types to apprehend the world. The distinction made between insiders and outsiders can best be understood in Schutzian terms as that which distinguishes (in an ideal-typical sense) 'consociates' from 'contemporaries': the former are those with whom we share a 'community' of both time and space; the latter are those to whom we are bounded only temporally; we inhabit the same world but may never meet. Consociates are directly encountered and known to us in terms of their particular, concrete characteristics. By contrast, 'the contemporary is only indirectly accessible and . . . can only be known in the form of *general types*' (Schutz 1980: 181; original emphasis). Such is the reason why insiders can regard outsiders (and subculturalists understand conventionals) as abstract, anonymous and homogeneous. As Mitchell observes, 'the process is one by which superficial relationships between people are determined by certain major categories within which no distinctions are recognized' (1971: 28).

Mitchell's observations are, however, only partially informed, since we do not always perceive as an undifferentiated mass those with whom we have such 'categorical relationships' (ibid.). As Ritzer correctly notes, Schutz's world of contemporaries is a 'stratified world' (1981: 169), existing at different levels of abstraction. Subculturalists are, in other words, quite able to perceive varying degrees of differentiation *within* the mainstream. In (E) we saw Neal speak of conventional people as a general category. Extract (B) in the next chapter will provide an example of what we might usefully term a middle-range analysis, where specific types of groups are invoked to symbolize conventional dress and lifestyle. Elsewhere in Neal's interview he was quite aware of the individual differences amongst conventional people, even to the extent that he began to challenge my own suggestion that they formed a specific group, wanting instead to accord them the same freedom from 'pigeon-holing' that he would wish for himself. At each of these levels – general category, middle-range and individual – conventional people are still regarded as a 'type', but to a different degree of specificity, for 'while style is often a group phenomenon, it is also an individual matter . . . The issue of group versus individual analysis depends on the detail with which lifestyles are classified . . . Ultimately, it could be argued, every individual's lifestyle is unique . . . Any definition of lifestyle should therefore not exclude the possibility of individual as well as group analysis' (Veal 1993: 242–3).

Let us now turn to examine subculturalists' descriptions of their own groups, where Veal's principle of differing levels of analysis can again be observed. To illustrate this point, let us first look at a recent empirical British study (Miles 1995; Miles *et al.* 1998) that examines the meanings that young people give to consumer goods, and how such purchases are central to the formation of their identities. Miles and his colleagues discovered that teenagers discussed their consumption experiences in a way that suggested their awareness of the similarity and predictability of fashion, while at the same time seeing their purchases as the expression of a personal and individual choice. One female respondent replied that their choice of consumer goods allowed you 'to fit in with everybody. To fit in more and show what you are really like' (1995: 16), while another said of their chosen item, 'it says that I like to be different and not have the same clothes as everyone else' (1998: 89). The authors conclude that the differences that exist within generally similar goods allow consumers to maintain their individuality (to 'stick out') yet still be socially accepted and 'fit in' within the wider peer group.[5] They additionally argue that their findings are compatible with the perspective on fashion taken by Simmel. According to Frisby (1985b: 62), Simmel tended to see modern fashion 'as a dialectic and ultimately a compromise between two tendencies: adherence to and absorption in a social group on the one hand, and individual differentiation and distinction from group members on the other'.

Yet I would claim that this relation between individual distinction and group conformity must be understood, not only within groups, but also in terms of comparisons across groups. Although empirically interrelated, these dimensions can be separated analytically. A within-group distinction is a comparison of the individual to their peer-group. An across-group distinction is a judgement by a group's members of their unconventionality in relation to other groups. Both dimensions can be observed in my own interviews. When, for instance, I asked a mod-scooterist, Curly, about the meaning behind his style he gave an answer similar to that of Duncan in extract (A) of this chapter – 'being an individual'. When pressed to expand upon this, Curly replied, 'seeing yourself as someone different than other people. You're a minority, you see.' Here, we have an across-group distinction where affiliation to an unconventional minority still allows a subculturalist to be 'an individual' in relation to the mass conformity of the conventional majority. As Jeff, an ex-skinhead, put it, 'you dress the same as all the other smoothies and casuals, so you are a member of an even bigger group. So how can you criticize me and say I'm not an individual, when I'm more of an individual than you are? 'Cos like there's 50 thousand skinheads in Britain, there's 20 million smoothies. So who's the individual?' (see also Widdicombe 1993: 111).

But Curly also recognized that 'seeing yourself as . . . different' necessarily involves being 'influenced by a certain type of music and clothes' through which this difference is expressed. His friends, Dave and Loz, phrase it as 'everyone having their own look' within the 'basically similar', or 'being an individual within a group of like-minded individuals'. This is a within-group distinction where subculturalists are quite aware of the socially shared dimension to their individuality – the individual look *within* the group. It is the diversity of this group that enables it to accommodate a range of looks and tastes, allowing each member to maintain a sense of simultaneous similarity and difference. 'Stylization creates decipherable lifestyles on all levels, from large collective cultures down to microcultures and even the personal habitus of each individual' (Fornäs 1995: 110). This allows one both to fit in and yet stand out within a group, the purpose of which is to be different from the accepted norm, or to not fit in on an across-group distinction.

Using the arguments of Thornton (1995) we suggested that the manner in which subculturalists express their distinctive individuality could be held to be deficient on two counts: that it fails to recognize differentiation within the conventional or consider the socially shared dimension to subcultures. We have now demonstrated that neither of these arguments is supported by the interview data. Subculturalists, by employing ideal-typical conceptions of both their own and outsider groups, can make comparisons within and between such groups to varying degrees of specificity. This does, however, ensure that the mainstream can continue to be typified and homogenized in order to emphasize subcultural diversity and difference. Not only does this finding refute our second hypothesis, that a de-differentiation (Lash 1990) of the conventional/subcultural divide has eroded the ability of subculturalists to make comparisons with outsider groups and maintain such boundaries, but it carries the same implications for all social groups, owing to the reciprocal nature of this process of subjective perception and homogenization. My own group, of which I am an insider, and that I regard as heterogeneous, is someone else's outsider group.[6] As Schutz phrases it, 'each partner has to be content with the probability that the other, to whom he is oriented by means of an anonymous type, will respond with the same kind of orientation' (Schutz 1980: 202).

There is clearly a lesson here on how subcultural style is likely to be regarded by outsiders to that group. Barnard (1996: 30) contends that it is the material act of wearing particular items of clothing that 'constitutes the individual' as a member of a certain subculture. Subculturalists could therefore stand accused of dressing in ways that seemingly contradict their verbal claims for individuality and rejection of group identification. We saw, for example, how Duncan (extract A) placed great importance on individuality, even suggesting that a punk is freed from the necessity of looking like one. Yet in my view Duncan visually conformed to the 'mohican and tartan bondage trousers' uniform worn by all the other punks in his group. Equally, Beth (extract D) and Neal, in (E), reject the very labels that, in my opinion, their dress codes appeared to signify. But what, in fact, is happening in such cases is the phenomenon that Schouten and McAlexander observed when conducting research on the HDSC (Harley-Davidson subculture), that mere contemporaries are initially apprehended as homogeneous types. 'To outsiders (including non-bikers and aspirants to the subculture) or to newcomers in the HDSC, the various biker groups may appear as virtually indistinguishable, even stereotypical' (Schouten and McAlexander 1995: 49).

In other words, my own status as a social researcher, with all the qualities of reflexivity and rigour that that implies, did not prevent my initial, visual assessments of certain subculturalists taking the form of abstractions produced from my outsider location.[7] Of course, those with an insider perspective would clearly reject this stereotypical characterization and maintain their individuality on two dimensions: one, on a within-group distinction, stressing internal group heterogeneity, and making reference to the very real material differences in dress codes and cultural tastes within the subculture; and two, on an across-group distinction, which allows for a recognition of the subculture as a collectivity, but would still establish their minority status (and hence individualism) when compared to conventionals. To again take Duncan (extract A) as an example. His understanding of the meaning of punk, 'being yourself, freedom, doing what you wanna do', is likely to be defined against the conformity and restriction of both conventional and subcultural norms, and is not contradicted by his allegiance to a punk look (or, by extension, lifestyle), since, from his own insider perspective, this is also heterogeneous and diverse. Duncan might well have replied to my homogenization of his group using the words of the punk quoted by Lull (1987: 227), 'We might look the same to outsiders, but there are big differences between us.'

There are clearly different perceptions of homogeneity and heterogeneity involved here, but we cannot simply claim that one is right and the others wrong. While dress is an aspect of material reality, and different styles and group practices may be more or less homogeneous or heterogeneous, we are unable to perceive this reality independently of our constructs and inter-pretations of it. As Barnard also points out, 'each reader . . . brings their own cultural experience and expectations to bear on the garment in the production and exchange of meanings' (1996: 31). Style is ideal-typical, and our values inevitably come into play through the process by which we all abstract different features of social groups in relation to our own position. There are, then, no objective appearances and group structures against which a subjective subcultural sensibility can be dismissed as *a priori* superficial, erroneous or ideological. On the contrary, as Schutz argues, 'the *starting point* of social science is to be found in ordinary social life' (1980: 141; original emphasis). One very important starting-point is the value that subculturalists place upon individuality and freedom, for this theme underpins the typologies they construct of the social world, and it is upon their typologies that social scientific accounts should be constructed.

Liminal Subculture

We have seen how the conception of subculture as both widespread and individualistic is achieved through the material and cultural practice of wearing a style that allows one both to fit in and stand out within the group. But subculturalists consistently define a subculture in more than just stylistic terms. We therefore need to explore the meaning of diversity in other areas, and deal here with the issue of musical tastes. That 'youth subcultures tend to be music subcultures' (Thornton 1995: 19) has provided a focus for a number of empirical studies (for example, Frith 1983; Kotarba and Wells 1987; Hansen and Hansen 1991; Locher 1998; Sardiello 1998). Research by Lull (1987: 236) and Widdicombe and Woofitt (1995: 140) further reports that the interest in a particular music is primary, preceding and leading to a related subcultural affiliation. The interviewees in extracts (F) and (G) also suggest that affiliation is conditional upon a liking for a specific musical genre, but use this assumption to resist a categorical identity on the basis of their widespread tastes.

(F)　*SUZIE AND MAGS*

DM:　*Do you think of yourself as belonging to some type of people because of the way you dress? Or identify with some type of people because of the way you dress.*

M: *Not really.*

S: *Not generally. I suppose if you put us into any group we're more ... we fit in more with the metal crowd and stuff than anything else, but that's it. We're definitely not goths.*

DM: *Right, so I mean would ... do you think of yourself as being a heavy or anything? Or a metaller?*

M: *Not really, I mean ...*

S: *We're into industrial stuff.*

M: *Yeah, it's more of a ...*

S: *At the moment, but the image we put across, people categorize us in that image. Usually it's quite deceiving, 'cos I mean I like stuff from you know Bjork to Carcass and stuff like anything between that. So I mean it's just, I've got a very wide music range. I don't like just one kind of music, I like loads, so I don't really dress to fit in with a certain type of music. I just dress how I want to dress, really.*

(G) OLIVER

O: *I dress a bit Mod-y, I like that style, but I wouldn't call myself a proper Mod or anything like that, because I don't want to define, limit myself to one, you know, one sort of music, because you know I like sort of house music as well. I used to be a raver (laughs) ... er ... well not a proper one 'cos I've never really been a proper anything. It's just sort of halfway, not a halfway house between everything, but sort of an amalgamation of the things I like, basically. I don't seem to be ... doesn't seem to, you know ... I don't know, sort of going 'I'm this and I've got to like this and I can't like that.' I don't know. I prefer listening to things and well, 'I like that.'*

DM: *If you don't think of yourself as a ... OK: you're making a distinction between yourself and a proper mod or whatever they are. What do you have to do to be a proper mod? In other words, what haven't you done that they do or vice versa? Or what do you think is the case?*

O: *Spend a lot more money on clothes, wear, I don't know, wear more of the right clothing and sort of listen exclusively to soul music, garage and things like that. Probably more soul music, but Small Faces, etc. etc. But I must say I have a great fondness for soul, but I also like sort of other things, classical music – Satie, you know.*

Figure 3. Oliver

(H)   *GARRY*

DM: *Do you think of yourself identifying with a certain type of group of people or whatever because of the way you dress?*

G: *Er, yeah, I suppose so.*

DM: *What is it?*

G: *Punk-ish (laughs).*

DM: *Ish? Right. Would you claim you are a punk? I mean would you go so far as to claim 'look I am a punk'?*

G: *Yeah; only, 'cos it's a convenient form of reference, if you know what I mean.*

DM: *Right. Do you think of yourself as being a punk?*

G: *Er . . . that's the nearest sort of name that I can put to it, if you know what I mean. I am what I am, really.*

In extract (F) we find the assumption that named identity is warranted given a correspondence between wearing a certain style and liking a specific and related musical form. This is precisely the reason why Suzie's 'very wide music range' enables her to reject such an identity. Again, in (G), a reason for Oliver claiming he has 'never been a proper anything' is his refusal to be restricted to one particular type of music.[8] After this I reversed the logic of the question and asked what he would have to do to be a 'proper mod' (and thus presumably for a clear mod identification to be acknowledged). Oliver had initially distanced himself from a specific identification by reference to his 'amalgamation' of tastes, and his reply logically confirms that those who do claim such an identification have a correspondingly more specific set of tastes: a need to 'listen exclusively' to particular types of music, to wear 'the right clothing', and to engage in the prescribed ritual activity of acquiring the right dress code, the description of which ('spending a lot more money on clothes') recalls the element of 'conspicuous consumption' that, according to Hebdige (1974), lies at the heart of the 'meaning of mod'.

Garry (extract H) is slightly more willing than the preceding three interviewees to acknowledge a subcultural identification. Even so, Garry's identification is qualified by the suffix '-ish', conditional on the 'convenience' rather than the exact relevance of its application, and is thus made to sound somewhat incongruent with what Garry actually perceives himself to be. From the substance of previous extracts, we might safely assume that this discrepancy could be explained by reference to Garry's wider tastes compared to the specificity of what the label connotes. It is also predicated upon a claim, present in (C), (E) and (F), that labels are imposed by outsiders rather than being a form of identification emerging from within. Moreover, given that subculturalists are consistently reluctant to endorse identifications that imply their tastes are restrictive, the word 'categorize' as used here by Suzie in (F) can only be pejorative, given its connotations of conformity and compliance to a clearly demarcated set of practices.

I would in fact suggest that (F) and (G) on one hand, and (H) on the other are in fact highly complementary, being two sides of the same coin. In the first two extracts, Suzie, Mags and Oliver appear to be comparing themselves with a very specific version of a relevant subculture, and rejecting a group identification on the basis that their own personal situation is not restricted to such a 'pure' model. But, as we have seen in the earlier sections of this chapter, this does not mean that they necessarily reject affiliation to a collectivity, only that labelling invokes a conception of a restricted model at odds with their own self-identity. What they may well do in such a situation is to accept the 'convenience' of the group label that happens to be closest to their own self-perception, while at the same time making clear the lack of fit through qualifying statements. Oliver's claim 'I dress a bit mod-y' is compatible in this sense with Garry's self-description in (H) as 'punk-ish'. One is therefore a type of mod, punk or hippy, but not a *stereotypical* mod, punk or hippy.

That certain subculturalists accept an identity not wholly incompatible with the label they resist is suggested in (F). In talking of categorization by others, Suzie says '*usually* it's *quite* deceiving' and 'I don't *really* dress to fit in with a certain type of music.' Through these qualifications she admits that attempts at categorization, and the correspondences between her style and musical tastes that give rise to these, are unlikely to be completely off the mark, and she has already indicated that neither she nor Mags would look completely out of place with metallers. Likewise, Oliver might draw attention to his eclectic musical tastes, but he still admits to his 'great fondness for soul', a musical genre that he claims proper mods should listen to 'exclusively'. We might also note how assertions of individuality are made in the last sentence of (F) by Suzie ('I just dress how I want to dress') and the final utterance of (H) by Garry ('I am what I am'). Yet none of these necessarily contradict group allegiance *per se*, for it is precisely the point that the 'widespread tastes' that are a defining feature of subculturalists' self-identity are seen to correspond with the expansive range of cultural forms and practices that make up a non-stereotypical conception of a relevant subculture.

This rejection of sharply drawn boundaries and resistance towards restriction derives, I suggest, from the quest for individual freedom from structure that so many subculturalists expressed. The implication is that such subcultures are characterized by inherently liminal tendencies. We can define liminality, following Martin, as 'literally being on the threshold, in no-man's land, between clear social identities' (1985: 50), and can usefully refer to such non-stereotypical subcultures as 'liminal subcultures'. Any one such collectivity would appear to have greater internal diversity and complexity of cultural forms than the CCCS theoretical orthodoxy would lead us to expect, leading to blurred boundaries and ambiguous classification. Yet it is still characterized by at least a minimum degree of distinctiveness from other, less similar, types of liminal subcultures. The above four subculturalists can themselves refer to quite different bases of relevant identity (metaller, mod and punk), and have indicated a non-stereotypical identification that, although not clearly delineated or unambiguously accepted, is not far enough removed from each of these to make them wholly irrelevant. This explains what would otherwise remain somewhat contradictory statements of the kind made by another informant, Paula – 'even then, though, I didn't like people calling me a goth, even though I was'.

It may at first seem a rather obvious finding that individuals profess to liking more than one kind of music. Yet certain subcultures are, after all, supposedly composed of people who dress in a highly visible style that signifies a special attachment to a specific musical genre. To discover that such individuals may embrace a plurality of musical affiliations has important implications for the manner in which sociological analysis has focused on the homological coherence of subcultural forms. Homology, as explained by Hebdige, is 'the symbolic fit between the values and lifestyles of a group, its subjective experience and the musical forms it uses to express or reinforce its focal concerns' (1979: 113). Furthermore, as we saw in Chapter 2, the internal homologies of a group are distinguished from other sets of homological relationships inhering in other groups through the manner in which sub-cultures are set in sharp opposition to each other. We can see this principle at work with reference to musical tastes, again, through the work of Paul Willis:

> The motor bike boys' fundamental ontological security, style, gesture, speech, rough horseplay – their whole social ambience – seemed to owe something to the confidence and muscular style of early rock 'n' roll. [By contrast] the originality and complexity of 'progressive' music not only matched the intricacy and inventiveness of the hippy life-style, but the unusual, bizarre and exotic sounds it made possibly matched and developed the 'head'-centred nature of the hippy culture and the general emphasis on expanded awareness (Willis 1978: 35, 159).

Yet what my own informants typically do is make reference to their 'widespread tastes', ensuring that their own situation diverges from or is not restricted to such a pure model. As we argued in Chapter 2, this does not mean that homologies cannot be discovered in liminal subcultures, nor that oppositional elements cannot form between them. Rather, it is to argue that this is but a partial account and that subculturalists can embrace a number of apparently exclusive stylistic and musical forms. Lull, for example, discovered that punks and skinheads 'listen to many of the same records and tapes and they attend punk shows where they freely interact' (1987: 245). Sid, one of my own skinhead informants, had previously been a punk, and used to listen to both punk rock and ska. His partner, Bea, also a skinhead, had once worn her hair long and had been into motorbikes, but even then had listened to all types of skinhead music. In Chapter 6 we shall present two detailed case studies involving such apparent contradictions, thereby satisfying Fornäs's call for subcultural analysis to direct itself more to the identification of 'heterogeneous and conflictual traits' (1995: 114).

Crossover Counterculture

Liminal subcultures can be conceptualized as groups that have begun to break out of the very boundaries through which they are defined; they are characterized as much by ambiguity and diversity as by coherence and definition. But while stylistic demarcation is not rigid, classification is not an impossible enterprise. As Widdicombe and Wooffitt discovered in their own interviews, respondents resisted a specific subcultural categorization, 'while not definitely denying the *potential* relevance of a subcultural identity . . . After all, the kinds of dress and appearance of the respondents invite a certain kind of categorical ascription' (1995: 104; original emphasis). But certain individuals in my study seemed almost to defy such attempts at definition. In the terminology of Kaiser (1990) 'appearance perception' was problematized, classification into subcultural 'types' rendered invalid.[9] Fornäs (1995) would attempt to account for this by his notion of 'antilogy': this is where the internal contradictions of any heterology have become overtly oppositional, a dynamic movement culminating in a new stylistic synthesis. My interviewees frequently explained it as the result of a 'crossover' between once-separate subcultures. Following the self-definition of Dave, another of my subcultural sample, I will refer to such people by the concept of 'crossover counterculture', designating (in his own words) an 'amorphous group' with 'no set rules' and 'blurring of boundaries'. This is not to suggest the existence of two clearly separate groups, liminal subculture and crossover counter-culture; rather, it is to conceptualize these as opposing ends of an ideal-typical continuum, with the latter displaying a greater degree of heterogeneity of its constituent parts.

(1)   PETER

P: *Yeah, I suppose I'm really quite individual. I'm half Chinese anyway. So as a starter that was a sort of . . . made things a bit . . . I always thought of myself as an individual anyway. Being half of something, you're never one or the other. So, then . . . um . . . really that sort of, by taking bits of being Chinese, in as far as hairstyle and things are concerned, and then . . . urh . . . mixed it with everything else really (laughs).*

DM: *So do you ever think of yourself as belonging to a certain group of people 'cos of the way you dress, or . . . ?*

P: *Er no, not really. 'Cos people do get confused by the way I look anyway. 'Cos I do ride motorcycles, so I look like I'm a biker, and then the clothes I wear are always baggy, so everybody thinks I'm*

Figure 4. Peter

*a skateboarder, and then it just sort of goes on and on like that,
and people just sort of . . . I suppose it's quite cosmopolitan really.
I fit in with just about everybody, really. There is always a certain
amount of bond between people who tend to dress individually.*

(J) DANIEL

D: *I find I relate to what's loosely called subculture. It always used to
be the weirdos. It started with the goths and then the hippies joined
in, and then you had like punk crossover as well, so the way I
look, I don't know. I think it's more on a social level. You sort of*

76

> *. . . the people who look the way I do think a certain way about the way the world works, so I associate with them.*

Peter, in (1), refers to his individuality and liminal (in-between) identity, but what is different about the basis on which these attributes are proposed compared to what happened in earlier extracts is the explicit emphasis on eclecticism. Peter's attitude towards style is suggestive of the sampling, mixing and matching sensibility by which Polhemus (1994) characterizes 'the Supermarket of Style'. The logical consequence of this postmodern pre-dilection to mix, match and plunder is to create greater scope for the construction of 'individually unique looks' (Kaiser 1990; Kaiser *et al.* 1991). On a 'continuum of uniformity', as conceptualized by McVeigh, Peter and similar interviewees would fall towards the end characterized as 'disordered, anti-standardized, anti-categorized and overtly individualistic' (1997: 198). We hear how 'people do get confused' by Peter's appearance, which perhaps indicates why the two styles through which people attempt to classify him (biker and skateboarder) are relatively dissimilar compared to, say, the options of metaller and goth in (F). Even then it seems that these are not the only possible candidates ('it just sort of goes on and on like that'). It is through this heightened sense of stylistic ambiguity that 'crossover counterculture' can be likened to the 'freak style' identified by Gottschalk: 'Unwilling to embrace any recognizable (sub)cultural style, Freaks subverted them all by combining them without centre, logic, or order . . . [This group] resists identification and classification' (1993: 368).

Even in such cases of stylistic ambiguity, affinity continues to be expressed with a wider collectivity of like-minded others: Peter talks of a 'bond', Daniel (extract J) claims to 'associate'. Yet Daniel's use of the word 'loosely' helps to distinguish 'subculture' in this context from its more specific, cohesive and coherent connotations, thus making clear the nebulous quality of the collectivity to which he 'relate(s)'. This is further emphasized both by its equivalence with another non-specific term, 'the weirdos', and by describing it as the end-result of a process whereby specific subcultural elements 'cross over' into once mutually exclusive stylistic domains. As this implies a tendency towards the formation of a wider group of more ambiguously dressed individuals who have the stylistic credentials to pass muster in a larger number of social milieux, it is interesting that the 'cosmopolitan' Peter claims to 'fit in with just about everybody really'. But this communitarian dimension to affiliation is not predicated upon a uniformity that obliterates and is antithetical to individuality, but a diverse unity (see extract B) that can encompass and accommodate individual difference. This is necessarily so, for it is individuality that is the basis of subcultural authenticity.

We can understand authenticity as that which defines the real or genuine members of a subculture. As we saw in Chapter 2, authenticity in the CCCS approach is located in a highly collectivist conception of subcultural resistance and theoretically imputed to those original members who constitute the subculture at the point of its inception. This presents a fundamental irony in the CCCS work, for it is exactly this homogeneous conception of subculture that my own informants reject as stereotypical and (by extension) inauthentic. The diffuse (or liminal) sensibility expressed by my subcultural sample is not, however, in any way suggestive of a post-inceptive inauthenticity, for it is through such sentiments that the whole *basis of* a subcultural response can be validated. A point made by Steve, a Preston interviewee: 'I would have said I was a punk or a mod, but the label always sort of like . . . if you were a punk it was always a contradiction to say I belong to this group of people, 'cos *what it's about* isn't' (my emphasis).

Much the same objection to the CCCS approach can be found in Widdicombe and Wooffitt's *The Language of Youth Subcultures* (1995). Here, the authors present interviews with members of various style subcultures to demonstrate how speakers typically resist group categorizations. Having examined how both academic and common-sense accounts of subcultures are based upon the assumption that affiliation satisfies an individual's 'need' or 'desire' for a collective identity, Widdicombe and Wooffitt argue that such perspectives patently fail to consider deeply felt notions in Western societies about individuality and authenticity. The origin of these concerns can be traced to humanist and existential discourses that emphasize the uniqueness of the individual inner self, and the importance of achieving authenticity through the realization and expression of this uniqueness. Group identifications are therefore resisted because they carry connotations of collective conformity, suggesting a concomitant loss of individuality that renders their members inauthentic.

Although this confirms my own findings, Widdicombe and Wooffitt do not consider the differences that may exist in this respect between subcultures and other groups in society. On the contrary, they are keen to emphasize that 'our analytic claims may be relevant to a wider community of persons that those whose accounts are examined here' (1995: 208). Andes (1998), however, makes the point that those subculturalists who transcend group identifications (such as the punks in her own study) have a particularly pronounced ideology of individualism, and that membership categories are likely to be a less sensitive issue for other types of groups. Individuality can, in other words, be considered a cultural value upon which different social actors can place varying degrees of emphasis.

Confirmation of this variation in individuality can be found in Jeffrey

Arnett's *Metalheads: Heavy Metal Music and Adolescent Alienation* (1996).[10] Arnett convincingly demonstrates that American youth involved in the heavy metal subculture have been socialized into a radical form of their country's dominant cultural belief system of liberal individualism. Compared to conventional youth, the metalheads are characterized by 'hyperindividualism'; they place a higher value on independence and lead more individualized lives, less integrated than many Americans into the collective ties and bonds of family, school, community and religion that act to balance the tendency towards cultural disintegration. 'American adults encourage their children towards independence, self-sufficiency and individualism from an early age believing that these are healthy goals for development. What is unintended, unanticipated, and often unrecognized is that, for some adolescents, independence easily becomes loneliness, self-sufficiency may shade into isolation, individualism may take an alienated form' (Arnett 1996: 17).

Subcultures can therefore be understood, somewhat paradoxically, as collective expressions and celebrations of individualism. We will take up these issues again in our concluding chapter. For now, we can raise the issue of whether this liberation from collective norms and values also entails (again somewhat paradoxically) a weakened sense of commitment to any one subcultural grouping. This form of reasoning finds its postmodern counterpart in the claim that contemporary subculturalists engage in a radical stylistic pluralism, embracing and celebrating the fluidity and ephemerality of different subcultural identities on offer. This is the theme of our next chapter.

Notes

1. References to the individualistic ethos of mod can be found in Barnes (1991).

2. Lull (1987: 228) also reports on such hybrids as 'psychedelic punk', 'Rasta punk', 'funk punk and 'punk funk'.

3. Moreover, this type of comparison was frequently raised in interviews by the subculturalists themselves long before the prompt occurred on my interview schedule. Conventional people can be also be referred to by the informants as 'straights' or the 'mainstream' (see Widdicombe and Wooffitt 1995: 168–74; Thornton 1995: 87–115; Pini 1997; Andes 1998; Tomlinson 1998).

4. This insider status should not be confused with the sense in which subcultures are regarded as 'outsiders' to the 'normalized' dominant culture. See, for example, Becker (1963).

5. Like many commentators on consumer culture, Miles and his co-researchers regard individual choices as somewhat illusory, placing more importance on the power of producers to shape consumer actions (see also the discussion of this research in Miles 1998). Again, this is not an 'objective' assessment, but one made from a

particular value position. For a different interpretation, see Lipovetsky (1994).

6. On the relevance of the insider–outsider distinction to groups other than subcultures see also A. P. Cohen (1986), Jenkins (1996) and Billington *et al.* (1998).

7. Similarly, despite Thornton's attempt 'to maintain an analytical frame of mind' (1995: 2) she does not avoid stereotyping clubbers, describing one such crowd, albeit in a partly knowing way, as 'pretty homogeneous' and wearing 'the acid house uniform' (ibid.: 88).

8. I am grateful to Nick Abercrombie for the observation that there may be a note of regret in Oliver's admission never to have 'really been a proper anything'. It may also appear that, through such a claim, Oliver is owning up to his own inauthenticity compared to the authenticity of 'proper mods'. But if this were the case he would be the only informant to imply that the most authentic subcultural tastes are those that are the most restricted and specific.

9. See, for example, the exercise in decoding in McCracken (1990: 62–7).

10. See also Arnett (1991a, 1991b, 1992, 1993). It is interesting to read Arnett's book in conjunction with the account given by Gaines (1991). Both authors see sections of American youth heading towards *anomie* and cultural disintegration.

5

Commitment, Appearance and the Self

I have had joy in helping Stephanie share in the exuberance and abandon of the New World, but in the process I have witnessed a flaw emerge, like a silent genetic disease knitted into her DNA, which has now inevitably unravelled at this later date. The flaw is simple: because Stephanie was not born here, she can never *understand* here.

'People in California meet people who they have not seen for two years', she says while driving home from Venice, 'and they say to each other, *"So who are you now? What is your new ray-ligion? What new style of clothes are you wearing these days? What kind of diet are you eating? Who is your wife? What sort of house are you in now? What different city? What new ideas do you believe?"* If you are not a completely new person, your friends will be disappointed.'

'So?' I ask.

'Do you not see anything wrong with this constant change?'

'Should there be? I think it's great I'm allowed to reinvent myself each week.'

Douglas Coupland: *Shampoo Planet* (1993: 237–8)

When I rummage through my wardrobe in the morning I am not merely faced with a choice of what to wear. I am faced with a choice of images: the difference between a smart suit and a pair of overalls, a leather skirt and a cotton dress, is not just one of fabric and style, but one of identity. You know perfectly well that you will be seen differently for the whole day, depending on what you put on; you will appear as a particular kind of woman with one particular identity *which excludes others*. The black leather skirt rules out girlish innocence, oily overalls tend to exclude sophistication, ditto smart suit and radical feminism. Often I have wished I could put them all on together, or appear simultaneously in every possible outfit, just to say, How dare you think any one of these is *me*. But also, See, I can be all of them.

Judith Williamson: *Consuming Passions* (1986: 91)

Part-timers

As one of the contributors to an internationally focused study of contemporary – read 'postmodern' – consumption practices and their implications
for self-identity, Langman writes, 'if the subject is not dead, s/he is more
likely decentred, fragmented, and differentially expressed and experienced
depending on context' (1992: 67). Likewise, Shields, as editor of the collection,
talks in his introduction of 'the multiple masks of a postmodern "persona"
who "wears many hats" in different groups and surroundings . . . their
multiple identifications form a private *dramatis personae* – a self which can
no longer be simplistically theorized as unified' (1992: 16). This mode of
theorizing has undoubtedly underwritten contemporary 'postmodern' perspectives on the increasing plurality, superficiality and ephemerality of
subcultural identities. The reference to 'multiple masks' and 'many hats'
suggests that looks are casually put on and cast off, enabling us to play with
our identities in a highly promiscuous fashion. This increases the potential
for any individual to enjoy a greater degree of stylistic freedom; to cruise
through the available images on offer, to engage in what Polhemus (1996)
has, in the context of clubland, termed 'Style Surfing'.

Our hypothesis to examine in this chapter is that subculturalists display a
superficial and transient attachment to any one style as they regularly
transgress the boundaries that serve to separate the conventional from the
subcultural and specific subcultures from each other. If we look back to extract
(A) in the previous chapter we can see that Duncan's emphatic manner of
claiming a punk identity is also a way of demonstrating his commitment to
the subculture. Claiming that he is punk 'through and through' conveys the
depth rather than the superficiality of his attachment. Saying how he has
been a punk for so many years also suggests the seriousness of his commitment
by drawing attention to the longevity of his affiliation. It is difficult to see
how such commitment could continue to be expressed if Duncan were to
change regularly between punk and other subcultural styles, or from
subcultural to conventional dress and back again, within the course of, say,
a few days or weeks. This chapter will examine such themes in the context
of simultaneous (synchronic) subcultural identifications and relatively short-
term mobility. A long-term (diachronic) analysis of subcultural change will
be a focus of the next chapter. The first two extracts of this chapter explore
the relationship of the subcultural to the conventional.

(A)   JIM, JANE AND SEAN

DM: *Do you . . . is there a degree of creativity about the way you look?
      I mean do you put a lot of thought and effort into it?*

Figure 5. Jim, Jane, Sean

Ja: *Definitely.*

Jim: *Individuality. You don't want anyone to dress the same as you.*

S: *Yeah, well even in the mod scene, if you start seeing lots of people dressing fairly similarly, you'd think, well I wanna be a bit differently to that. So that's the individual bit within the group sort of thing.*

DM: *Are there any occasions where you might look totally different? Do you tend to stick – OK, I know everyone has their own individual way of looking – but are there any occasions where you look totally different? I mean, do you always dress in the kind of general sixties style?*

S: *Yes.*

Ja: *Yeah.*

DM: *You never look any different?*

S: *Yeah. I can't understand people that would kind of like put some
        clothes on for the evening and then wear something completely
        opposite.*

Jim: *Part-timers.*

Ja: *Yeah, we look the same during the day as we do when we go out.*

DM: *What about different occasions? When . . . I can't think of one
        offhand.*

Jim: *Red Chrysanthemums. Red, er, what's the one?*

Ja: *Carnation.*

Jim: *Carnation. We were going out for this meal, and I was wearing a
        red carnation.*

S: *Not really relevant, though, is it?*

Extract (A) begins with an issue first discussed in the previous chapter: distinctive individuality within the group. We can see that this is regarded positively, one reason being that it allows individuals to recognize their location within stylistic parameters that would designate them as, say, mod, while distancing themselves from what they perceive to be a stereotypical version of the subculture. My second question has a temporal basis, to ascertain whether any one person might undergo a total change from one type of look to another and back again. This, by contrast, provokes a very negative response. One reason for this, I would argue, is because such a stylistic 'switch' takes an individual out of the range of dress codes that serve to mark allegiance to a particular grouping. Deriding such people as 'part-timers', as Jim does here, is a way of calling into question their commitment to the subculture.

> Different youths can bring different degrees of commitment to a subculture. It can represent a major dimension in people's lives – an axis erected in the face of the family around which a secret and immaculate identity can be made to cohere – or it can be a slight distraction, a bit of light relief from the monotonous but none the less paramount realities of school, home and work. It can be used as a means of escape, of total detachment from the surrounding terrain, or as a way of fitting back into it and settling down after a week-end or evening letting off steam (Hebdige 1979: 122).

Part-timers are those who, according to Hebdige, display allegiance only for the weekend; or, as Sean would have it, for just the duration of the evening. That such an individual might then re-enter the group by switching back to the required subcultural look would probably be taken only as further evidence of their dilettantism. We can, however, see that a change of style is admitted to in response to my prompt concerning 'different occasions'. I suggest, though, that this information is volunteered precisely because it is concerning a special occasion. Looking different is characterized as the exception that proves the general rule. One does not go out for meals as a matter of course, and 'dressing-up' for such occasions is not only acceptable but perhaps expected. And while Sean might feel the example of a red carnation is hardly relevant, it is relevant precisely because of the function that such a superficial detail plays in drawing attention to what is otherwise a general lack of change.

As the three informants dress in a mod style, it might be argued that the above claim is an easy one for them to make. The mod image is singularly closer to notions of conventionality than is the case for other subcultures, and is therefore unlikely to look completely out of place in such special circumstances. Let us look, then, at (B), the first part of which throws into sharp relief the comprehensive distinction between the interviewees' usual subcultural style and their conventional dress, but again mitigates possible accusations of partial affiliation by making reference to the latter as a rare and therefore acceptable departure from the former.

(B)   ANNE AND JULIE

DM: *Have you ever dressed in . . . have you ever thought of yourself being, or have you ever dressed in a way that was different?*

J: *Well, in about two or three weeks we're going to the Paradox for a hen night.*

A: *We're going on a Shaz night.*

J: *We're going to call it . . . it's called the Shaz night, and we're going, like, completely overboard.*

A: *We are going to . . . I'm taking all my piercing out, so I'm even going to bleach my hair and curl it into a nice bob for the occasion.*

J: *Fitted jacket, sheer tights, stilettos, the whole bit.*

A: *Stilettos, the whole works. Cover up the tattoos.*

J: *Gold lamé handbag. We're going to go for the whole Shaz bit.*

DM: *Doesn't that compromise what you are?*

A: *Not at all, 'cos we still know.*

DM: *(Later in interview) Do you ever buy from mainstreet stores?*

A   *Oh, I have done, yeah.*

J: *Yeah, yeah. Definitely, 'cos there are things that like . . . I mean like . . . I'm into vest tops a lot of the time, and it's best to get them from mainstream stores, and, I mean, if you just wear them*

> *differently; it's not really what you're wearing, it's the way you wear it, what you wear it with, and . . .*
>
> A: *It's like I bought a vest top last Sunday and matched it up with her lacy skirt, which is really nice.*

Anne and Julie talk of going to a nightclub for a hen night, thus signalling the occasion as a one-off event. Its 'conventional' status is made clear by referring to it as 'the Shaz night', Shaz and Trace being typical names used by subculturalists to denote 'trendies'.[1] The talk of dressing-up in a Shaz style, 'we're going completely overboard . . . the whole works', suggests an excessiveness bordering on the edge of parody, that this is at one level something of a joke at the expense of the clientele who are usually found to patronize such a place. There is more than a hint here of dressing-up in costume, the way in which one might for a fancy dress party. The reference to tattoos is important, for they can be displayed as 'marks of mischief' (Sanders 1988), a badge of commitment to subcultural values (Fox 1987; Moore 1994; Polhemus 1994; Schouten and McAlexander 1995), and covering them up is a way of effecting a temporary disguise of Anne's status. There was also a telling response to my question as to whether such a change of appearance would 'compromise what you are'. Anne's reply is 'not at all, 'cos we still know', which can only mean still having knowledge of 'who or what we are'. Lurie has said that 'to put on somebody else's clothes is to symbolically take on their personality' (1992: 24). It is this assumption that is being mitigated here by characterizing a conventional appearance as a misleading guide to, and a temporary masking of, what or who someone really is.

I later ask Anne and Julie whether they buy clothes from mainstreet shops. Instead of referring to the wearing of conventional clothes as an exception, as they did earlier, Julie states that vest-tops from mainstream stores are a commonly worn item ('a lot of the time'). Yet by claiming 'if you just wear them differently', she is able to differentiate herself from any conventional dressing people who might be wearing the same item. What is, in fact, being described here is their attempt at constructing a different look through a *bricolage* of conventional and subcultural elements: in this case a mainstream vest top with a goth-style lace skirt. So rather than the separation between conventional and usual wear seen in the first part of the extract, we find here the juxtaposition and combination of the two. As J. Clarke (1986) and Hebdige (1979) have argued, subcultural styles are constructed by the taking and recontextualizing of items from the dominant culture. If unconventionality of appearance is constructed in such a way, the wearing of specific elements that are of conventional origin is therefore unavoidable, and cannot be taken as evidence of being only partly committed. (As we will see in Chapter 7, there are good reasons why interviewees are unable to argue that full commitment is demonstrated by the wearing of a distinct set of items that are wholly subcultural.)

There is, though, a second reason given in (B) as to why Anne and Julie are different from conventional people who wear the same item. This is somewhat intangible, and concerns 'the way you wear it'. That this is different from 'what you wear it with' is attested to by the same distinction occurring in a number of different interviews (see also Widdicombe 1993: 104). But what is meant by such a phrase? The answer to this question lies in the next three extracts.

Hearts and Masks

In the first extract of the last chapter we saw that Duncan made a distinction between a punk appearance and the values underlying this, privileging the latter over the former. A similar feature appears in our next extract, (C), where Dougie claims that punk is not about what you look like, but what you feel in your heart.[2] In sociological terms, this suggests that the meaning of punk is internalized. People, in other words, express as part of their personality the particular values into which they have been socialized (Parsons 1951). The argument made in the last chapter, that those who affiliate to subcultures are likely to have been brought up to express the values of hyperindividualism (Arnett 1996), would explain why some of my interviewees claimed to have *always* had a feeling of inner difference to other people, *predating* their affiliation to a subculture (see also Fox 1987: 353; Widdicombe and Wooffitt 1995: 158; Andes 1998).

While it may be objected that everyone is individually different, such a claim was clearly phrased in terms of individual estrangement from the majority (Widdicombe 1993: 106), and can be understood through our concept of distinctive individuality outlined in the last chapter. The argument put forward here is along the lines of: all people are individuals with different attitudes, tastes and personalities, but some have more individuality than others (Kitwood 1980: 117–18). An example of this can be seen in (D) below. Robin is clear that this feeling of difference 'deep inside' must have preceded his entry into punk, since this was the 'whole reason why' the punk subculture, as a visible manifestation of distinction, 'appealed' to him, and why its emergence is characterized as 'something I'd been waiting [for]'. Note the way that, like Dougie, he defines punk in terms of his inner self, 'it was just like me'.

(C)   DOUGIE

D: *I mean that's what it's all about, punk, it's in your heart. It's not what your haircut's like or whether you've got big boots on. In my opinion it's just about the way you feel. I mean people might look at me and go 'oh, he's not really a punk rocker 'cos he doesn't wear punk rock clothes all the time', but it's in me heart. I mean I don't have to go out and impress anybody.*

Figure 6. Robin

(D)   ROBIN

R: *I mean the whole reason why the punk thing appealed to me, it
was just like me, something deep inside of me, and I just immediately went, 'yes, this is for me!' Like I said, it was almost something
I'd been waiting . . . something inside of me. Perhaps I felt different
inside; I must have done. But it is what you feel inside, because
you could wear identical . . . you could go out and buy more or
less – I mean obviously you'd have to do a bit of chasing around –
but more or less buy something that looks very similar to what
I'm wearing now, but you're the only person who would know
genuinely how you feel inside about it. The truth is – I'm not being
funny – is certain people can carry a certain image and some people
can't. Certain people look just totally out of place in what they're
dressed as and what they're trying to be.*

(E)   PETE AND ALISON

A: *I know people who just, who just . . . er . . . dress similar to us
because they want to, er . . . they're doing it for the image and
they'd probably answer the question in a completely opposite way
than we are because they're meant to be just doing it for the image,
'cos they think that it looks good. Therefore they adopt the style
of dress. It's not something that comes from inside to those. It's
more that they adopt, and they adopt . . . er, they adopt . . . er
liking a certain kind of music and they adopt certain attitudes.*

P: *Nothing's really them, their own. There's nothing to their appearance, to be something as they aren't really.*

A: *They're plastic. And it's very plastic. It's not real.*

P: *Done for effect rather than for any real reason.*

DM: *So you're trying to say you're not like that?*

A: *It's not really wearing a style; it's part of expressing yourself.*

P: *Yeah, it's an extension of yourself.*

A: *The look's part of me.*

P: *It's self-expression.*

Dress, according to Stone, is a vehicle through which a person 'announces
his identity, shows his value, expresses his mood, or proposes his attitude'
(1981: 193). As one of Tseëlon's informants phrased it, 'I like the outer me
to reflect the inner me' (1995: 50). It is this self-expression through style
that, in the second half of (E), leads Pete and Alison to each characterize
their appearance as an 'extension of', even 'part of' their persona. Of course,

as Robin (extract D) acknowledges, 'you' could wear a similar style to what he is currently wearing. But this would not necessarily be a genuine act, for the style may not be an expression of inner feelings. It is, in other words, whether or not 'it comes from inside' (extract E) that is the marker of authenticity and makes the difference between doing it 'genuinely' or 'falsely'.[3] Those who merely 'adopt' an unconventional appearance without possessing the necessary 'inner' qualities are regarded by Pete and Alison as 'plastic', 'not real'. What, in fact, we are seeing in these extracts is the use of a reference group – a subcultural 'Other' – against which the interviewees authenticate themselves. We might have reasoned from our discussion of Schutz (1980) in the previous chapter that this is a stereotypical characterization based on subculturalists who are contemporaries rather than consociates of the informants. Because their specific identities and personal characteristics remain unknown, they can be typified as anonymous outsiders on the evidence of only their appearance.[4]

That such contemporaries are judged by Robin as only 'trying to be . . . what they're dressed as' additionally implies that they have not successfully managed it. If you *are* something, then you don't by definition need to try. This form of reasoning allows certain subculturalists to be relatively unconcerned with their own stylistic expression.[5] Dougie (extract C), for example, is happy to admit that 'he doesn't wear punk rock clothes all the time'. Given that he *is* a punk – 'inside', there is no reason why he should 'have to go out and impress anybody'. Yet this effectively denies a correspondence between his internal and external states. So is he suggesting that on such occasions he is 'false'? I would argue not. As Geoff, a Preston interviewee, put it, 'there could be a bloke wearing a T-shirt and tennis shoes and he could be more punk than me'. That people dressed in ordinary clothes could be *more punk* than Geoff is hardly suggestive of their falsity – in fact quite the opposite. This is because, as we have seen, the possession of underlying attributes such as feelings of inner difference are valued more highly than the wearing of subcultural style. It was even conveyed that inner difference will 'show through' no matter what one is wearing. Ricky, a bonehead and ex-punk, to whom I suggested that the wearing of expensive clothes was hardly an expression of dissent, replied, 'but I wear them with attitude'.

The suggestion being made here is that subcultural allegiance is inscribed on and conveyed through the body (Bourdieu 1984) in ways other than dress. Brake is useful here, distinguishing between 'image' and 'demeanour', the latter consisting of 'expression, gait and posture' (1980: 12). Those who make a fetish of image to indicate their membership clearly risk the accusation of trying too hard, for subcultural affiliation is more authentically gauged through one's physical actions and bodily dispositions (so long as these remain *genuine* expressions of inner feelings). We can now go back to (B) and say that this is perhaps what Julie had in mind when she appears to claim that she wears conventional clothes in a different way to other people who might be wearing the same items. It is also why, in the eyes of Robin in (D), she should *not* appear false (i.e. not 'look out of place').

We have, so far, situated subcultural authenticity in an expressive concept of identity, where genuine membership is defined by the sincere expression of the self through subcultural practices. I want, however, at this point to raise, in order to circumvent, a potential criticism: that this particular notion of the self appears to rely upon what Lloyd (1999) has termed the 'substantialist' and 'spatial' dimensions of identity. The substantialist dimension assumes that identity comprises, or is founded upon, an inner 'core' self, a fixed essence (see Billington *et al.* 1998: Ch. 2) that pre-exists one's acquiring of social characteristics. As Widdicombe and Wooffitt put this with regard to subcultures, 'authenticity is established by reference to the emergence and maintenance of a true or inner self which just happens to reflect, or mesh with, the underlying values of the group' (1995: 157). If this, essentially speaking, is what one *is* (i.e. punk at heart), then it also presupposes what one is not; indeed, what one cannot be (i.e. mod, skinhead or goth at heart). Hence, the substantialist dimension implies the spatial dimension, the construction of boundaries that demarcate clearly defined identities. It assumes the existence of an 'Other', in possession of their own substantialist identities against which we define ourselves.

From this point of view, the sense of self that subculturalists articulate appears to involve a tightly fixed and bounded identity. If style is an expression of this self, then subcultural identity will also be rigid and unchanging. Yet, as Evans has remarked, 'people actually do move through subcultures' (1997: 180). This suggests a need to retheorize the self, to dispense with the substantialist conception and establish a more fluid and de-centred identity that can account for subcultural mobility and movement. One way in which this process of retheorization has proceeded is to envisage subcultural identity as 'performative'. It is in Judith Butler's work on gender (1990, 1993) that we find an understanding of identity as a 'performative enactment' (Lloyd 1999: 197). Put simply, gender is not a categorical fixed property of a person; rather, it is constituted through our 'repetition' of a series of, never wholly identical, practices. There are three implications that arise from this: (i) 'gender is not simply an aspect of what one is, but it is something that one *does*, and does recurrently, in interaction with others' (David Bell *et al.* 1994: 32); (ii) the gendered self does not precede the performance; rather, as Lloyd puts it 'performativity produces that which it names' (1999: 201); and (iii) the constant differential construction of gender leads to an open and fluid, rather than a fixed and determinate, identity.

It is not difficult to see why Evans (1997) has discovered in Butler's work a useful model by which to reconceptualize subcultural identities as 'constantly mutating'. In referring to Barnard's contention that 'it is not the case that an individual is first a skinhead and then wears all the gear, but that the gear constitutes the individual as a skinhead' (Barnard 1996: 30), Evans draws a direct analogy with Butler's notion of performativity, suggesting that skinhead is not something that one is, but what one does. There is, in this account, no underlying self, no subcultural essence, that pre-exists the performance; rather, subcultural identities are constantly created and recreated in an ongoing process of enactment.[6] At this point the model is highly suggestive of subculture as mimesis and masquerade, in which nothing lies concealed behind the various masks and veils. Subcultures become no more than the sum of their representations, an interpretation not so far removed from postmodern theories of subjectivity where subcultural identities can have no substance beyond the endless succession of styles through which the self is constituted. It is but a short step here to recasting performance in the language of pose and facade, thereby suggesting a 'theatrical attitude' indicative of inauthent-icity (see Wilson 1998).

Yet to conceive of subcultural identity in this way is to propose a model at odds with subculturalists' own conception of their authenticity. Widdicombe and Wooffitt have, for example, convincingly demonstrated that members of subcultures consistently portray themselves as 'being' punk (or hippy, skin, goth, etc.), thereby constructing themselves as genuine in opposition to superficial members who are merely 'doing' (or performing) punk (1990: 274). Moreover, it is not acceptable simply to dismiss, as Ryan and Fitzpatrick do, 'the idea that there is . . . a "self" that is "authenticated" by this process of reflexivity' (1996: 172). There are two reasons for this, which address the criticism raised earlier. First, the above claim for genuine membership is designed to address the issue that subcultural identity is constructed by possession of the required attitudes and values, not merely adopted by performing the requisite actions and dressing in the appropriate fashion, as Barnard (1996) appears to believe. In this sense, a claim to feel punk 'inside' does not denote an essentialist self, but an internalization of values acquired through socialization – a process that, in a very real sense, precedes subcultural performativity and leads certain individuals rather than others to affiliate to particular subcultures.

Secondly, a sense of self has equally real implications for how performance is stabilized and anchored. Appearance is not, as postmodern theory suggests, composed of free-floating signifiers, but appears to be constructed according to socially acquired tastes and preferences. As we will see in extract (I) of this chapter, while style is, indeed, something you put on, it is also regarded as 'part of you'. Having established the relationship between self and style in this way, it is understandable that rapid and comprehensive changes would pose problems for self-identity. This does not, however, mean that informants utilize a conception of the self that is static, unified and tightly bounded. As we shall see with the example of Matt in Chapters 6 and 7, informants resist interpellation into named subcultural identities precisely because this invokes a homogeneous, stable and uniform notion of a subculture that conflicts with the lived reality of their own practices. Indeed, I intend to demonstrate in the remainder of this chapter that subcultural forms are characterized by fragmentation, partiality and change. If authenticity is achieved by the genuine expression of the self in appearance and actions, then the self must also be mobile, complex and multi-faceted.

Fragmentation, Synchronicity and Schizophrenia

We have so far been concerned in this chapter with the relationship between the subcultural and the conventional. It was hypothesized that a plurality of available styles had reduced commitment to a subcultural identity as individuals regularly and pleasurably transgressed the subcultural–conventional boundary. What we found, by contrast, was that individuals perceived in this way were derided as both superficial and part-timers, and invoked as a subcultural 'Other' against which the interviewees could assert the authenticity of their own affiliation. This self-authentication was achieved by emphasizing how inner feelings were more important than appearances, or that the wearing of conventional items was an infrequent departure from a subcultural norm, or a necessary element in the creation of subcultural style through *bricolage*. These second and third forms of mitigation can again be seen in the next extract, but within the context of the relationship that individuals have to different subcultural styles.

(F)   PETER

DM: *OK, do you always tend to dress in this way nowadays? Are there occasions when you will look different?*

P: *I've got clothes from every period really, so I can look completely different at any given occasion, really. I have complete outfits that will make me a completely different person. You'd think I was just someone completely different. I've got some like original 50s clothing which is 50s jeans, could be a college jacket, or I wear*

50s box jackets occasionally. Or to be completely different I could look virtually, like, Charlie Channish really. I've got all the chino gear and the Panama hats and everything if I had to. So I could be just any number of people really. See, I've never really followed any trend but I've got clothes from every trend that's been (laughs), it's really funny. So I just dress how I want to dress really. I just throw it all together. I really just tend to mix and match. I just take whatever I like. I just take it and wear it, you know, just mix and match it anyway, so I don't really care what I'm wearing. Yeah, I just put it all together; yeah, I just mix it all up from different things. As I say, I could be anyone of a number of different people (laughs). I don't really consider whether it's one thing or the other. But (laughs) most of the time, most people will probably think I'm a punk (laughs). And then other ones will think 'he could be a biker'. Like I say, I could be any number of things all in one go, couldn't I?

What catches the eye in this extract is the range of diverse styles to which Peter refers, and that the phrase 'completely different' occurs four times in the first few lines along with one use of 'complete outfits'. That this is indicative of a comprehensive short-term change between distinct unconventional styles is interesting, for we have seen how similar suggestions of movement between subcultural and conventional styles are mitigated as a result of negative inferences about part-time affiliation. There then follows, however, a concerted effort to suggest that such complete change is, or would be, an infrequent departure from a more usual mode of dress. Note how Peter says that he wears '50s box jackets *occasionally*' as opposed to, say, usually or quite often. The words 'I can look . . . if I had to . . . I could be' could also be interpreted as demonstrating the potentiality rather than the actuality of certain courses of action. It would seem strange to talk of a typical or common form of behaviour in this way. It is also relevant that Peter's clothing is first described in a general way ('original 50s) and then separated into three more specific items ('jeans . . . college jackets . . . box jackets'). This may appear a small point, but it is a precursor for the strong emphasis that Peter then places on his ability to 'mix and match'. The effect of this is further to undermine his initial references to being 'complete', for at the end of the extract he is claiming that he is likely to 'be any number of things *all in one go*'.

This emphasis on fragmentation is further reinforced by Peter's haphazard dress sense. We can visualize how the act of taking off one complete outfit and selecting another to wear would require at least some minimum degree of conscious thought and careful selection in order to maintain adherence to the stylistic totality and purity of the specific look in question. Boundary maintenance is something to be worked at. Yet Peter's selection of items for wear is characterized by a carelessness and lack of thought ('I just throw it all together . . . I just take it and wear it . . . I don't really care what I'm wearing . . . I don't really consider whether it's one thing or the other'). What Coupland terms 'decade blending . . . the indiscriminate combination of two or more items from various decades to create a personal mood' (1995: 15), is, I feel, entirely appropriate for Peter. His claimed lack of thought and care is indeed indiscriminate, while the notion of a personal mood chimes perfectly with the emphasis he places on the creation of an individual look through the combination of items from previous styles. As he puts it 'I've never really followed any trend but I've got clothes from every trend that's been. I just dress how I want to dress, really.'

As we can ascertain from the quotations by Langman (1992) and Shields (1992) that appear in the first paragraph of this chapter, the fragmentation of the postmodern subject is assumed to be a consequence of its multiple identifications across different social sites and consumption practices. This 'decentring' of the subject, the challenge to the notion of the unified self, can also be found as a central concern in post-structuralist schools of thought that conceptualize the self as differentially positioned or 'articulated' by multiple and contradictory discourses, of class, gender, sexuality, ethnicity and age (Coward and Ellis 1977; Laclau and Mouffe 1985; Hall 1989). As Weeks (1990) puts it, 'each of us live with a variety of potentially contradictory identities which battle within us for allegiance'. In the view of Miles and his colleagues (1998) the problem with both postmodern and post-structuralist approaches is that the theory is formulated at a level of abstraction far removed from the everyday contexts in which identities are negotiated and managed. The influence of these perspectives in contemporary sociology and cultural studies has led to a situation where 'discussions of identity and more specifically the relationship between identity and consumption, have tended to operate in a theoretical vacuum' (Miles *et al.* 1998: 84).[7]

A study that provides a rare exception to this state of affairs is that by Tseëlon (1995). Although Tseëlon's female informants are not subcultural, they nevertheless provide a range of fascinating answers to questions about the relationship between their appearance and subjective identity. Particularly relevant here are Tseëlon's attempts to ascertain whether certain looks reflect a real self, or different aspects of the self (ibid.: 49–53). Although the responses are complex, it is possible to isolate three ideal-typical answers: (i) a conception of a 'real me' when dressed in a certain way; (ii) that different looks reflect various moods or aspects of the self; and (iii) that there is no 'real me'. None of these are mutually exclusive, and elements of each can be found combined in the same informant. This leads Tseëlon to advocate a conception of the self 'as both unitary and multiple' (ibid.: 53). It can be argued that this is not inconsistent with my own findings in extract (F). While Peter marginalizes certain styles as exceptions to the norm, suggesting a more consistent look (or set of looks) relevant to a central aspect of his identity, the 'multiplicity' of this centralized style is itself produced through fragmentation, thus suggesting a differentiated identity rather than plural identities.

What this more specifically suggests, contrary to theory, is that identities are differentiated and/or marginalized rather than multiple, holistic and central to a persona. Why this should be so can be partly explained by a conversation I had with a woman, Marie, not in my subcultural sample, but who nonetheless dressed in a manner that would have made her eligible to be. She told me that she once used to dress in a number of clearly distinct, different styles (punk, goth, retro fashions) across the course of any week or so. Although this allowed her to experience several separate, virtually synchronic identities, she had to abandon this pursuit because it induced in her a feeling of 'schizophrenia'. What she now did was to select 'bits' from each type of look, and consequently felt more 'comfortable' with this practice. There is, then, a subjective recognition of a point at which the multiplicity of stylistic identity presents a problem to one's subjectivity. It is ironic that Jameson (1991: 27–31) understands schizophrenia to be a postmodern symptom resulting from a disorienting and fragmentary sense of time, meaning and perception. MacCannell also assumes 'a fragmented consciousness' to entail 'schizophrenia at the level of culture' (1992: 220). Kellner similarly equates 'highly unstable identities' with 'a totally fragmented, disjointed life' (1992: 174). Yet, for Marie, instability and schizophrenia is produced by a plurality of unified, holistic identifications, and it is fragmentation that provides relief from this disorienting condition. Clearly, if subculturalists do find the plurality of styles on offer a cause for celebration, they appear to utilize these in a partial and marginalized manner.[8]

'Feeling Comfortable'

'The seasons of life follow one another, and one must change one's face as one changes one's clothes' (Berger 1968: 127).

We have, to this point, been primarily concerned with consistency of affiliation, the degree to which subculturalists view their membership as either full- or part-time. But commitment can also be gauged according to another temporal dimension, that of duration (long-term affiliation). Although empirically related, these two dimensions can be distinguished analytically. One can, for example, continue to move in and out of subcultures with a high frequency, yet still demonstrate a more durable commitment to any of these than someone whose membership is consistent, but short-lived. Here we will begin to focus also on durability, for according to Lash and Urry, 'the thesis of a postmodern political economy is one of the evermore rapid circulation of subjects and objects' (1994: 13). In this '"throwaway society", in which there is a strong emphasis on the volatility and ephemerality in fashion, products, labour processes, ideas and images' (ibid.: 245), is the potential for the disposability of style a cause for celebration? In the accompanying 'accelerated culture' (Coupland 1995), is the new, novel and up-to-date positively embraced? Some answers to these questions are to be found in the next two extracts.

Figure 7. Jane, Sean, Jim

(G)   JIM, JANE AND SEAN

S: *I don't know. You've got to wear something. You just wear what you like, really. I mean to me a fashion victim is someone who follows fashion every other week, like.*

Ja: *Someone who changes every month, sort of thing.*

S: *With whatever is current. Basically we think people that just follow fashion, they're silly really. 'Cos I mean they are not just making a choice themselves. Whereas we've just made the choice of what we want to do, and we just carry on with it. No big deal. Just think for yourself, really.*

Ja: *That is, you've just got to learn to think for yourself, and not follow what everyone else is doing.*

(H)   JOHN

J: *With punks I think it is just a complete waste of time. I mean like we were walking into a pub the other night, and there were these three people walking the other way with, like, bleached hair, and it was all spiked out and whatever, and like chains, the works, and like looking really sort of like, 'I'm from 1977 and if you don't watch out, 'cos I'm going to spit on your Granny, whatever.' You know, it was like that, and I mean it looks so ridiculous. I think that is really outdated, though, looking like punks.*

Extract (G) provides some reasons why stylistic ephemerality is regarded negatively. Sean and Jane perceive their own mod-related style in terms of individual expression ('wear what you like . . . think for yourself') and long-term commitment to that expression ('we just carry on with it'). By contrast, those who 'follow fashion' are characterized by transient tastes ('every other week . . . changes every month') and a collective orientation ('follow what everyone else is doing . . . they are not just making a choice themselves'). Clearly, fashion is itself defined as a short-term trend. The assertion that such people change 'with whatever is current' suggests the following of fashion irrespective of the type of style involved, and is meant to contrast with the specificity of choice made through individual selection. Such comments are obviously intended to be derogatory, for the term 'fashion victim' clearly conveys the actions of those so described as a result of manipulation by external forces rather than individual volition.

Yet a look at extract (H) immediately tells us that long-term commitment to an unchanging look can be regarded with equal derision. John's references to 1977 and spitting are a comment on the futility of attempting to strike a rebellious pose through a punk style so durable it is now clearly 'outdated' and missing the point. The real point here, at least according to John, is that the style has now become a *stereotype*, suggesting uniformity, conformity and predictability. 'I've always hated the idea of a uniform. If you have any kind of movement at all, you should reject things like that. You're not moving, plus it's sterile' (Lydon 1994: 71–2). Extracts (G) and (H) taken together suggest that both transience and permanence are potential markers of the superficial and inauthentic. Such judgements are again based on unknown contemporaries, and any person is likely to avoid the imputation that they can be characterized either way. As Tseëlon discovered in her own study of attitudes to dress, 'while women admitted that they would not want to look "dated" they strongly rejected the idea of looking like "fashion victims"' (1995: 30).

Clearly, if both short-term change and stylistic permanence present potential problems for the authentic expression of self through style, a third option must exist whereby authenticity can be re-established. We find this in extract (I).

(I)   PETE AND ALISON

A: *It appeals to me because I feel comfortable with it. If I wore anything else I wouldn't feel – I wouldn't be able to relax.*

P: *Yes, I feel comfortable. I wouldn't feel comfortable any other way. I just could not dress any other way.*

A: *It's like you put it on 'cos it's part of you.*

P   *I just tend to have evolved from thing to thing. I don't, haven't made any conscious effort. It just happens.*

A: *There's two words I really hate and that's 'always' and 'never'. I'm really into change and progression and development. I'll always be myself. I hope I'll always have the respect for myself to be myself and to express myself, but that may change. It may not; I don't know.*

P: *Yes, I can't imagine myself dressing or being any other way than what I am, no matter how old I am. I mean it's not to say that I won't change, but I can't imagine any other way. I haven't even thought that far forward. But that's not to say . . . but that's not to say I won't be. I mean if something comes along that I feel comfortable with that would make me change the way I dress or the way I think, then fine. But I can't foresee anything at this present time.*

DM: *Right, but you're not the kind of person who says 'I'm always going to be like this whatever happens'?*

P: *No, no, that would be stupid, because you don't know what's going to happen.*

Here, as was also the case in (E), appearance is virtually subsumed into the self. Consequently, Pete reports feeling 'comfortable' with his appearance, and finds it difficult to envisage feeling the same way if dressed in other styles. Yet while this would logically lead to expressions of permanent commitment, there is unmistakably a positive emphasis placed on change in this extract. How can continuity and change be reconciled? In an article on contemporary developments in subcultural studies, Evans (1997: 183) finds it apposite to cite Venturi's (1977) aesthetic judgement, 'I prefer "both-and" to "either-or."' We find the same sentiment expressed in this extract. By resisting the two categories of 'always and never', Pete and Alison escape from the inevitability of *either* the new (never continue, always change) *or* the outmoded (never change, always continue). Yet this, on the other hand, legislates for the possibility of *both* continuity ('I can't imaging myself dressing or being any other way than what I am, no matter how old I am'), *and* change ('It's not to say that I won't change' . . . 'you don't know what's going to happen'). The reconciliation of these two eventualities is achieved through the formulation of change in evolutionary terms ('progression and development') while continuing to hold to the principle of 'genuinely' expressing one's self through appearance ('I'll always express myself, however that is'), suggesting that authenticity of commitment is guaranteed when appearance has *gradually* evolved in tandem with the changing persona (see also Widdicombe and Wooffitt 1995: 145). In this respect it is important that Pete talks of change in both his outer and inner self ('the way I dress and the way I think'). It is precisely this gradual symbiosis that would allow him to remain 'comfortable' throughout such a situation.

Our analysis of extracts (G) to (I) has important implications for the way in which researchers such as Fox (1987) and Sardiello (1998) claim to distinguish between authentic and inauthentic subcultural members according to such criteria of commitment as consistency and durability. According to Fox, the crucial difference between 'real punks' and 'pretenders' is whether membership is full and permanent or part-time and temporary. The former group, the most highly committed, are a small number of 'hardcores'; the latter, those on the 'periphery' of the subculture, are the more numerous yet only superficially attached 'preppie-punks'.[9] Fox observes how the 'hardcores' had demonstrated their complete conversion into a punk identity by making severe and long-lasting, sometimes permanent, alterations to their physical bodies; through, for example, the display of swastika tattoos in highly visible places or the cutting of their hair in a drastic 'mohawk' style. Preppies, by contrast, wore their hair and clothes in such a way as 'to look punk sometimes and conventional at other times . . . this obvious ability to change roles kept the preppies from being considered real or committed' (1987: 361).

Although Fox constructs a picture of the subculture from the subjective perceptions of the subculturalists themselves, she appears to be suggesting that the punk subculture is objectively stratified in this way. Yet this presents a quite misleading account, in that the 'preppie punks' appear only as viewed through the eyes of the 'hardcore' members (and Fox herself). So what Fox is actually describing here is the way in which members authenticate their own commitment as 'hardcore' by invoking a subcultural 'Other', interpreting the positive sentiments towards change expressed by certain contemporaries as evidence of their ephemerality and superficiality. It is telling that Fox provides no quotes from the 'preppies' themselves; but those so denigrated would no doubt have characterized themselves in the same manner as Pete and Alison in (I), as being open to gradual development (thereby incorporating both change and continuity) rather than merely rapid change. They would not have seen their stylistic partiality and supposed transgressions of the subcultural–conventional boundary as evidence of a part-time status, but on the contrary as clear indication of their subcultural commitment through any of the three ways seen in extracts (B) and (C) of this chapter (the wearing of conventional style is a temporary departure that does not affect what one really is; it is an unavoidable effect of *bricolage*; it is less important than attitude).

Moreover, we can go further and suggest that the 'preppies' would most likely have thought the hardcore style to be an inauthentic uniform indicative of trying too hard, and the expressed commitment of 'hardcores' as suggestive of stasis and stereotypicality, rather as we saw in (H). For if tattoos and mohawks or similarly severe body modifications were clear signals of permanent authentic membership for the 'hardcores', they can be equally indicative of inauthenticity from the viewpoint of others subculturalists. See, for example, Andes, who quotes Lester, a punk respondent, complaining, 'I visualize punk and I see dozens of mohawked morons running about with spray paint, writing "Anarchy" and "The Exploited" all over the place' (1998: 227). Robin (extract D) also related the tale of a punk who was 'mutilated from scarification' through 'really sad Sid Vicious tattoos' and going bald through constantly dying his hair and soaping it into spikes. All of this, together with his 'fluorescent lime green leopard skin trousers', made him in Robin's eyes, 'just look sad, because he is still definitely trying to be a tourist punk rocker in London'. Robin's advice: 'Mick. Wake up! It's 1994, you've got nothing to prove any more.'

From this, it should be evident that there are no 'hardcores' and 'preppies' in any 'realist' sense, only members who construct themselves as the former and their contemporaries as the latter, a process which, as our earlier discussion of Schutz (1980) should have indicated, is reciprocal in its effects.[10] This is not to claim that there are no differences between individual members of a subculture in terms of style, tastes and values. As Fox remarks 'the punk style codes were somewhat diverse' (1987: 348). Indeed, heterogeneity facilitates conflicting interpretations of members' authenticity. This issue will be explored further in Chapter 7. For now, we can be content to add superficiality, rapid change and stasis to homogeneity and specificity as indicators of the inauthentic. What, though, does this allow us to make of Polhemus's experiences of clubland?

> Unlike those who feel and express a consistent commitment to a particular subculture, "Clubbers" delight in promiscuously "cruising" through all manner of clothing and musical styleworlds – one month (or, indeed, one evening) plunging headfirst into the 70s ... the next going Gothic or Techno or Fetish or New Romantic or Punk or Cowboy/girl or Hawaiian. It is this "surfing" (as in "Channel Surfing" or "Surfing the Internet") that most tellingly identifies "clubbing" as a post-subcultural phenomenon. And which, in so doing, defines this world and those within it as Post-Modern' (Polhemus 1996: 91).

As described and illustrated in his book, *Style Surfing* (1996), Polhemus depicts a world inhabited by people who, with their quick-fire turnover of discrete, holistic identities, appear very different to my own subcultural interviewees. The exceptional shallowness and superficiality implied in such transient attachments is perhaps best captured through what Grossberg defines as 'authentic inauthenticity', an attitude that valorizes 'poses', but with the self-knowledge that all such identities are no more than empty images (1992: 209–34). Perhaps this really is a scenario where style is simply not anchored in any underlying sense of self.

We should be wary of such an interpretation because of the way that Polhemus engages here in the same conceptual confusion that, in his previous book, *Streetstyle* (1994), characterized his description of 'the Supermarket of Style'. On the one hand, this is identifiable by its postmodern stylistic eclecticism and fragmentation, precisely the features that led me to compare it to my own concept of 'crossover counterculture' in the previous chapter. Yet its members also undergo comprehensive short-term change between clearly identifiable styles, '"Punks" one day, "Hippies" the next, they fleetingly leap across decades and ideological divides' (Polhemus 1994: 131). But these are clearly two, conceptually distinct, options. And so it is with his description of clubland. For despite his identification of clearly demarcated clubber identities, Polhemus also refers to its visual 'eclecticism, fragmentation, surreal juxtapositions and synchronicity' (1996: 97). Undoubtedly it is this latter identification that, along with claims for a more gradual rate of change, is likely to be advocated by the clubbers themselves. Perhaps Polhemus is partly guilty, as indeed other researchers have been in their own studies, of homogenizing and inauthenticating informants from an 'outsider' perspective. There was not, in any of my interviews, a single unambiguous case of anyone claiming to engage in the fleeting, comprehensive stylistic changes that Polhemus describes.

Evans has rightly observed 'that, in subcultures, more than anywhere else, identities are fluid, mobile and on the move' (1997: 180). The interview data unmistakably support this assertion. Stylistic change is regarded positively – an important criterion of authenticity. But change is best understood in transformative terms, as a gradual, partial and evolutionary process, not as sudden shifts in whole identities, as some postmodern commentators would have it. Our hypothesis that opened this chapter cannot be supported. Appearance is not free-floating, available to be put on and cast off as a mere whim. To engage in such acts would be evidence of one's superficiality and inauthenticity, for style is viewed as an expression of one's inner self. References to 'flatness or depthlessness, a new kind of superficiality' (Jameson 1991: 9), 'a costume party' mentality (Fox 1987: 361), and the 'putting on' and 'casting off' of 'hats' or 'masks' (Shields 1992: 16) have therefore only a limited applicability even as metaphors.[11] Drawing attention in this way to surface and image at the expense of depth and persona functions only to refer to the 'falsity' of subcultural 'Others'.

Nor are the inauthentic connotations of pose and performance apt for anything other than those occasions when the point is 'pretending to be what I am not' (Tseëlon 1995: 47), when the wearing of conventional style is a misleading guide to what an informant 'really is'. This is not, however, to suggest that subculturalists employ a conception of their self that is unified, essentialist and unchanging. On the contrary, a wholly static self would, like its reflection in style, be viewed as stereotypical, restrictive and inauthentic. As Tseëlon suggests, the relationship of appearance to the self is more complex than that suggested by 'simplistic true/false dichotomies' (ibid.: 51). Something of all these points can be seen in our final extract (J).

(J)   MATT

M: *It's really difficult. I mean, would you say I was a hippy or a punk, traveller or . . . you know, I'm all those things. But I'm also, like, it's a different bloke; that was the laundry (laughs), do you know what I mean?*

DM: *No, I know what you mean.*

M: *I wish it was as simple as that. It would be great to, like you know, Batman you know. Like I watched Batman last night. Batman puts on his, on his gear, you know, he's Batman, you know.*

From one perspective, Matt's past subcultural identities are portrayed as styles he has merely 'cast off', so to speak ('it's a different bloke, that was the laundry'). Yet, he also realizes that the relationship between style and self is far more complex. Through the use of the present tense the past is characterized as, at the very least, residual rather than irrelevant ('I'm all those things'). Crucially, this continuing intimate relationship between self and appearance must still pertain for emergent styles and identities. The whole allure of Batman in this extract is the ability of multi-millionaire Bruce Wayne to suddenly 'put on' his Batman outfit and assume a different persona. But while such feats are possible in fiction, in the real world we can only remain envious – 'I wish it was as simple as that.'

Notes

1. 'Trendies' or 'townies' and 'casuals' are labels used by subculturalists to denote respectably dressed working-class young people: what, in Chapter 4, I referred to as a 'middle-range' conventional group. Thornton (1995: 99–101) remarks how this particular group is usually 'feminized' (i.e. referred to as female) as a way of further denigrating the 'mainstream' culture to which it refers. Extract (B) certainly suggests that this is so in the case of dance culture, but in other contexts trendies were just as likely to be male ('Trev and Kev' or 'lads in suits and ties'). Conventional reference groups could also be middle-class male adults ('city suits', 'businessmen'). These cultural stereotypes are obviously historically specific. 'Sharon and Tracey', who personified the mainstream in Thornton's study, are perhaps connected with the 'Essex girl' image of the 1980s. Back in the 1970s, two groups against which punk defined itself were the 'footballs' and the 'discos' (Mick 1976: 2, cited in Henry 1989: 106). See also Note 10, Chapter 7 on how subcultural 'Others' are typically feminized.

2. This exact phrase is also used by a punk in Andes (1998: 228).

3. See also Widdicombe (1993: 104–8) and Widdicombe and Wooffitt (1995: 144–5).

4. This is one reason why the 'insider' (or ex-insider, or partial insider) status of some social researchers, such as myself (ex-punk), Kathy Fox (ex-punk), Sarah Thornton (ex-clubber) and Belinda Wheaton (windsurfer), does not, I suggest, prevent us from unwittingly inauthenticating some of our informants, either explicitly, through our own descriptions, or implicitly, through the eyes of other members. See Fox (1987), Thornton (1995), Wheaton (1997).

5. See, for example, Arnett (1993; 1996: 59–62), Andes (1998: 216–17), and Sardiello (1998: 135).

6. This seems to have much in common with another understanding of 'perform-ance', found in the 'dramaturgical sociology' of Erving Goffman. In *The Presentation of Self in Everyday Life* (1976), Goffman's concern is to demonstrate that the self is not a stable, internal entity, but is continually constructed in an ongoing process of social interaction. 'The self is not simply "present" but must be presented to others. Self-presentation is a "performance"' (J. Wilson 1983: 130). In this sense, Goffman also appears to offer a deconstructive model of identity (Tseëlon 1992b, c). The most recent application of Goffman's work to the understanding of subculture and clubculture is provided by Malbon (1998), who observes how clubbing is an experience that is 'physically performed'. Individuals act out the role of clubbers by presenting a sense of self through participation in particular clubbing rituals, of dress, dancing, and drinking, in shared interaction contexts (1998: 276). See also Malbon (1999).

7. There are studies of subcultural identity (Roman 1988; Ryan and Fitzpatrick 1996) that combine theories of decentred subjectivity with the use of ethnographic methods. Yet these theoretical judgements about identity operate as a privileged realist text providing the agenda for surface observations. The purpose of qualitative data is to give life to the inter-group tensions and social conflicts arising from multiple identities that are pre-given by social structural variables of class, gender and sexuality, rather than being used to demonstrate how any individuals concerned might subjectively define their own senses of self, negotiating and resolving these contrad-ictions. Furthermore, despite the obvious potential for addressing the question, no consideration is given to how subjects might handle multiple *stylistic or lifestyle* identifications.

8. See on this point Jackson's (1995) comments on research by Miller (1987). Although Miller examines how council tenants on a London estate engage in *bricolage* to invest consumer goods with new meanings and create a range of diverse lifestyles, 'he seems not to recognize the possibility of *multiple identities* within the same individual' (Jackson 1995: 215; original emphasis). This study suggests, however, that multiple identities are expressed *through bricolage* in terms of hybridity and partiality.

9. Fox also identifies an intermediate group, the 'softcores', less ideologically serious than the hardcores, but more committed than the preppies to punk as a way of life. I have omitted softcores from the discussion purely for clarity of exposition. Sardiello (1998) recognizes similar distinctions within the deadhead subculture between (in decreasing order of commitment) 'hardcore', 'stable' and 'new' deadheads.

10. For example, as Sardiello says of 'new' deadheads, 'no one wanted to be identified with this group, but many of these same people made reference to the existence of the category' (1998: 134) – presumably because they inauthenticated other members in this way, and vice versa.

11. I am grateful to Justin O' Connor for pointing out that the idea of style as a mask, enabling an individual to take on a new role, to establish a different sense of

self, can be found in conventional subcultural theory. Here, subcultures provide a space for the exploration of identities outside those ascribed by the dominant culture. Thus, for example, taking on a punk identity allows a female to escape the restrictions of appropriate feminine behaviour (C. Miles 1993, 1997). Riding a motor bike and donning a leather jacket is 'to create for oneself a persona or temporary alter-ego' (Schouten and McAlexander 1995: 53; Stuart 1987). Yet interviewees typically claimed that their own subcultural membership allowed them to put into practice an escape from conventions and labels that, to some extent, they had always themselves felt like expressing. In this way the subculture facilitates the expression of the 'true' self, and had this topic been pursued in the interviews the informants might well have argued that it was in the period before their subcultural affiliation (i.e. when dressing conventionally) that their appearance and actions had not been a faithful counterpart of – had, in fact, masked – what they really were inside.

6

Change, Continuity and Comparison

One afternoon, at the Virgin Record Store down Kensington High Street, I see this group of little mates which is like one of those mixed assorted liqueurs, because you've got a rather bad one of everything. There is, for instance, a Nouveau Mass-Mod, 1979 style, who's got on every obvious thing you ever saw . . . His mate is Two-Tone, which is to say dressed exactly, but exactly, like the boy on the cover of the Selector E.P . . . One girl is plasticine punk . . . and *her* mate is a high yellow girl with the most enormous bouffant, a B52 . . . And the point is . . . that they're all mates and by any of the laws of nature ought to be at each other's throats, for any of a hundred reasons to do with the old inextricable laws of teenage society and *dressing the part*. The problem is that the old laws are clearly being mucked about with something criminal.

Peter York: *Style Wars* (1980: 42)

At 7.30 p.m. on a Friday night, Rhygin and I enter Darcy's and meet several other skinheads. Through the evening we both see, and talk to, several people apart from the usual group. Those we encounter are mods, skinheads, ex-mods, ex-skinheads, teddy boys, rockabillies and trendies . . . One, Wilson, has been, at different periods in his stylistic career, a rude boy and a mod. He is presently a ted . . . Another, Duncan, returned from a teenage visit to Scotland as a skinhead with 'no hair'. Later, he became a mod. He now dresses in a more mainstream style . . . A third, Ron, is a public servant of four years' standing who has been, at varying stages, a skinhead, a mod, and a soul boy . . . What do these seemingly disparate persons have in common with one another and with Rhygin?

David Moore: *The Lads in Action: Social Process in an Urban Youth Subculture* (1994: 83)

'There Was No Such Thing as a Punk': Continuity Through Change

As part of the CCCS approach to style and subcultural identity, Clarke draws on the well-documented hostilities between different youth subcultures to demonstrate that 'one of the main functions of a distinctive subcultural style is to define the boundaries of group membership as against other groups. This is usually thought of as being a reaction to other groups within the youth, sub-cultural arena (e.g., Mods vs Rockers; Skinheads vs Hippies and Greasers etc.)' (1986: 180). At the heart of this analysis lies a conception of internally cohesive subcultures with sharply drawn lines of demarcation and a strong sense of boundary maintenance, which finds its empirical confirmation in the study of hippies and bikers undertaken by Willis (1978).[1] It is, however, difficult to see how such a model allows for the possibility of individual members experiencing stylistic mobility between different subcultures, other than through the sort of short-term comprehensive change that, in the last chapter, we found to be a marker of inauthenticity. We might postulate that certain members are less committed to the subcultural ideology and lifestyle, and for these individuals the style is not so strongly rooted in an underlying sense of self. Yet we have also discovered that attempts to stratify members according to their strengths of affiliation are fraught with problems. All individuals portray themselves as no less committed and genuine than any other members.

This chapter is therefore concerned with the possibility of diachronic mobility for individuals between subcultures, and examines how such change is accomplished. We will be examining interview extracts to find evidence for the following hypothesis: that stylistic mobility relies upon weakened boundaries between different subcultures and precludes the formation of what Clarke terms '"negative" reactions to other groups' (1986: 180). The first two extracts involve a transition between what are commonly regarded as two highly incommensurable subcultures. In (A), Matt, whose extract concluded the last chapter, discusses his transformation from hippy to punk.

(A)   MATT

M: *I mean, I started off as a hippy, do you know what I mean? I was fourteen in 1973 and I was fifteen in 1974 and I was taken in by that whole thing. Acid and stuff. You know I took acid when I was very, very young. Oh yeah, I wanted to be a hippy when I was about fourteen.*

DM: *Yeah, would you say you were?*

M: *Well I went to free festivals and stuff in the early seventies, if that makes you a hippy then . . . And then punk happened and I got into punk. But it was like it was a revolution inside my head as well as because I had all the hippy influences from the 1960s 'cos I had a brother who is five years older and I looked up to and I was* into all that music and stuff, and then punk happened. All my friends were punks. And . . . um . . . so I took on board the punk, you know. I moved up to Scotland, and the old hippies didn't know what to make of us 'cos we were eighteen or nineteen and we all looked like punks but we were hippies. And then during the 1980s it all went a bit dead, and then in about 1987, 1988 all the traveller things started happening and that was, you know, I was looking really straight round about that time, and I started seeing all these people that were, you know . . . because punk was dead and it seemed like I could have identified with these people. Do you know what I mean? It was like something that I needed to do for myself again, only to reaffirm that statement that I made when I was sixteen or something.

DM: Were you a punk?

M: Well no. I was a hippy-punk.

DM: Right. It's getting very confusing.

M: But I didn't know I was a hippy-punk. Do you know what I mean? I didn't know I was a hippy-punk. You know, I got fucked off when the word 'hippy' became acceptable again. I actually fought against that. I didn't want to be called a hippy.

DM: Right.

M: But I'm quite prepared to accept the fact that I probably am a hippy (laughs).

DM: Listen, this is really interesting, because I used to be a punk, and what was the most interesting thing about being a punk was that it was very anti-hippy. 'Cos I remember all this, we hate all this progressive rock fucking crap and we hate Pink Floyd, and we hate Led Zeppelin and we have three-chord wonders and all that.

M: Well yeah, yeah, yeah, yeah, yeah, all that happened. We threw it all out. Let's face facts.

DM: Well how did you become a hippy-punk? Because that seems to me a contradiction in terms.

M: Well, mushrooms. Mushrooms.

DM: Didn't you feel like a contradiction between being a hippy and a punk? I mean, when the two things . . .

M: Well, I didn't know I was a hippy-punk. What it was was all the people who had grown up through the 1960s and seen all that and they landed and found themselves growing up in the 1970s suddenly became . . . and were really fucked off with the whole thing. It was crap, you know, and not as bad as it is now; but at the time it seemed like it wasn't going the way it should be going, and they *got labelled as being punks. There was no such thing as a punk. I mean I was a punk; but as far as I thought I was, I was trying to be a hippy. Do you know what I mean? You know, I was a punk, but I didn't know that. Can you understand that? I mean I had no idea I was a punk. I thought I was a hippy (laughs). There was no uniform when punk happened. There were no punks. There was no such thing as a punk. There was just a bunch of people who were pretty disaffected by their upbringing and stuff who had seen the whole 1960s revolution happen. You know, as a child lived through it all and that, you know.*

Of particular importance in both this and the next extract is the emphasis placed on commonality, continuity and the integration of different elements across subcultures. This undercuts the sense of opposition between the subcultures in question and also ensures change is achieved gradually. In (A) we find this to be accomplished through four different substantive themes: style, drugs, attitudes and music. Looking first at style, we should initially note how the influence of Matt's older brother provides a link back to the hippy culture of the mid-1960s. The reference to 'that whole thing' suggests that this culture consists of a whole constellation of elements. These appear to be music, attitudes and activities (taking 'acid' and going to 'free festivals'), but, significantly, style is not mentioned at this point in the extract. Change first appears in the dialogue when Matt talks of his initial involvement in punk. A distinction, rather than a historical connection, is now made between 'the old hippies' and Matt and his friends. The reference to the latter group's teenage years serves to underline this separation. It is only at this point that style is first mentioned – as the sole indication of this change ('we all looked like punks'). Yet Matt goes on to say 'but we were hippies'. The word 'but' is clearly used to denote the misleading nature of appearances in this case, and to indicate the source of confusion for the 'old hippies'.

We saw in the last chapter how subcultural appearance should be a genuine and sincere expression of an inner self. The lack of this correspondence implied falsity – that one was not engaging for the proper reasons. A look back at extract (E) in that chapter will show that attitudes, music and possibly even activities could also be perceived as having being 'adopted', denoting insincerity. Yet it was style, the most visible manifestation of affiliation, that was more commonly cited in this respect. It is therefore significant that Matt omits style when discussing indications of his affiliation to the hippy subculture, but mentions it when needing to draw attention to a disjunction between what it indicates (punk) and what actually lies underneath (hippy). Change, in other words, encompasses continuity. In a number of significant aspects other than style, Matt was still a hippy. Indeed, the subcultural category of 'punk' is claimed to be wholly an effect of labelling. This process also reproduces the category as a stereotypical and homogeneous 'uniform', accentuating its differences from other cultural movements, such as hippy. For me, hippy-punk is an oxymoron, hence my persistent questioning as to how Matt ever managed to become such a thing.[2] Yet by claiming 'I had no idea I was a punk. I thought I was a hippy', Matt locates his involvement as having occurred prior to this labelling process. This allows him to resist a stereotypical attribution, removes categorical distinctions, emphasizes similarity across subcultures rather than differences between them, and allows the suggestion of continuity within change.

The second theme by which continuity is achieved is the use of drugs. Matt justifies his identity as a 'hippy-punk' with a reference to mushrooms. Bearing in mind the previous mention of 'acid', this can only mean 'magic mushrooms' and implies a continued use of hallucinogens, drugs that are typically associated with the hippy subculture. On this issue, Willis (1986) has mapped out 'a sub-cultural pharmacology': the symbolic role of particular drugs in certain subcultural groups. Consciousness-expanding drugs like acid and hash are homologically related to the countercultural concern with the exploration of the self, while barbiturates and amphetamines play only a marginal role, their typical associations being with other groups.[3] Other drugs can be explicitly rejected as antithetical to a hippy attitude. The hippies observed by Young (1971) drew correspondences between the lifestyle of the heroin user and that of the 'straight' world they themselves opposed, so incongruent was the drug to their own expressive ethic. The importance of Matt's justification therefore lies in the inference we can draw from it: although having become a punk, Matt must also still be a hippy because he continues to take hallucinogenic drugs.

This might so far sound as though Matt is describing himself in terms of traditional subcultural homologies, which suggest a restrictive set of predictable practices. But we must remember that Matt's identity is partly punk. What is therefore missing in (A), and what we should have expected if cultural oppositions were being drawn, is an explicit contrast with drugs more obviously favourable to a punk aesthetic, such as speed. There undoubtedly exists the potential for such a claim. As Mignon reports, 'punks were, more explicitly than the mods, adepts of amphetamines. The target was the easy-going nature of the hippy, symbolised by hashish or drugs involving control such as LSD' (1993: 190). Calluori similarly comments that 'the drugs of consciousness restriction (e.g. heroin, glue sniffing, amphetamine sulphate) were the preferred pastime' of punks (1985: 53), while Burr (1984), in a homological analysis of empirical data showing heavy barbiturate use amongst punks, suggests there is a symbolic fit between the destructive effects of this particular drug and the punk ideology of nihilism and despair. So while (A) justifies the hippy component of the hybrid through the traditional use of hallucinogens, any expectation that this would clash with the central aspects of a very different cultural system, in this case punk, is left unacknowledged. Such an answer is clearly designed as an alternative to admitting that the hybrid is actually a contradiction, and allows for the understanding that punks could break out of their ascribed homological restrictions and also take consciousness-expanding drugs.[4]

Thirdly, by referring to 'a revolution inside my head' in the context of his initial involvement in punk, Matt manages to draw attention to attitudinal change while remaining wholly unspecific as to the attitudes in question. It is important that this phrase links a discussion of punk to Matt's hippy influences. From this, we might surmise that two apparently conflicting subcultures can share ideologically common ground that overrides any differences in this respect. At a further point in the extract, this inference is made explicit through a remark concerning generational continuity. It is the cohort of people brought up in the 1960s, old enough to remember the radicalism of that period, who carry such values into adolescence and the next decade. Yet, rather than hippies being succeeded by punks, one specific value system replacing another, this anonymous 'bunch of people' are referred to only as the 'disaffected'. Generality takes precedence over specificity, continuity over change.

This emphasis on the commonality of attitudes is carried through to the late 1980s. Change has again taken place, for Matt is dressing conventionally ('straight') at this period. We should realize from the last chapter that these acknowledgements of outward conventionality do not affect what a person really is inside (i.e. unconventional at heart). That this is also the case here is evident from Matt's identification with the travellers who were emerging at this time. It is particularly significant that this identification is premised upon the death of punk, for it might be assumed that Matt would still hold to punk ideals and values even if no longer wearing the style. Yet there is no sense of incompatibility in the extract between what, on the face of it, might appear to be two very different groups – punks and travellers. It is, rather, their shared status as unconventional movements that allows Matt 'to reaffirm that statement that I made when I was sixteen'. Generality again provides continuity within change.

References to music are the fourth and final way in which a sense of opposition is undermined. After his initial remarks about hippy culture, Matt claims 'I was into all that music and stuff.' My reason for bringing up the subject later in the extract was to highlight what to me seemed a fundamental contradiction. The back to basics, no-nonsense aesthetic of punk rock is often defined in explicit opposition to the self-indulgences of 'pomp-rock', a hangover from the hippy era (G. Clarke 1982; Coon 1982). According to Laing (1985) and Home (1996), punk is a musical genre as much as a youth subcultural (life)style, so it is hardly plausible that Matt 'took on board' punk without developing a taste for the music.[5] Moreover, there are no examples in the interviews of any respondent accepting a label while claiming not to affiliate to the related musical genre. Yet how could a punk affiliation be compatible with a liking for such dinosaurs of progressive rock as Pink Floyd and Led Zeppelin? Perhaps Matt underwent a change in musical tastes, as his reply to my query about punk being anti-progressive rock suggests ('yeah, all that happened'). But this is not so straightforward an answer as it might at first appear, for two reasons.

The first of these concerns the depersonalization of Matt's answer. We have seen in the last two chapters that subculturalists resist collective and restricted attributions by highlighting their own diverse tastes. Here, Matt appears to invoke the notion of the collective ('we threw it all out') as a stereotypical entity from which his own individual case is to be excepted. In other words, stereotypical punks undertook this complete musical conversion (which could also be indicative of rapid change), but this leaves open the possibility that Matt personally did not. A continued appreciation of 'hippy' music could have co-existed with an immersion into and liking for punk rock. The second reason is that 'hippy' music is as much a stereotypical designation as 'punk rock'. Middleton and Muncie rightly call progressive rock 'a particularly heterogeneous genre' (1982: 77–8).[6] Exactly what was 'thrown out' and what remained (even to be incorporated as musical influences on punk) is a moot point. Either way, the possibility for continuity must remain. In received subcultural wisdom, punk was the rising avant-garde that finally put paid to the progressive rock legacy of hippy culture. The hybridity of these two movements is a contradiction that requires an element of continuity as its only possible means of resolution.

'A Natural Progression': An Integrative Sensibility

In (B) we again meet Robin, whom we first encountered in extract (D) of the last chapter. Like Matt, above, Robin similarly carries his previous influences across subcultures. But we find here an additional emphasis upon how the subculture in question (again punk) itself harks back to previous stylistic influences: teddy boy, rocker and biker. These two aspects of continuity feed off each other and help to undermine what Hebdige understands to be a fundamental 'antagonism' and 'incompatibility' between the punk and teddy boy subcultures (1979: 123).

(B)   *ROBIN*

R: *When I was ten I thought I was a teddy boy, even though, I mean I like Showaddywaddy and Elvis, and then obviously when this thing called punk rock came around . . . At first I thought it was a bit weird because like you said it did just seem a bit like chaotic noise, but like you said, the more you got to hear it, the more you started liking it. So from that point of view, yes, I would have said I was a punk rocker until very recently. I mean I've only had my natural hair colour for about two years, and actually even then it*

Figure 8. Robin

wasn't a deliberate decision. It was a case of the girl who used to dye my hair, she went on holiday to America, and when she came back I didn't really see much of her any more, and obviously, as you can imagine ... by which time my roots were getting longer and longer and I just went 'that's it, I've had enough', sort of thing.

DM: Do you still think of yourself as being a punk?

R: I think inside I do, yeah. Maybe some people did do it from a fashion point of view, and obviously to me, there's an old quote, 'punk's not a fashion: it's an attitude', and it's how you feel inside and how you genuinely believe and how you think.

DM: Let me ask you something that's always occurred to me, that you have a kind of rocker look about you.

R: Oh yeah, well that ... to me it was almost like a natural progression, because as I got older, obviously ... just from being narrow-minded punk rock as it were, meaning any other music is shit. Then you start saying, 'Well hang on a minute. Where did the Clash get their influences from? Where did the Pistols get their influences from?' Paul Simonon out the Clash, he was like the bass player, he was the coolest guy, and it was more to do with ... like, he started wearing a quiff, then he started wearing 1950s-style jeans and shirts like the old bowling shirts and stuff, and I really liked them. Obviously I was always aware of, like, say, bands like Elvis and that, Gene Vincent and Eddie Cochran, but like I said, it's obviously my whole sort of mind opened to other sort of musical influences and musical styles and types. But as far as my image now goes, yeah, I mean the whole thing with the punk movement right from the beginning you always wore drape jackets and teddy boy shoes, which was obviously sort of a mickey-take at first of the teddy boys. That there was a lot of violence between the two sort of groups, but yeah, I've always loved drapes and creepers and that, and all the time I was a punk I've always had creepers. So like I say, it was a natural progression to me. Especially mixing with older people and friends had older brothers who were riding round in Crestas and Ford classic cars and they were into rock 'n' roll, and then obviously I got into bikes and obviously the whole idea of the British rocker, obviously the way I'm dressed at the moment is obviously 'cos it's to do with the British biker scene. Typical proverbial, like motorbike boots, leathers, chains, but the chains are a throw – a cast-off thing from the punk thing, anyway. I mean punks were ... you always wore leathers anyway. You know, the motorbike boots, again, Sid Vicious wore a pair of jackboots and

> *a biker's leather jacket. So it was always the little, the hints of the biker, the rocker thing in there. But from the tacky side of punk, like the green hair and that, that lost its appeal. Getting away from, like I said, the bondage trousers and the splashed paint T-shirt and that. To me it was a natural progression from being a punk rocker to just lopping off the word punk and becoming a rocker. It's to me it's just a natural, it's purely down to do with age.*

DM: *You know the sort of ideas of youth culture used to be very distinct, it was separate. So if you were a punk, that's what you were and you didn't want to be anything else. It seems to be that you've got this kind of rocker stuff, this sort of ted stuff and the punk stuff. How do you manage that?*

R: *It's not really, it's like I said it's not a split wardrobe. It's not like I have my punk bit and I have this bit, because I don't. To me, I don't. To me I'm very, very slightly different to what I was, you know ... probably my last bastion of being a punk was when I was still, I was clinging on to my dyed hair, that was really, like ... but it's not like, it's not as if I suddenly think 'God! I'm a different person', because I don't. I'm exactly the same. I wear my 1950s, you know, I wear my Levi's and I wear my Levi jacket and I wear my Clash T-shirt, and I wouldn't call that, I wouldn't say that's me dressing in my punk outfit, you know. And I've still got my quiff. I do wear my bondage trousers, but like I say I would wear that with a drape because that's what I wore – worn it with a drape in 1978–9 with creepers – so that hasn't changed.*

Throughout the extract, Robin emphasizes how elements of the biker, rocker and teddy boy subcultures fed into punk 'right from the beginning ... it was ... always in there'. Exactly how the complex cultural contestations and interconnections between, amongst other things, art-school bohemianism, hippy, glam rock, mod, rocker, teddy boy style and 1950s rock 'n' roll fed into punk is a history well documented by Savage (1992). It is not that Hebdige is unaware of aspects of this genealogy, far from it. He does, however, view the punk propensity for cultural plunder, particularly of all things Edwardian, as heavily steeped in irony. Such an interpretation at first appears to be affirmed in the extract, where the wearing of teddy boy gear by punks is described as initially a 'mickey-take'. Initially, this would accord well with the violent clashes between the two groups to which Robin also refers.

Yet much mitigation then takes place, which undercuts this sense of opposition. Robin states how he has 'always loved drapes and creepers', and clearly sounds as if these are worn out of a genuine sense of passion and respect for what the items 'originally' signify rather than for any sense of punk-induced irony. This point is reinforced by citing the influence of older people who were also into 'classic' rock 'n' roll culture, while, earlier in the extract, Robin makes clear how his awareness of and liking for 1950s music preceded his involvement in punk. Even the incorporation of rock 'n' roll elements into punk rock is interpreted as veneration or an act of homage. Paul Simonon of the Clash is regarded as 'the coolest guy', not least because of his taste in 1950s fashion, a style Robin 'really liked'.

On the other hand, Robin does seemingly offer up his own dialogue of change through exclusion and accentuation of difference. His style also includes what is termed its 'tacky side' ('green hair . . . bondage trousers and the splashed paint T-shirt'). It was likely to be principally through these prototypical punk images that Robin's stylistic identification with the subculture initially originated, for in claiming that he would no longer call himself a punk, Robin attributes this directly to the fall of 'my last bastion . . . clinging on to my dyed hair'. Discarding the punk element therefore entails 'becoming a rocker': a subtle but nonetheless emphatic shift in identity. Furthermore, while all these different cultural influences were deemed to be in place from the very start of punk, Robin retrospectively characterizes his younger self as 'narrow-minded . . . meaning any other music is shit'. Only with age has his 'mind opened' to a greater appreciation of punk's cultural and musical heritage. All this somewhat interrupts the narrative of continuity begun in the previous paragraph.

Yet what is potentially a tale of modification and opposition is again undercut by a refusal to interpret this in terms of any radical or sudden transformation, as Robin maintains a sense of continuity in the areas of attitudes, style and self-identity. While the 'tacky side' of the punk style may have 'lost its appeal', and 'rocker' rather than 'punk' now appears to be the choice of terminology, the importance of style is dismissed in favour of inner feelings and beliefs. In terms of these, Robin still continues to feel punk 'inside'. This allows for a continuing commitment to punk in the face of a declining interest in the visual aspects of the subculture. Note also how such an attitude is left unspecified (thereby combating any sense of restriction) and should be 'genuinely' held rather than merely adopted for effect (thus signalling authentic expression of this inner self). Many aspects of appearance have anyway remained unchanged since the late 1970s (1950s style, quiff, Levi's, Clash T-shirt, bondage trousers worn with creepers and a drape), and, what is more, the self-concept is declared to be unaltered ('it's not as if I suddenly think "God! I'm a different person", because I don't. I'm exactly the same'). I suggest there are two reasons for this continuity of self, which follow on from the conclusions of the last chapter.

The first is the emphasis on *gradual* incorporation and dissociation (note the presence of 'suddenly' in the above disclaimer). The literal fading away of the dyed hair ('my roots were getting longer and longer') is as protracted an event as Robin's original initiation into punk rock music ('the more you got to hear it, the more you started liking it'). There is, in other words, a gradually declining interest in the stereotypical, restrictive and inauthentic (the tacky punk style) and a concomitant widening of cultural appreciation. This movement is referred to as a 'natural progression', exactly the same phrase used by an interviewee in Miller (J. Miller 1995: 194) for describing his transition from rude boy to skinhead. The second reason for the lack of disruption to the self-concept is the fragmented (perhaps *integrative* is a more apposite word here) sartorial sensibility. Punk is combined with rocker with 1950s rock 'n' roll with biker, but 'it's not a split wardrobe'. The integrative sensibility of gradual growth and expansion over time brings to mind the words of other subculturalists. Jan predicted that he would experience change ('the bigger picture of what I want to do') only after his present style had become a 'limitation'. Mike reckoned that, 'I might mould my image slowly towards what I prefer at the time . . . if there was any change it would be slow and barely perceptible'. In (B) it is all the more so, because all the elements were in place – and not with any sense of dissonance – from the very outset.

'It's Not Like an Identity Crisis': Change and Partiality

Extract (C), below, demonstrates three reasons why an apparent transition between different named subcultures is possible without encountering problems of incompatibility. These are to do with partiality, external attribution and widespread tastes. As we examine each of these we need to be aware how making oppositional comparisons with subcultural reference groups does not hinder, but facilitates the ease of Paul's transition. The first thing to observe is how group labels are made relevant to only a partial aspect – the hairstyle – of that particular look ('little bits as a psychobilly', 'practically a goth'). The response to my query as to how long Paul has been dressing as a punk is made by reference to his mohican, for it was only through his hair that such a categorization was stylistically verifiable.

(C)   *PAUL AND DOUGIE*

DM: *How long have you been dressing in a punk way?*
P: *Erm . . . sort of since I was fifteen, but I've had little bits as a psychobilly and as a Airy-Mary Jesus and Mary Chain, and practically a goth, but don't tell anyone that. Erm . . . I've only*

had the mohican for five years. Before that it was a psychobilly, and when I was little and still at school it was sort of shaved round and sticking up on top, so I don't know what that is.

DM: *When you were a psychobilly or nearly a goth or whatever, in the same way as you now think 'I'm a punk', did you think then 'I'm a psychobilly' or did you have this kind of identity with whatever you are?*

P: *No, not psychobilly, no. I've always liked the same sort of music. I mean I always had my punk records, but at the same time I did have like the Jesus and Mary Chain records and the psychobilly stuff as well. And I've always gone and seen all of those types of bands. But no, the only reason I have had a psychobilly was an in-between haircut, getting from having a long fringe to a mohican or something, and I never ever thought of myself or anything like the psychobillies I knew, who were all mad bastards with bottles in their heads and mopeds and all of that, so no, not really.*

DM: *What about with goth?*

P: *But with goth, well no, 'cos I didn't like the . . . I hate goths, 'cos they are so miserable and they smell and they sit there looking like they don't want to be there, and white faces, and they're just anti-social, miserable. This is generalizing horribly, but that's what a lot, that's what a lot of them are, and I've never felt like that at all. All that black fingernails and make-up and all that. I didn't like any of that. When I had all that hair, it wasn't . . . I never . . . I wasn't really thinking of myself as a goth. I wasn't. I was still jumping about on stage and we were playing lively music. It's just that I had a stupid back-to-front haircut and people called me a goth more than anything. Erm . . . it was . . . it wasn't me trying to be a goth at all, and I mean we used to get all this stuff about 'urh, what do you sound like then?' I expect, you know, people thought we were going to be the Cure or something like that, and we were still playing punk music.*

DM: *Was it difficult from sort of changing from being a psychobilly to a . . .*

P: *No, not at all. You just grow and shave hair. That's all. And really it was no difference at all. I had the same clothes, I had the same mates, I went to the same places and the same gigs. I played in the same band. One week I had different hair.*

D: *It grew that quick?*

P: *Yeah, if you cut it off it does (laughs). It's not like an identity crisis or anything like that at all.*

We discovered in the last chapter that, contrary to what both sociology and our own assumptions might have led us to believe, some subculturalists did not hold style in high regard. As Paul himself admitted elsewhere in the interview, 'I'm not really that bothered about clothes to be honest, I mean, you know, I could be any old student. I got a boring T-shirt, boring jeans and boots on, and that's about it.' This general lack of interest in wearing a complete ensemble appropriate to the particular subculture in question allows affiliation to be visually demonstrated by only partial aspects of the style. Another interesting consequence of partiality is the way it allows the psychobilly hairstyle to be defined as a transitional 'in-between' stage. This not only suggests that change is gradual and continuous rather than abrupt and comprehensive, but demonstrates the non-intentionality of this particular feature, a point that is reinforced by the next claim.

This is, secondly, that it is people other than Paul who define him in this way. Although the punk identity may be self-attributed, this is not the case for psychobilly or goth ('people called me a goth more than anything'). We first encountered in Chapter 4 the idea that labels are identities imposed from outside the subculture, and that the resistance expressed towards such labelling is a consequence of their stereotypical associations. This is evident in (C), where Paul invokes stereotypical attitudes of both psychobilly and goth (aggression and depression respectively) and stereotypical features of goth style ('black fingernails . . . make-up . . . white faces') in order to dissociate himself from such identifications ('I've never felt like that at all') and point to his own divergence from the collective goth look.

The third issue we also first encountered in Chapter 4, and it is the rejection of a label on the grounds of widespread musical tastes. Although Paul likes psychobilly music this does not lead him to affiliate with this subculture, for, in terms of both records and live gigs, his taste for this genre co-existed with punk and a liking for the Jesus and Mary Chain. This allows a continuity in musical identity to confound stereotypical associations of music with appearance. Having been classified as a goth, Paul relates how his band is expected to play appropriate music (sounding like the Cure). Yet the label is a misidentification, based on only a partial aspect of his appearance ('a stupid back-to-front haircut') and his band continues to play punk rock. The outcome of all this is that change is not experienced as contradictory or difficult precisely because so little actually changes. Moreover, that which does undergo change is transformed in a gradual piecemeal way. And while the change of hairstyle described in the final lines of (C) occurred somewhat rapidly – within 'one week' – this accentuates the sense of continuity in all other areas. The fact that partial change does not provoke an 'identity crisis' recalls the example of Marie in the last chapter, where fragmentation alleviated her feelings of schizophrenia brought about by wholesale stylistic pluralization.

In his ethnography of British-born Australian skinheads, Moore describes the transition from skinhead to mod style, or from rockabilly to rude boy, as something that takes place 'slowly . . . as time passes' (1994: 26). By using the word 'throughout' to discuss her stylistic transformations over six years, Anne, in (D) below, also suggests constant gradual movement rather than discrete, comprehensive change. Intriguingly, she has 'always' managed to remain 'basically the same', despite the 'lots of different ways' in which she could have been categorized during this substantial period of time. This achievement is possible because, as with Paul, above, categorizations are redefined and new hybrids formed on the basis of slight shifts in stylistic elements – cut, colour and combing of hair, length of skirt, and, interestingly, the locale or 'scene' frequented.

(D) ANNE AND JULIE

A: *I mean I've changed like gradually throughout the past like six years and that. I mean I've always been, you know, basically the same, and you know, if you look back on photos you think, 'Well, I was a bit of a crusty then, oh I was like. . .', you know.*

J: *A bit of a hippy.*

A: *A bit of a hippy then, wasn't I? You know, and at the time you never notice the classifications, but you do change gradually, and I am sure with me, like with us, it will be a gradual change. I mean I suppose you could have categorized me in lots of different ways throughout the past, like, six years. Like I started off, like, in the goth–hippy-type thing. I had, like, long sort of . . . really long hair that was sort of reddy, sort of normal shades of red, rather than this. And I used to, like, back comb my hair, but sometimes I didn't, and wore long skirts and lots of black, and so I was more sort of . . . I was sort of around that. And then I was sort of like hanging around on the goth-rock scene, so I was probably more of a rock-chick-type thing.*

DM: *Did you, when you were like that, did you think of yourself as a . . .*

A: *No, it's only looking back that you really notice it.*

The self-attribution or rejection of labels by reference to only specific and partial elements of appearance would seem to ensure that subcultural identification remains a wholly subjective process. As Miller quotes an interviewee, 'people probably couldn't tell I was a Mod unless they were one or had been one, then I suppose it's the hair and the little touches that you'd recognize' (J. Miller 1995: 185). The same fine details that make one individual claim, say, a hippy-punk identity could conceivably enable someone else to see themselves as, for example, a goth-metaller.[7] A visual example of this point is the cover of Beatrix Campbell's *Wigan Pier Revisited* (1985 Virago paperback edition). What are the subcultural affiliations of these five young women? On page ii, the author describes them all as New Romantics. Yet, from my perspective, the second and third from the left more clearly resemble goth and punk respectively. But on what basis would any of them accept or reject such a classification? And more importantly, what would it take – a change of hairstyle or colour, bleached leggings discarded for a long black skirt or a short leather one, to change between any of these identities?

Figure 9. Wigan Pier Revisited

A final, but crucially important, feature of (D) is how subculturalists authenticate themselves not only relative to a subcultural 'Other', but to a prior situation in their own biography. We can, looking back ourselves, observe this in a number of earlier extracts. Robin's transition from punk to rocker in (B) is conveyed in terms of a 'natural progression' from relative restriction to widespread appreciation, and is clearly linked to a process of personal maturity ('it's purely down to do with age'). Jim, in extract (B) of Chapter 4, is also adamant that his past expressions of permanent commitment to a group identity (implying stasis and a collective stereotype) could be put down to his youthful narrow-mindedness, and that he has, with age, come to appreciate the 'self-destructive' implications of labelling ('I used to say "mod till you die". That was when I was younger').[8] What Anne has further realized in (D) is that self-classifications (such as 'I used to be a mod') are often unrecognizable (and thus unacknowledgeable) at the time, becoming pronounced *only* when viewed retrospectively ('it's only looking back that you really notice it').

We have already remarked upon Schutz's (1980) distinction between the world of 'consociates' and that of 'contemporaries' in explaining why conventional and subcultural 'Others' are perceived as homogeneous abstractions. But Schutz also referred to two other abstracted realms of reality, the worlds of predecessors and successors (denoting past and future relations). It is the first of these that is relevant to extract (D), for Schutz argued that we also make sense of our past relationships through ideal-types (ibid.: 182). And while Schutz was concerned with how we perceive others, it appears from Anne's comments that we have an ability to consider our own past identity retrospectively in this way. This seems to allow any past point in one's biography to be characterized as inauthentic relative to a subsequent situation, while the inauthenticity of this past can be recognized only with hindsight. If styles that are judged at the time to be partial and complex can be perceived retrospectively as categorical typifications, this clearly raises questions about the status of the benchmark against which postmodern fragmentation is measured, a point that is taken up in Chapter 8.[9]

We began this chapter with a puzzle. The CCCS model of subcultures – internally cohesive and homogeneous – clearly facilitated the maintenance of boundaries between different style groups. But how could this be reconciled with the existence of individuals undergoing stylistic mobility between apparently incommensurable subcultures? Our hypothesis that this would preclude the expression of negative sentiments towards other subcultural groups is not supported. While subculturalists who undertake such change do not regard boundary maintenance as pertinent to their own personal situation at the time, they continue to express their authenticity through opposition with a subcultural reference group (or a previous group identification of their own), the inauthentic features of which are themselves constituted through subcultural boundaries and oppositions. One's own refusal to heed boundaries therefore continues to be expressed, somewhat paradoxically, through self-exclusion from the sensibilities of a stereotypical group for whom, it is implied, such oppositions continue to be relevant.[10]

This continuing negative portrayal of other groups presents subculturalists with a potential contradiction. As we first saw in Chapter 4, their own self-characterization as independent-minded and open to alternatives is contrasted with a stereotypical view of conventional (and subcultural) reference groups as, basically, unquestioning and predictable. Elsewhere in the interviews this translates into crude dichotomies such as open-minded against narrow-minded, permissive versus intolerant, even peaceful compared to violent. So it is not particularly surprising when subculturalists are occasionally found to voice their explicit dislike of such groups, as we see in (E) below. These openly hostile sentiments, if not the stereotyping, clearly undermine the very claims to open-mindedness that subculturalists make, and dissolve any such distinction made on this basis between themselves and the 'Other' whom they so deride. One way in which this problem is resolved is by remarking upon individual exceptions from the rule that are based on ties of friendship or acquaintance – what, in Schutzian terms, are called consociate relationships.

(E)   LUCY

L: *I would say 'Oh, those trendies are real twats', or whatever. But if I was with my friend, like Gabby or whatever, she's my friend, I wouldn't hate her, but I would hate them as a group. See what I mean? So I wouldn't hate one of them on their own, but I would hate them so I wouldn't voluntarily go up to them, see what I mean? I wouldn't go up to them. But like, if I knew them, then I wouldn't hate them.*

Here, the different manner in which the anonymous group and the personally known individual are held in regard is so clear as to make extensive commentary superfluous. The example given is trendies, but similar remarks were made about various subcultural groups. Moore (1994) likewise discovered in his own research that Rhygin, his main skinhead informant, had formed friendships over a number of years with several individuals from a variety of subcultural groups (see the quotation from Moore at the beginning of this chapter). These individuals, who can be considered past or present consociates, were treated by Rhygin according to their personal characteristics, while other, unknown members with the status only of contemporaries were regarded as cultural stereotypes. 'Such assumptions ... explain the apparent contradiction in a statement like "I hate mods!" when contrasted with the speaker's actions while talking to a known mod who is an ex-consociate (Moore 1994: 88).

It is clear that 'such assumptions' also provide an explanation for the observations made by York (1980: 42) – which again appear in one of the quotations heading this chapter – and raise doubts as to whether York witnessed the emergence of a novel development.[11] Over sixty years ago Wirth (1938) conceptualized the urban as a space characterized by density, cultural hybridity, and a high frequency of social contacts amongst a variety of different groups – precisely the features we now associate with aesthetic modernity, and the conditions under which group boundaries are likely to become blurred and numerous consociate relationships formed. Yet Wirth also realized how the 'impersonal, superficial and transitory' (ibid.: 12) quality of the relationships forged in these circumstances would lead them in all probability to be viewed through the prism of anonymous types. The social conditions of the past could, in other words, have been as favourable to the formation of inter-subcultural friendships as they were to the creation of conflicts. Furthermore, increasing heterogeneity and fluidity can still continue to reproduce group antagonisms through promoting negative, stereotypical perceptions of the 'Other'.

Attitudes, Values and Beliefs

A claim made by Robin in extract (B), one commonly found throughout the interviews, was that a subculture was not (or not only) a style or fashion, but an attitude (see also Lull 1987: 226). As Moore puts it, 'visual style is more than a set of clothes to be discarded at will, rather an attitude to life given expression in apparel and behaviour' (1994: 36). Yet these same subculturalists rarely, if at all, specified what such attitudes consisted of, nor identified values they might hold that would differentiate them from other types of subcultures. Paul (Extract C), for example, invokes the attitudinal stereotypes of psychobillies (aggression) and goths (depression) only to emphasize the irrelevance of these to his own identity. This does not necessarily mean that subculturalists do not hold specific and coherent values, only that they are more likely to identify (and attribute to 'Others') those they do not hold. But it might suggest less ideological coherence to subcultures than has commonly been supposed.

This finding clearly differs from what we might have expected from the CCCS approach, in which attitudes and values not only mark out subcultural difference from conventional society, but also serve to set subcultures in opposition to each other. Yet, as we saw in Chapter 2, this 'pure' and 'abstract' (G. Clarke 1982: 8) CCCS concept of subculture was, in part, the product of a methodology in which specific subcultural attitudes were imputed through a semiotic reading of style and homologically related to the subculture's 'historical problematic' in a form of 'literary ethnography' (Blackman 1995: 4). Although Paul Willis's commitment to first-hand ethnographic field work methodologically sets him apart from this mode of enquiry (McGuigan 1992: 97–8), I have, nonetheless, argued that the portrayal of internally coherent yet opposing world-views of hippies and bikers in *Profane Culture* (1978) owes much to Willis's interpretative skills in homological analysis. As was argued in Chapter 4, it is not that homologies may not be present, but that attention has been directed towards their discovery to the neglect of identifying what Fornäs (1995) terms 'heterologies' and 'antilogies'.

Subsequent studies carried out in Britain, America, Canada and Australia, using both interviews and participant observation, have, in fact, found subcultural belief-systems to be complex and uneven.[12] In some cases, values tend towards ambiguity, or findings are produced that are themselves somewhat imprecise. Fox discovered in her ethnography of an American punk subculture that 'these values were ambiguous at best, but included a distinctly antiestablishment, anarchist sentiment' (1987: 352). Moore concluded that 'in the skinhead subculture one can hold almost any belief, even running contradictory to a general skinhead view' (1994: 52). Gottschalk (1993) more carefully catalogues the fragmented world-view of American countercultural 'freaks'; they:

> Quoted Zen proverbs, evoked Camus, Burroughs, Bukowski, Bataille, Jerry Rubin, Abbie Hoffman, radical environmentalism, the Sex Pistols, Frank Zappa, and Bob Marley (among others), but they neither organized these into a coherent and integrated ideological system nor expressed any concern about the lack of such a system ... the Freak 'story' was a collage of ideas, an assemblage of political, ideological and aesthetic positions originating from different points in time and space (Gottschalk 1993: 364–5).

Ambiguity clearly allows, at a certain level of generality, for ideologies to be diffuse, heterogeneous, and expressed across different styles. Burr, in a British study, had no problem distinguishing between anarchic punks and racist skinheads; yet he was also able to claim that 'neither has evolved a coherent, interrelated and systematized system of belief or well developed philosophy which is articulated in everyday speech' (1984: 932). This lack of specificity enabled Burr to homologically relate both groups' usage of the same drug, barbiturates, to their shared, negative ideologies of 'alienation' and 'despair', thereby providing a contrast with the work of Willis (1978, 1986), discussed above, in which homological analysis is employed to identify cultural oppositions between subcultures.

Even the more specific subcultural attitudes and values identified by ethnographers do not necessarily indicate group cohesion and demarcation, for two reasons. First, these could arguably serve to bridge as much as to separate different groups. Two sets of reactionary values that usefully illustrate this point are the 'patriotism', 'xenophobia' and 'machismo' of American bikers (Schouten and McAlexander 1995) and the skinhead traits of racism and homophobia (Lull 1987) or 'monoculturalism' and 'manliness' (K. Young and Craig 1997). Second, these may not be uniformly expressed within any one particular subculture. What Schouten and McAlexander (1995) claimed to have identified are typical working-class biker values, which are redefined and reinterpreted across various biker sub-groups in accordance with class and gender differences. Young and Craig's more general assessment is that 'the Canadian skinhead movement is both complex and multi-dimensional, and accommodates, albeit in often intersecting and contradictory ways, a range of behavioural and ideological opportunities for the members of its various branches' (1997: 179). This also sits comfortably with Knight's assertion, in the British context, that the skinhead alliance to politics is 'uneven and transitory' (1982: 33).[13]

We are left with the sense that the ideological distinctions that were thought to set particular subcultures in opposition have been over-emphasized. Attitudes and values articulated across different style subcultures can be as fundamental to identity formation as any logically patterned belief-clusters that serve to demarcate them. This can produce sets of shared ideological configurations that, to outsiders, may even appear contradictory. For example, the same uneasy combination of libertarian ideology and racist sentiments has been identified in subcultures as apparently diverse as bikers (Schouten and McAlexander 1995) and punks (Sabin 1999b). Why, then, should certain individuals not move from punk, to skin, to biker, and even to hippy? (Would a researcher other than Willis (1978) have found an ideological compatibility – a libertarian emphasis on personal freedom – between the same samples of bikers and hippies?) Subcultures in fact break out of restrictive homologies at all levels. We saw in Chapter 4 that ambiguity can also be stylistic, while individuals from different groups may also have overlapping musical tastes.

Subcultural 'Others', on the other hand, are invariably perceived as homogeneous, internally coherent and externally demarcated, for as unknown contemporaries they are judged only by reference to general cultural categories. But those so classified likewise classify the classifiers. There are, in other words, less differences (or more similarities) between subcultural groups than there are perceived to be. Were this not the case – if subcultures actually were characterized by specific and mutually exclusive styles, attitudes and tastes – it would be difficult to understand how change such as that discussed in this chapter could occur at all; or how Moore (1994) could find individuals who had taken various pathways through skinhead, punk, soul boy, teddy boy, rockabilly, rude boy, mod and causal styles, or Young and Craig report that, 'without exception, the skinheads in this study had been members of other youth subcultures including punks, skaters and White Power skinheads before becoming "non-political" Oi! skins' (1997: 184). As Kotarba and Wells reflect on discovering a surprising amount of sub-cultural mobility in their own fieldwork:

> Ethnographic research like this points to both the usefulness and the promise of a postmodern conceptualization of youth and rock music. For example, we found that many patrons at Roma's moved from one style to another without significant consternation or consequence, certainly more movement than one would expect if these styles were tied rigidly to structural memberships such as class and ethnicity, as subcultural theorists argue (Kotarba and Wells 1987: 415).

That the characteristics of homogeneity, fixity and demarcation, as emphasized in the CCCS approach, appear increasingly irrelevant is amply demonstrated by recent attempts to reconceptualize subculture using different criteria. Widdicombe and Wooffitt (1995: 218) draw on Willis's (1990) concept of 'proto-communities' to capture the sense of fluidity and flexibility suggested in such a 'bond' or 'association'. Moore (1994) likewise defines the Australian skinhead subculture as 'labile', prone to instability of form, changing membership and transient relationships between subgroups. My own attempt to cover what I saw as the increasing gap between my empirical evidence and an outmoded orthodox understanding of subculture was through the employment of Maffesoli's (1996) concept of 'neo-tribe', designating a diffuse grouping with insubstantial boundaries and 'affinity based on heterogeneity' (Muggleton 1995). All these conceptual innovations improve on the CCCS approach through their ability to map more accurately the lived reality of the subcultural world. The way they achieve this is by importantly creating what we might term a 'collective space' where individual difference and freedom is allowed to flourish. Indeed, if we are to move beyond exercises in conceptualization, then individuality, mobility and diversity are central characteristics upon which any adequate explanation of subcultures must be founded.

Notes

1. See also Brake (1977) for an empirical study of the social and cultural distinctions between hippies and skinheads.

2. On the incompatibility between hippy and punk see Nehring (1996: 272) and Steele (1997: 287). Lull, however, notes 'the uneasy alliance' and 'intricate association between these two groups' (1987: 248), while Goldthorpe (1992) and Osgerby (1998: 106) also remark on shared themes. A brief extract from an interview with a 'punk hippy' appears in Widdicombe and Wooffitt (1995: 164).

3. For example, Hebdige (1974) examines the centrality of amphetamines to the 'meaning of mod'.

4. Lull (1987: 233) provides an account of marijuana use amongst punks.

5. Weinstein (1991) also understands heavy metal to be a music-based subculture, and the same point might also be made about Glitter or glam (Taylor and Wall 1978; Cagle 1995). See also Sardiello (1998) on the deadhead subculture which centres upon the band The Grateful Dead.

6. See also Willis (1978: Ch. 7). Of the five 1960s tracks selected by Middleton and Muncie (1982) to demonstrate how this genre exemplifies countercultural style, I regard two, those by Procul Harum and Donovan, as more akin to commercial pop songs, while two others, by Pink Floyd and The Beatles, are prime examples of inventive psychedelia that count among my all-time personal favourites. But then, when I use the term progressive rock, I refer to fifteen-minute guitar solos, the period from about 1970 to 1976, and bands like Yes, ELP, Barclay James Harvest and Pink Floyd without Syd Barrett. Lydon has a similar definition (1994: 236–7).

7. For such reasons, a quantitative assessment of the degree of stylistic mobility experienced by my subcultural sample would not produce any valid or reliable figure. Nor were informants always as willing as Anne, in extract (D), to classify such past identities retrospectively. It is therefore not possible to assess accurately Evans's (1997) proposal that females are more subculturally mobile than males. The evidence in this chapter should, however, be enough to refute the suggestion that 'men tended to stay locked into one subculture' (ibid.: 181).

8. See Kitwood (1980) and Brown *et al* (1986) on the positive correlation between age and individuality.

9. This means that we should also regard with caution those attempts to identify the different stages of affiliation to a subculture through which individuals pass (see Schouten and McAlexander 1995; Andes 1998). Andes, for example, argues that an individual member initially embraces a group identity only to transcend it at a later stage. Yet what she is actually discovering is how individuals authenticate their present situation in relation to a supposedly stereotypical past.

10. As Martin puts it, 'the opposition to boundaries must erect a new boundary between its adherents and the boundary-conscious structures outside in order to protect the open pattern inside' (1985: 41).

11. See, for example, Frith's research into early 1970s youth culture (Frith 1983: 207).

12. Of course, a wide range of methods have been employed to identify subcultural ideologies, but there is no space for a detailed discussion of all of these. Questionnaires have been used to provide quantitative data on the values, attitudes and personality characteristics of various subculturalists (Brown 1973; Gold 1987; Hansen and Hansen 1991). Various forms of content analysis have also been applied to fanzines (Lamy and Levin 1985; Henry 1989: da Costa 1995) the underground press (Levin and Spates 1970; Nelson 1989), band names (Levine and Stumpf 1983) and lyrics (McDonald 1987; Gross 1990; Arnett 1996). But evidence suggests we should be cautious when extrapolating from textual content to the subjectively held meanings of the subculturalists themselves (see Gross 1990: 125; Kotarba and Wells 1987: 415). For discussions of lyrical content in punk variously informed by genre theory and literary and critical theory, see Home (1996), Davies (1996), and Laing (1978, 1985).

13. Baron (1997) also found a political consciousness in a sample of fourteen male Canadian skinheads that could best be described as 'fragmented', consisting of racist, radical non-racist and apolitical views. These case study findings are hardly conclusive, but neither are they inconsistent with more general claims for an increasing disjunction between style, ideology and identity. To stay with the skinhead subculture as an example, Redhead argues that 'subcultural theorists' claim for a homology – or fit – between a skin haircut, DocMarten boots and fascist leanings has long ago been refuted' (1991a: 145). Indeed, in certain British cities in the 1990s, such a style is more likely to signify Gay hypermasculinity than working-class homophobia (Bell *et al.* 1994).

7

Resistance, Incorporation and Authenticity

What we did was we opened the doors, and so all these endless punk imitators suddenly flooded in and dissipated the whole point of it, because they became clone-like. Now they totally missed the whole point, that this was all about individual expression and personality. These are the things that count in life for me, but most of the punk outfits didn't appreciate that at all. They allowed the likes of the *Daily Mirror* to dictate a uniform. *The* leather jacket; *the* safety pin; *the* torn jeans; *the* bovver boots; *the* spiky hair. And it became hideous.

> John Lydon on the Sex Pistols and Punk Rock: 'Mavericks',
> (BBC Radio One, Feb. 1995)

Our politics were clear in 'Anarchy'. We weren't political in the sense of saying: be a Socialist, be a Tory, be a Communist. We were political in the sense that we didn't even entertain the idea of politics, it was below us. It was anarchy in its purest sense: self-determination. We couldn't, we felt, do much about changing the system, but we weren't going to let the system do anything to us. We wanted to live our lives how we wanted to live them – and we went out and did it.

> Glen Matlock: *I Was a Teenage Sex Pistol* (1996: 163)

Defusion and Diffusion

In any examination of subcultural authenticity and resistance, a consideration of the role played by the media and commerce is indispensable. That this should be so is primarily because of the way these two pairs of factors have been almost completely counterpoised in the CCCS approach. In a two-way process, authentic stylistic resistance occurs through *bricolage*, an act of transformation by which a new and original style is formed through plunder and recontextualization as a challenge to the hegemony of the dominant culture. It is this radical creativity that, so the theory goes, is then co-opted and incorporated through media and commercial exploitation, after which those who take up the style are reduced to the status of mere fad-followers.

We discussed the initial part of this process in Chapter 2. The latter part, as sketched out by Clarke (1986: 185–9) and Hebdige (1979: 92–9), itself involves two interconnected movements, defusion and diffusion. Through defusion, the subversive potential of subcultural style is sanitized, commercially, through the commodification of subcultural forms: the turning of gestures and signs of refusal into mainstream fashion – 'a pure "market" or "consumer" style' (J. Clarke 1986: 187). Diffusion is the actual geographical and social dispersal of the style from the original nucleus of innovators to new and mass publics, mediated through television and tabloid reports. In both cases, the process assumes an underground, yet internally-cohesive, clearly defined, self-contained resistance movement, untainted by the world of media and commerce until its discovery and dissipation by the institutions of dominant society – 'the element of commercial reaction which attempts to universalize, at a purely stylistic and consumption level, the innovations made by distinctive youth cultures, while simultaneously defusing the oppositional potential of the exclusive lifestyles' (J. Clarke and Jefferson 1978: 157).

As we saw in Chapter 3 the increasing power of media and commerce in a postmodern society hastens this process of incorporation (Connor 1991; Redhead 1991b), further negating the potential for authenticity and resistance. McRobbie (1989) and Thornton (1994, 1995) more radically demonstrate how the forces of media and commerce are, from the very outset, proactive in subcultural formation. If the postmodern thesis is fully realized we might expect subculturalists to exhibit a celebratory attitude towards style, fashion and the media rather than to view their affiliation as a normative or political gesture of resistance or rebellion. This is our hypothesis, to be supported or refuted by the data. Although the two themes of media and commerce are obviously interrelated, I will deal with them separately. First, let us consider the media. Here there are three interrelated questions: (1) How do subculturalists view the role of media and commerce in the construction of their own identity?; (2) How do they view the role of the media in the construction of others?; and (3) Are different media allocated distinct roles in the above processes?

(A)   MATT

M: *If you actually look at the photographs of the Sex Pistols gigs there is like not a punk in the audience, they have all got long hair. They have all got, like . . . if you look at the real photographs, nobody knew what a punk was, there was no uniform. There wasn't a punk uniform. Maybe I might be wrong. There might have been people*

> *who actually thought they were punks, but um, I'm not so sure,*
> *you know, I think punk became a label possibly after Johnny Lydon,*
> *Johnny Rotten said . . . er . . . told . . . er . . . Grundy to fuck off.*

In the first extract we again find Matt, who opened the last chapter. He was then engaged in the process of authenticating his punk identity by virtue of his involvement having occurred prior to the labelling process by which punk was publicly named and identified. Not only, then, does his inception predate the point at which punk became a uniform, but he was initially unaware of his identity as a punk. As corroborative evidence he points to photographs of the Sex Pistols' gigs. It will become clear that these are the gigs taking place before the end of 1976, before punk became a focus of mass media attention. The people in the audience on these photographs not only fail to look like 'punks', they are more likely to resemble hippies or, at the very least, sport the general youth fashion of the time ('they have all got long hair').[1] As Matt points out, at this period in time 'nobody knew what a punk was'.

What is significant is the way the mass media are deemed to be fully responsible for the sudden transformation of this situation. The watershed is precisely identified as the Bill Grundy interview with the Sex Pistols. Broadcast on Thames Television in the early evening of 1 December 1976, this infamous encounter brought national notoriety to the group and punk rock in general. It is only after this event that punk becomes labelled, the style becomes identifiable as a 'uniform', and people think of themselves *as* punks. This not only clearly defines the subculture's identity, but the perceived movement towards homogeneity sharply demarcates it from the remnants of residual cultural movements such as hippy. This further implies that those who become punks in the wake of this event are inauthenticated, not only through their uniformity of look and rapid conversion (attributable to one specific instance of media exposure), but by the very fact of media-influenced affiliation itself. As Osgerby has perceptively argued, 'any sense of a coherent punk "movement" or punk "identity" was largely the outcome of media simplification and commercial marketing strategy' (1998: 111).

In one obvious sense, (A) follows the pattern of events set out by the CCCS work: the mass communications media are evacuated from Matt's own (authentic) inception, but construct those who enter the subculture after the Grundy interview as, for all intents and purposes, inauthentic 'followers'. Yet, as the Osgerby quotation suggests, this appears to reverse the CCCS construction of subcultural cohesion. Rather than self-contained and clearly defined subcultures being diffused and dissipated by media attention and commercial exploitation, authentic inception is characterized here by a lack of cohesion and demarcation, with the media playing a homogenizing and clarifying role. It might appear that Matt's views are more consistent with those expressed by Stanley Cohen in his seminal text, *Folk Devils and Moral Panics* (1973, 1980). As Trowler and Riley say of this work, 'its principal theme [is] that youth subculture must be seen as a media creation rather than as a reaction by the working class section of youth to their economic and social environment' (1985: 157). Similarly, according to Thornton, 'scholars of "moral panic" assume that little or nothing existed prior to *mass* media labelling' (1995: 119; original emphasis).

These, it must be said, are somewhat oversimplistic readings of Cohen, who was careful to stress in the final chapter of his book that a conventional socio-structural account is required to explain the origins of such subcultures – 'the mods and rockers did not appear from nowhere' (Cohen 1973: 191). It would be more accurate to see this as an origin in which the media are not allocated any explicit or significant role. Only in the process of societal reaction do the media really come to prominence, the effect of which is to homogenize and polarize the two subcultures. In (A), then, Matt appears to be proposing a more radical version of Cohen's thesis whereby mass media coverage does not simply intensify weakly drawn differences between already existing groups, but *actually creates the very notion* of a subcultural identity itself.

Mass, Niche and Micro Media

That media effects are imputed to others is unsurprising, given the oft-made equation between mass media influence and a lack of capacity for critical and independent thought in those so swayed. However, this does suggest the need to examine whether subculturalists have in mind different types or forms of media, and if these are regarded as having varying implications for the construction of authenticity or inauthenticity. Relevant to such an analysis is Sarah Thornton's (1995) study *Club Cultures*, discussed in Chapter 4. In her discussion of the media (see also Thornton 1994), Thornton poses two questions. First, in what way are the media involved in the actual development of subcultures? Second, how do 'subcultural ideologies' (1995: 121) – the subjective perceptions of subcultural members – construct the role of the media?

In answering the first of these questions, Thornton takes issue with Cohen (1973), who defines media solely in terms of the regional and national press. She argues instead for an internally differentiated understanding of 'the media', distinguishing between micro, niche and mass media. Thornton proposes that such distinctions undercut any simple opposition between media that are indigenous and those that are exogenous to subcultural movements. Nor, therefore, can their relationship to subcultures be viewed in terms of a linear process of increasing incorporation. Such a proposal is justified by three claims. First, that negative mass media coverage does not act as a mechanism of defusion and diffusion, but on the contrary, can help to render subcultures subversive and increase their longevity. Thornton notably diverges here from the CCCS view of the media-subculture relationship. Second, that niche media – the music press and style magazines – are often staffed with people previously or currently subcultural members themselves. Such media actively help to compose and structure stable subcultural entities from real yet nonetheless nebulous movements and cultural fragments. Third, that micro-media, such as fanzines, listings, posters and flyers, are also integral to the networking process of assembling individuals *as a* crowd for a specific purpose and imbuing them with a particular identity (see figures 10–12 for examples of flyers collected during my own fieldwork). Moreover, in an ironic reversal of subcultural ideologies, the tabloid mass media can often be well ahead of certain micro-media in their coverage of new developments in the subcultural arena.

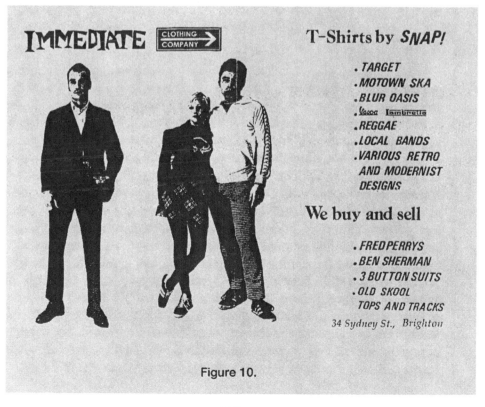

Figure 10.

Figure 11.

Clearly, Thornton's conclusion, 'that subcultures are best defined as social groups that have been labelled as such ... Communications media create subcultures in the process of naming them and draw boundaries around them in the act of describing them' (1995: 162), does not allow any space for a non-mediated subcultural identity. A point which, at one level, a number of my interviewees are happy to concur with; for as Oliver put it, 'everybody's influenced by the media'. However, this is precisely to raise Thornton's second question of how subculturalists position the media (or different aspects of it) in relation to their own affiliation. In much the same way as my own interviewees, Thornton's informants proclaimed their authenticity through comparisons with two types of reference group. First, against a feminized nightclub mainstream which bears more than a passing resemblance to the 'trendie' venue and its Shaz inhabitants talked about by Suzie and Mags in extract (B), Chapter 5. Secondly, against a subcultural 'Other' – inauthentic clubbers known, somewhat bizarrely, as 'Acid Teds' (ibid.: 100).[2] There are really, then, two aspects to Thornton's second question: how do her clubber informants regard their own relationship to the media? And: how do they see the role of the media in the construction of these inauthentic 'Others'?

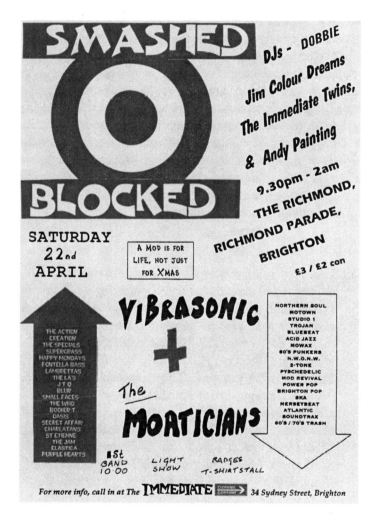

Figure 10.

Predictably, in line with Matt in (A), we find that 'Others' are denigrated as mass-media-influenced. Sharon and Tracey, who personify the mainstream, set their cultural standards by 'Top of the Pops', while 'Acid Teds', and their feminized equivalent 'Techno Traceys', take their cues from *The Sun* newspaper (ibid.: 109). And as we might also have expected, the clubbers invert this relationship when referring to themselves, disparaging the mass media (a sure sign of 'selling-out'), yet championing micro-media such as fanzines as an authentic, grass-roots means of communication, thus confirming an earlier finding by Lull, that flyers and fanzines were 'trusted sources of information' (1987: 244) for the punks in his study. This varying regard given to different aspects of the media can, in fact, be detected in (A). Note how Matt characterizes the visual evidence of those first gigs as 'the real photographs', thereby suggesting their authenticity, presumably in relation to the 'falsity' of the mass media. Yet this is too easy a conclusion to leap to. Such remarks may be more of a comment on the people portrayed and constructed by the media than it is on the media themselves, for such a distinction seems to derive from the dichotomy between 'genuine' and 'false' members, first outlined in Chapter 5. It would also be necessary to see how subculturalists deal with the complications that arise when, unlike Matt, they would find it difficult to claim that their own inception preceded not only media attention but the very naming process of the subculture itself. Let us look then at (B) which deals not with punk, but with mod.

(B)   OLIVER

DM: *I mean – you know – the difference between being genuine or whatever you want to call it and not being a fad-follower. And yet I'm wondering that someone else might see you as a fad-follower and what your defence would be. Because I can't see what it is that you have which fad-followers don't. Or at least, I don't know what it is.*

O: *Yeah, I see what you mean. I don't know, because I got into dressing like this through sort of hanging around with people like it. And although everyone's going . . . you know, there's been that piece in that music paper, Select, about the mod revival, and there's like Blow Up, which is a mod club, and everything like that . . . but I don't know. I was sort of dressing quite sharp before I read about those, and it's more about watching Quadrophenia or something like that.*

This extract opens with a reference to the distinction between real members and mere followers. Here, I put it to Oliver that there is nothing that obviously seems to place him in the former group rather than the latter. What we can observe in this extract is how three potential admissions of inauthenticity are counteracted by their framing within claims for authenticity. First, Oliver states that his style has emerged though peer-group interaction. While this could be interpreted as an admission of copying (following the dictates of others), the point of this statement is to highlight how the style came about through face-to-face contact rather than the influence of the media. Secondly, he does not deny knowledge of the contemporary mod revival, nor of his interest in associated media coverage. Yet he plays down any possible accusation of influence by chronologically placing his initial involvement as having preceded such developments ('before I read about those'). Note also that he does not acknowledge 'mod' as a group label relevant to his identity, but merely says that he was 'dressing quite sharp'. His alternative source of influence ('it's more about watching *Quadrophenia* or something like that') also provides the third potential admission of inauthenticity. Not only is this an explicit acknowledgement of media influence, but a particularly significant one given that *Quadrophenia* is not merely a cult film, but was popular in major cinemas at the time of its release. It could conceivably be regarded as more akin to a mass media text than *Select*, the music paper whose influence is mitigated, and which Thornton would clearly regard as an example of niche media.

But as Oliver is attempting to situate his involvement as having occurred before the, then current, 1994 mod revival, mitigation need take place only with regard to contemporary media influences. As *Quadrophenia* was originally released in 1979, it would normally be cited as having helped precipitate the 1980 mod revival. While we would therefore have expected 1980 mods to have denied such an influence at the time, Oliver was then only eight years old, and too young to be involved. It is precisely this point that allows him to cite the film as an influence rather than, say, current music papers, for he can now safely claim he saw it well before the origins of the 1994 revival. In other words, there are significant time lags between the 1980 revival and his own viewing of the film, and from then until the emergence of the 1994 mod subculture. This minimizes the likelihood of others who were similarly influenced becoming mods through viewing the film at the same time as Oliver, and emphasizes his individuality and authentic origins. An additional inference might be that contemporary revivalists are also too young to have seen the film, and would therefore have been influenced by other, more current, media material. The point is the manner in which the age of the film, Oliver's personal biography and the dates of the two revivals intersect, providing a historical conjuncture that allows this particular person to cite this specific film at this moment in time while retaining his authenticity in relation to a media-influenced collective other.

Many subculturalists fully recognized the pervasiveness of the media and the inevitability of its influence on people's lives. But consistently with findings in the previous chapters, media effects were most usually attributed to others or retrospectively to a point in one's own past in order to authenticate a more recent situation. Subculturalists did not, however, consistently differentiate along a scale of decreasing authenticity between micro, niche and mass media in the expected manner. This is because claims for authenticity are primary; the media can then be illustrative of this. In other words, one's own heterogeneity and originality is first contrasted to the relative lack of such qualities in a subcultural or conventional 'Other' or past situation. Various media are then positioned and defined as mass or otherwise on the basis of this contrast. Their relative 'massness' is therefore derived from the homogenization of the 'Other', not in terms of any pre-defined formal qualities. This means that admissions of media influence by subculturalists can in no way be considered a postmodern celebration of the media, for such references are most likely to take the form of mitigation. The claims for authenticity that they seek to establish are necessarily conditional upon the 'mass media'-influenced inauthenticity of others.

Fashion and Commercialism

Empirically, the worlds of media and commerce are clearly interrelated; they are also theoretically combined in accounts of defusion and diffusion. In this chapter they are separated for analytical purposes to highlight their similar implications for subcultural authenticity. Echoing the manner in which respondents perceive their relationship to the media, the homogeneity of a look is not a quality of the style itself, nor a function of where it is purchased, but depends on how it is situated within a description of the wearer's authenticity.

> (C)   *MARC AND PAULA*
>
> M: *Yeah, there are definite categories of people around. It's just that I don't really like categorizing myself.*
>
> P: *There are a lot of people who do, like, belong to (indecipherable on tape). I think there are a lot in Brighton. Like recently there's been an upsurge of quite young girls, sort of between thirteen and sixteen, who think it's cool to be crusty, basically. I don't know if you've noticed that; it's quite obvious. And if you go around these pubs, you see them. There's loads of underage drinking. And they've got sort of like a uniform of holey tights on, I dunno.*
>
> M: *They're like us really.*
>
> P: *Well, yeah; but in certain cases they're trying to belong to a certain group, and that's really obvious. Like, you know they're obviously copying something that . . . you know. I think it's a phase they've got caught in, really.*
>
> M: *You just have to look at what most of the sort of High Street shops are doing. I was looking through some magazines the other day and Top Shop are bringing out their traveller look because now*

they think it's trendy to look sort of crusty in a way. So they're bringing out new clothes, basically for probably your thirteen- to sixteen-year-olds. I can see people do think this all has some sort of bearing on fashion.

(D) SUZIE AND MAGS

S: *I got very fed up with all the clothes that I was wearing and buying cheap and wrecking being sold for huge amounts of money to people that had probably never heard of . . . they'd heard of, like, Teen Spirit, but hadn't heard of Mudhoney or any of the other, like, grunge bands that were fairly big then, and were just buying stuff from Top Shop and stuff and thinking they were great and it got on my nerves and I thought 'I'm not wearing this any more.'*

M: *Got really pretentious.*

S: *'Cos I was being lumped in a group with them which wasn't on really, so.*

M: *When the grunge look became fashionable, well, that was a piss- off. Before that, people used to have – rip you apart for it, really – and then all of a sudden the catwalk said it was fashionable and it was cool, do you know what I mean?*

Extract (C) begins with a familiar sentiment. Marc resists categorization, but feels that it is applicable to others. Paula then nominates such a category – 'crusty'. Those designated by this term are claimed to be identifiable by their uniformity of appearance. That the description of this style could equally be applicable to the two interviewees makes this a potentially dangerous accusation. The irony is not lost on Marc ('They're like us really'). But Paula has already mitigated such a response in two ways. The first is by describing the emergence of this group through the words 'recently' and 'upsurge'. The transformation into 'crusty' has, in other words, been both rapid (superficial) and contemporary (after the original impulse), in contrast to which the interviewees can claim that they have been dressing in this style for a long time (which makes them innovators rather than followers), and that their own transition was gradual (suggesting an evolving, developing self). Paula's second mitigation, that this group 'think it's cool to be crusty' is premised on the distinction made in Chapter 5 between subculturalists, like the crusties, who merely adopt an image, and people, such as Marc and Paula, who wear style as a genuine expression of internally held attitudes.

Following Marc's comment, Paula commences to reinforce these initial negative group references. 'Trying to belong to a certain group . . . obviously copying something' implies a deliberate attempt by the crusties to follow a collective look, while the remarks about a 'phase' suggest that this is to be a short-lived, superficial attachment. The final claim is that the group look has been purchased from a High Street store, Top Shop, which renders it nothing more than an immediately obtained youthful trend. Just as 'preppie punks' were denigrated as 'pretenders' with a 'costume party' sensibility (Fox 1987: 361), the crusties are perceived to be interested only in subculture as fashion. As such, they resemble what Baron terms '"poseurs" (those youth who had adopted the subcultural style but did not participate in the subculture)' (1989b: 231). For other examples of this distinction between genuine and fashion-oriented members see also Andes (1998); Kotarba and Wells (1987); Lull (1987); Roman (1988); Sardiello (1998); Tomlinson (1998) and Widdicombe and Wooffitt (1990, 1995).

Although slightly older and of a related rather than identical style, Suzie and Mags in extract (D) would come close to the type of people who are disparaged by Marc and Paula in (C) for their fashion mentality. Of course, as we might expect, they also impute a fashion sensibility and related negative attributes to a comparative 'Other' through which to authenticate themselves. Suzie sets herself up (singular) as a creative innovator ('buying cheap and wrecking'). This is contrasted with those (plural) who merely buy the style, presumably 'ready wrecked', after it has become an expensive fashion. Note again the use of Top Shop as a symbol of a youthful, female fashion mentality. Also, observe the description of this 'Other' as 'pretentious', used in other interviews as a synonym for both 'plastic' and 'false'. Suzie's refusal to wear the style after this point is to differentiate her individual self from this inauthentic collective. Her complaint about 'being lumped in a group with them' could easily be a direct riposte to Marc and Paula. Mags also bemoans how the turning of grunge style into fashion by 'the catwalk' (note the impersonal, collective noun) has divested it of its shock potential and ability to provoke a critical reaction ('before that, people used to . . . rip you apart for it'). Moreover, this transformation is deemed to have occurred 'all of a sudden'. In other words, those taking up the fashion would have undergone a rapid change, denoting their superficiality. By contrast, Suzie and Mags can imply that their own inception occurred gradually, took place prior to this incorporation, and thereby signified a more individualized stylistic radicalism formed in opposition to mainstream fashion and mass consumption.

Interestingly, Suzie also invokes music to make claims about her authenticity. Those who constitute the reference group are thought to have heard of *Teen Spirit*, a reference to a hit single by Nirvana, but not any other grunge bands, despite the fact that some of these, such as Mudhoney, are described as having been 'fairly big then'. However, this is not to endow such bands with the popularity and renown that ensues from a top-selling hit single; for what, then, is the point of the contrast with *Teen Spirit*? The implication is that such bands were big enough for anyone *genuinely* into grunge to have heard of. The fact that certain people were not aware of them, yet had heard a successful chart single by a grunge band, is a comment on their taste for only the commercial element of such music. The falsity of grunge 'fashion' is clearly being equated here with the superficiality of commercially successful grunge music, both being contrasted with a depth metaphor: music (or style) as an genuine expression of and belief in inner feelings. Dancis expresses this difference with regard to punk music as, 'a band that has adopted a punk image and sound because it has become marketable, rather than because they believe in what they're doing' (1978: 63). This is one reason why, in the eyes of Lull's San Francisco punks, 'rock music that makes a lot of money is suspect, and songs that are rotated regularly on commercial radio stations do not gain approval' (Lull 1987: 243–4).

What is being privileged here is the artistic integrity of the underground compared to the mass commercialism of the mainstream. In Thornton (1995: 109, 122–9), we find, for example, the association of the denigrated mainstream with 'Top of the Pops' and various forms of 'chartpop'. For Thornton's clubbers, commercialism is a sure sign of 'selling out', a threat to one's sense of exclusivity, esotericism and cultural capital.[3] But Thornton also recognizes the irony that 'nothing proves the originality and inventiveness of subcultural music and style more than its eventual "mainstreaming"' (1995: 128). On one hand, there is the desire to protect the scarcity of subcultural capital and thereby retain one's originality; on the other, the need to have this affirmed by a larger following, losing in the process what Wai-Teng Leong has termed 'the power to be different' (1992: 32). Oliver indicated as much when he said, 'It's [the mod revival] not very big at the moment, and therefore, you know, you hope it's going to get big almost, but in a way you're glad it's not, because it would be full of people who would be jumping on the bandwagon.'

The oppositions brought into play in these extracts – between alternative and commercial, minority and majority, originals and followers – are those that in the CCCS approach distinguish 'the first wave of self-conscious innovators' (Hebdige 1979: 122) from the merely fashion-conscious. We examined the theoretical basis of this distinction at the beginning of this chapter, where we also made reference to subsequent modifications of the theory that have attempted to demystify the concept of pure stylistic innovation. Of these, we have already outlined Thornton's (1995) arguments that the media are as responsible for the definition and demarcation of subcultures as they are for their defusion and diffusion. A parallel thesis is provided by Frith and Horne (1987), and Seago (1995), who examine how the art schools provided an entrepreneurial ethos and designer dynamic, a strand of bohemianism that fed straight into the innovative world of streetstyle, counterculture and subculture, yet is absent from so much theoretical analysis. The relevance of this to punk is given in Jon Savage's (1992) cultural history *England's Dreaming*, certain passages of which suggest that the 'creation' of punk as a distinctive style owes as much to the entrepreneurial impulse of Malcolm McLaren and Vivienne Westwood, and the adoption of these designs by the Sex Pistols and others, as it does to the creative originality of disaffected youth.[4]

Now let us attempt our own theoretical re-evaluation of what occurs 'after the subculture had surfaced and become publicized' (Hebdige 1979: 122). We could assume this necessarily leads to the passive and collective acceptance of a commercially produced style. Or, alternatively, we could propose that such commodified subcultural styles, whether purchased new or obtained second-hand, continue to be customized and subverted. 'Just as the innovators can construct new meanings for clothes or other symbols from the dominant culture, so too can other members adapt and change the subcultural items for their own purpose and needs' (Andes 1998: 213). Why, then, should the option of further adaptation leading to heterogeneity be any less subversive than the actions of the original innovators? The answer, of course, is that it isn't, particularly when one further considers that some of the original adapters may also have adopted. In other words, as Wai-Teng Leong realizes, 'it is difficult to establish empirically the difference between adapters and adopters of style, between innovators and followers' (1992: 46). What is being suggested here is captured by Cagle's concept of 'out-there subculture':

> Unlike Hebdige's subcultural innovators, out-there subcultures take styles from mass-mediated sources (out-there) and appropriate them in a subcultural manner. Thus the out-there subculture is not pure in that it takes particular images given to it by commercial sources that have already incorporated innovative subcultural styles. Out-there subcultures, however, may engage in the recontextualization of an already commercialized (incorporated) style, but in so doing, they also engage in an act that symbolically resists the supremacy of dominant/mainstream culture (Cagle 1995: 45).

Cagle is proposing not only that those who make use of incorporated styles can do so in a different cultural context to that of the original innovators and thereby maintain a sense of 'otherness', but that they may additionally engage in acts of stylistic *bricolage*, further individualizing the ensemble in question (1995: 42, 97, 218). As Andes discovered, subculturalists do indeed view themselves as authentic by virtue of their individualistic innovations and adaptations, for 'regardless of when [their] involvement took place in the history of the subculture' (1998: 219) they always construct themselves as originals relative to an 'Other' who, it is claimed, merely follows in their wake, adopting mass versions of subcultural fashions. To illustrate these points let us now look at (E).

(E) *PAUL AND DOUGIE*

P: *Yeah, I mean I'd never had any what you might call punk gear really, any bondage stuff, anything like that.*

D: *We used to make it myself. Sew zips on.*

P: *I never had anything. Exactly. All I ever had was tatty, crappy clothes, and always wrote all over my T-shirts and drew on the jacket and that, and it's all, it is just do-it-yourself stuff. It's not deliberately modelled on anything.*

DM: *Did you ever buy punk stuff, like, off the peg I suppose is the best way of putting it?*

P: *No, never ever at all. The most punk gear I've ever done is paint jackets and draw on T-shirts, it really is. I've never, I chucked bleach all over my jeans, I suppose, that's about it. If you see someone who, it just looks like they've just gone out and spent two hundred pounds in London on the right punk gear and someone's put the safety pins through it for them and someone's put the studs on for 'em and that, that's not right, is it? What's the fun of that?*

We find here a number of binary oppositions in play. First, punk style is personally constructed through customizing ordinary clothes ('paint jackets, draw on T-shirts')[5] rather than having a look that is 'ready-made' to look 'subcultural' ('I never had any what you might call punk gear'). This also constructs a second distinction between, on the one hand, heterogeneity and partiality through *bricolage*, and on the other, a look that is holistic, or wholly subcultural. Third, this is therefore the difference between adapting ('do-it-yourself') and adopting ('someone's put the safety pins through it for 'em'). Also, fourth, between the original ('all I ever had') and the latest ('just gone out and . . .') immediately obtained style. Fifth, this distinguishes the old and cheap and personal ('tatty, crappy clothes . . . my jeans . . . my T-shirt') from that which is expensive, fashionable and purchased over the counter ('spent two hundred pounds in London'). Sixth, all of this also amounts to an attempt to produce something individual and unique rather than that which is merely an copy ('it's not deliberately modelled on anything') or which is meant to fit in with the dictates of the collective ('the right punk gear').

What are outlined here are sets of correspondences that, although congruent, can be selectively applied for the purpose of inauthenticating a comparative 'Other'. Let us again take the study by Fox (1987) as an example, not because it is deserving of sustained criticism, but because it is particularly illuminating on how certain members use style as such a means of inauthentication. Here, the dress of the 'preppies' is disparaged by the 'hardcores' on three main counts. First, they are considered to be into punk only as a fashion. Second, this partly derives from their purchasing of 'punk outfits from Ms. Jordan's [an exclusive clothing store]' (ibid.: 361).[6] Third, as we noted in Chapter 5, their malleable appearance is indicative of a part-time affiliation. By making adjustments to the style, they can change roles and pass muster in both punk and conventional society. We hear how, 'Mary, a typical preppie punk, put her regular clothes together in a way she thought would look punk. She ripped up her sorority t-shirt. She bought outfits that were advertised as having the "punk look". Her traditional bangs transformed into "punk" bangs, standing straight up using hair spray or setting gel' (ibid.: 361).

Yet it is precisely through the reordering and customizing of conventional items that authentic subcultural style is actively created. So one can readily admit to purchasing clothes from commercial stores, because the point is not what you wear or even where you buy it from, but what you wear it with or what you do to it. This is the whole basis of *bricolage*, and this is what Mary is actually doing when transforming the meaning of her regular clothes. What could be more subversive than the desecration of a sorority T-shirt, apart perhaps from mutilating the Stars and Stripes? And why is this any different from 'original' British punks mocking and customizing school shirts and ties? – an action that Marxist theorists, had they thought about it, would have interpreted as symbolic resistance against a dominant institution. Perhaps the bone of contention is the newness of the clothes worn. But, to continue with the above line of argument, surely it is logical to view the abuse of expensive new clothes from an 'exclusive' store as an infinitely more potent gesture of defiance towards bourgeois conventions than the spoiling of one's old tatty hand-me-downs? Moreover, the obvious alternative to both partiality and adaptation is to buy ready-made outfits, indicating homogeneity and adoption. Yet this is also exactly what Mary is accused of!

Clearly, there is something contradictory in such allegations. In fact, it doesn't take much imagination to construct the 'hardcore punks' as equally inauthentic through much the same accusations. We saw in Chapter 5 how their badges of permanence – the mohawk and tattoos – can equally indicate stasis and stereotypicality. Fox does not precisely delineate the style of the hardcores compared to that of other punks. But we hear that, for the scene in general, leather jackets were favoured wear (for a choice, considered opinion on this item, see the John Lydon quotation that opens this chapter). She also notes, as does Lull (1987), that Army and military wear, along with T-shirts and unkempt jeans, are commonly worn gear for punks. Again, depending on the combination of items, this might invite the criticism that what is worn does not differ considerably from conventional wear (T-shirt, jeans), that it is not particularly punk (army boots and jackets), that it is newly purchased from outlets specifically for the purpose, and so on. To give another example applicable to almost any subculture, a band T-shirt might for the wearer be revered as a sign of authentic affiliation to a particular group or to the music in general. Yet it is precisely because of this that these and many similar items, ostensibly indicators of permanent and genuine membership, hold the potential of being dismissed by others as expensive new purchases, the sign of a fashion mentality, of buying into the subculture.[7]

It is again important to stress that the wearing of 'conventional' items, or the purchasing of them from particular shops, is not, *in itself*, an admission of inauthenticity. What is important is the manner in which this is included in a claim for the wearer's heterogeneity and originality. Similar sartorial behaviour observed in others (and observed by others in oneself) can, however, be interpreted quite differently, as evidence of a fashion sensibility and of the wearer's having purchased 'ready made' subcultural 'outfits'. Hebdige is therefore correct when he observes that 'the distinction between originals and hangers-on is always a significant one in subculture' (1979: 122), but he fails to realize that this dichotomy has no objective basis or temporal logic.

Politics and Lifestyle

Although the extracts so far presented in this chapter appear to demonstrate resistance to the media and commercial incorporation of the subculture, it is not media influence and the commercial purchase of clothing, in themselves, that have negative connotations for authenticity, but the imputation that these have produced a tightly bounded, homogeneous group identity. We can therefore agree with Widdicombe and Wooffitt (1995: 206, 213) that subculturalists are resisting stereotypical characterizations of their affiliation, a process particularly evident in extracts (C) and (D). This type of resistance cannot, however, be a causal factor in the emergence of subcultural phenomena, for typifications can only be produced and resisted after the subcultures to which they apply have originated and become recognizable. As we saw in Chapter 4, it is individuality that is the basis of subcultural affiliation. Can expressions of individuality therefore be considered a form of resistance?

Our postmodern hypothesis would, in fact, state that subcultures would be apolitical cultural forms rather than gestures of resistance.

> *(F)*   DUNCAN
>
> D: *Yeah, I don't like society as it is. I'm just me. I don't care what other people think. And I look how I look 'cos I wanna. I listen to what I want to 'cos I wanna, and not 'cos someone else does. And that's just me. I mean if that's being a rebel, then, yeah, I'm a rebel. But I don't like the word and I don't consider myself a rebel. I'm just me. If people like it, great. If they don't they know where to go.*
>
> DM: *Um, are you kind of political?*
>
> D: *No. Anti-politics.*

Figure 13. Duncan

DM: *Is there anything about the attitudes of the majority of people that you don't like?*

D: *Well their attitude probably will be, if someone said 'Oh, you've got to do this, why don't you do like this to get a job, why aren't you doing this, you should go home, have a normal hair cut'. And my answer is, 'Fuck off.'*

(G)   PAUL

P: *I will happily sit and argue politics if I have to, but that's not why I look like this. It's not a political statement or anything. I hope if it says anything at all, it is that there ought to be some kind of freedom of expression, freedom of speech and dress, and you don't all have to be the same, you know. The only thing that you are really saying with a haircut is that I don't want to conform to the most basic kind of standards that society sets in tie-wearing offices. It's not really even anti-system is it, I don't think, having a mohican?*

Cashmore recycles conventional wisdom when he writes, 'Youth subcultures are ways in which young people come to terms with the social order as they understand it, and they frequently articulate a dissatisfaction with the world as it stands' (1984: 17). This dissatisfaction was expressed to varying degrees amongst my own sample, yet it was typically asserted in conjunction with a general reluctance or inability to see the meaning of subcultural membership in political terms.[8] Some informants took an anti-political stance, an example being Duncan (extract F), whose dislike of 'society as it is' finds a highly individualized expression. Others, like Paul (extract G), held political opinions but were easily able to separate their subcultural affiliation from such considerations. If there is a statement being made in these two extracts, it is not a challenge to the system, but a liberal declaration of freedom of expression, including the right to dress in ways contrary to dominant social conventions.

It may be argued that this is itself a political opinion; this rather depends upon our definition of the term. Young and Craig (1997), for example, discovered that when skinheads claim to be non-political, it is not they do not hold any personal opinions that can be construed as 'political'; rather, they are declaring their indifference to or lack of sympathy for overt political agendas and organized political groups.[9] The Glen Matlock quotation that heads this chapter tells a similar story, and suggests that punk 'politics' is best understood in terms of personal 'self-determination' (Matlock 1996: 163). 'An absolute sense of individuality is my politics', is how his (once) fellow band member John Lydon puts it (1994: 324). A number of metalheads interviewed by Arnett also redefined the political in this way. '"I'm a personal anarchist", said Dan, when asked to describe himself politically. "You should do what you feel is right and what you believe in. Anything goes until it goes so far as to hurt others"'(Arnett 1996: 128). As we saw in Chapter 4, this subcultural value system is a heightened expression of the dominant Western ideology of liberalism. Baron quotes Marchak (1975) on the point 'that "radicals" in a liberal society tend to be become more liberal – i.e. libertarian or anarchist' (Baron 1989a: 306).

From this perspective subcultures do not so much challenge as 'reinforce the prevailing set of norms' (Ehrich 1993: 31). They are no more a resistance to bourgeois hegemony than an extension of its liberal premises. Yet for this very reason they tend to exhibit resistance to all forms of collective and holistic belief systems, irrespective of the particular political content of those beliefs, for these are viewed as ways of imposing authority, conformity and uniformity. It is not therefore surprising that Duncan (extract F) and others express their individuality in anti-political terms, nor that Gottschalk's American countercultural 'Freaks' 'are suspicious of organized political movements, ideologies, categories, science or . . . "mono-theory" and "mono-culture". Freaks can believe in no absolute truth, heroes, myths or answers. Their main common denominator is a caustic rejection and criticism of "mainstream society"' (1993: 369). Lahusen similarly found a significant section of Basque punks to be similarly opposed to all collective ideologies, whether conservative or alternative. Such anarchic punks proposed 'anti-order' rather than 'alternative order' (1993: 271). Baron likewise discovered that 'there is no coherent ideology in the [Canadian] punk subculture that would facilitate organized political resistance . . . If anything, punk ideology is libertarian. The types of resistance engaged in reflect this libertarianism. The members are into "doing their own thing" which means no restrictions' (1989a: 305–6).

This is not to say that subculturalists would necessarily view their actions as constituting resistance, for this might imply that their affiliation is a calculated gesture of dissent rather than an expression of their inner self. As Duncan (extract F) puts it, 'I don't consider myself a rebel. I'm just me.' To state otherwise would suggest a concern with the opinions of others, and Duncan couldn't be more clear on this point – 'I don't care what other people think.' Yet his expressions of personal freedom are simultaneously defined against the expectations and dictates of others, and his full message is 'I do what I want and not what others tell or expect me to do', a logical counterpart to the meaning of punk offered by him in the first extract of Chapter 4. Duncan's retort when asked about the attitudes of others, is, in effect, a way of saying 'I don't have to explain myself to you.' This is a more radical gesture that any of those imputed to subculturalists (and other subordinate groups) by sociologists armed with collective categories, emancipatory discourses and theories of objective interests, for in its purest form it amounts to a complete and utter refusal to take any side but one's own.

An anti-structural subcultural sensibility is unlikely to facilitate political organization with a desire to enact social change. Certain academics since the CCCS have, in any case, opted to assess the degree of subcultural resistance, not through positive attempts to change the system, but negatively by reference to the extent of members' alienation and withdrawal from conventional institutions and lifestyles. There is in these studies an echo of Donnelly's (1985: 558) suggestion that the more individuals are committed to full-time occupations in conventional society, the more ephemeral their subcultural roles, and vice versa. A clear example of this approach can be found in Baron's (1989a, b) ethnography of Canadian west coast punk subculture. According to Baron, 'some members are totally committed to a lifestyle of resistance. They are alienated from dominant goals, rebel at home and school, and live on the streets engaging in illegal activities to survive. At the other end of the spectrum are those who display resistance in only one of these areas (e.g., school) or whose resistance is muted (e.g., live at home)' (1989a: 311).

An assessment of commitment according to lifestyle can also be found in Fox's (1987) ethnography. We drew upon this in Chapter 5 to demonstrate how appearance could be used as a criterion of full- or part-time subcultural commitment, but we also hear how the hardcores in Fox's study expressed their commitment to punk as a 'permanent way of life ... This lifestyle consisted of escaping the system in some way' (Fox 1987: 353, 354). By contrast, the preppies could be considered as having retained connections to a more secure existence: they were likely to live with their parents, still be at school, or have jobs 'within' the system. It was this persistent prevarication between punk and conventional society that rendered them only partly and transitorily committed. As one hardcore expressed his contempt of preppies, 'All I know is that I live this seven days a week, and they just do it on weekends' (ibid.: 363).

With gradations in between, this distinction between full- and part-time (or, what amounts to the same thing, core and marginal, real and pretend, permanent and ephemeral) members also appears in empirical studies of subcultures undertaken by Kinsey (1982), Webb (1996), Wheaton (1997), Moore (1994) and Sardiello (1998). Yet, just as I argued in Chapter 5 in relation to style, there can be no 'core' or 'marginal' members in any objective sense, only those who are defined as such by the researcher. Indeed, because subcultralists can have conflicting views as to what constitutes 'core' affiliation, different researchers can identify opposing criteria of 'core' commitment depending on which members' views they are privileging. Moore (1994: 19), for example, is typical in defining 'core' skinheads as those whose unemployed status allows for a total commitment to the subcultural lifestyle. Yet, in complete contrast, Young and Craig (1997) elevate Moore's 'weekend' skinheads (those with mainstream jobs that curtail their subcultural activities) to the status of central (and by implication 'proper') members, a designation validated with respect to the value system of the subculture itself:

> We learned early on in the fieldwork that membership really meant being a weekend deviant . . . In other words, membership entailed a certain amount of mobility between the subculture and the mainstream, or what one subject called 'normal life'. This was clearly demonstrated in the case of the much discussed work ethic. Since it is subculturally meaningful to be employed in conventional jobs, temporary modification of many of the traditional accoutrements of the subculture while pursuing work (wearing shoes other than the intimidating Doc Marten boots, concealing tattooed body parts, allowing the requisite cropped hair to grow out) is condoned behaviour (K. Young and Craig 1997: 184).

It is not that one of these two conflicting views is 'wrong'. We could, in fact, construct any number of (ideal-typical) subcultural models, each based on different criteria of resistance or 'core' (or authentic) commitment, and use these to assess the empirical situation. This means, in principle, that there could be as many types of subcultural resistance (or ways of demonstrating core commitment) as there are members who hold these different definitions. What typically occurs in practice, however, is that the academic imposes an *a priori*, holistic and objective standard of resistance – commitment to a lifestyle outside conventional society – against which the great majority of subculturalists are inauthenticated and marginalized because they do not measure up to this (actually very particular and partial) definition. This leads to the absurd suggestion that the only genuine article is that which many members would regard as a negative stereotype: the unemployed punk or skin, living on the street or in a squat – a definition that also appears largely irrelevant to certain contemporary subcultures (rave, mod) and previous generations of punks and skinheads.

There can, in any case, be no justification for imposing an external, unitary meaning by which to assess 'core' membership. Stratifying members according to their commitment to what they 'should' be doing runs absolutely contrary to typical indigenous meanings of punk, metal, biker and other subcultures as 'individual freedom'. To circumvent the potential criticism that this emphasis on individuality itself involves applying such a general principle of 'core' affiliation, I would argue that, first, this is a value derived from the constructs of the typical subculturalist, not a minority view imposed upon the majority; and second, that it allows for some variation of response. There are many ways in which one can find, as some subculturalists phrased it, a 'niche within the system where I can do my own thing' – by, for example, valuing work that allows for creative expression over that which demands greater compliance to rationalized routines, or using the family (a room of one's own) as a personal space where one can find isolation from external pressures (see Arnett 1996: 98). Indeed, living outside the system is likely to place greater restrictions on one's freedom, which is one reason why this apparently 'core' subcultural lifestyle can be regarded as stereotypical by other members.

To again make the point clear, there is no reason why we cannot select any criteria of commitment and gauge the sentiments of subcultural members accordingly. What is illegitimate is to take this, inevitably partial and one-sided, construct as an objective portrayal of subcultural stratification. To do so is to privilege the views of only certain members whose lifestyle coincides with the analysis's conception of what 'core' resistance should be. Some of the problems arising from this procedure can be seen from the social characteristics of marginalized members. My own extracts confirm the various observations of Fox (1987), Roman (1988), Baron (1989a, b) and Sardiello (1998) that poseurs and peripheral members are likely to be relatively young, often female and/or from middle-class backgrounds. Hardcores tend to be older and established on the subcultural scene, working-class in origin and male. The gender distinction is easily understandable. According to subcultural theory (McRobbie and Garber 1986; Powell and Clarke 1986) the 'marginality' of females in subcultures is a result of their structural centrality to the family. By defining the focal point of hardcore subculture as the street or the squat, Fox (1987) and Baron (1989a, b) select a masculine criterion of commitment that necessarily 'marginalizes' the subcultural participation of females.

The relation of class to full- and part-time membership is more perplexing, for middle-class marginality and a working-class 'core' inverts the schema proposed by the CCCS authors: 'middle class culture affords the space and opportunity for sections of it to "drop out" of circulation. Working-class youth is persistently and consistently structured by the dominating alternative rhythm of Saturday night and Sunday morning' (J. Clarke *et al.* 1986: 60–1). While this anomaly can be partly explained by the changing cultural, social and economic conditions of youth since the publication of the CCCS work, my major contention is that certain types of people (teenagers, females and the middle-class) are more likely to be subjectively inauthenticated by other members, and this one-sided view is objectified by the analyst. For example, in my own interviews I found travellers to be disparaged simply on the assumption that they came from well-off, middle-class families. Crucially, the bone of contention was not to do with travellers only intermittently living a lifestyle independent of conventional institutions; it was rather that their backgrounds were seen to provide them with a potential 'escape route'. Whether or not they took advantage of this connection to conventional society was not known, nor was this the issue. For as Widdicombe and Wooffitt put it, 'it is not what a person does that makes her a genuine person, but what informs or motivates her actions' (1995: 157).

The point, then, is how this assumption about class background enabled the activities of travellers to be characterized as insincere, and indicative of a part-time affiliation. No doubt rather different class-based assumptions, for example, 'that only *true punks* are unemployed' (Price 1977: 2; original emphasis, cited in Henry 1989: 67), have fed back into academics' construction of hardcore characteristics. Younger members are likewise regarded as part-timers or transitory because of the assumption that fashion is equated with youthfulness.[10] Moreover, any claims they make to the contrary would be viewed as nothing more than (to cite an interview example) 'their youth talking'. Of course, such perspectives can be contested. I have already indicated that the characteristics of the typical 'core' (i.e. working-class) member can be regarded as a stereotype, or in punk terminology, a cliché. Older members are also particularly vulnerable to the accusation of stasis and stereotypicality. The bottom line in any case would be that one's actions were, in fact, a sincere expression of an inner self. Individuals will, like Daniel, always attempt to convey themselves as 'people like me who *are it*; they are not so much doing it'. It is this wholly subjective and binary distinction between being (genuine) and doing (false) – see also Widdicombe and Wooffitt (1990) – that overrides any other considerations of authentic affiliation. To let Robin have the final say on this issue - 'I don't think it's a case of commitment. To me, you are what you are anywhere.'

Notes

1. See, for example, the photograph in the centre pages of York (1980) of the Sex Pistols playing the 100 club in 1976, and at the two males in the background either side of Steve Jones. The same point was made in the Granada television programme 'Mark Radcliffe's NWA', broadcast on 22 July 1996, one item of which was to commemorate the twentieth anniversary of the Sex Pistols playing the Lesser Free Trade Hall, Manchester. One of the original audience reminisced, 'this wasn't like a punk gig. The audience was just like us really – hippies.'

2. Tomlinson (1998: 207) likewise remarks on 'bubblegum ravers'. See also Rietveld (1993) on 'Acid Teds'.

3. For an application of this to rave, see Tomlinson (1998). Its relevance to rap music is discussed in Blair and Hatala (1991) and Blair (1993).

4. But as we saw in our discussion of the media, subculturalists do not wish to be so clearly defined and labelled. Unsurprisingly, then, we find John Lydon, the singer with the Sex Pistols, claiming to have been an original *bricoleur*, and that McLaren only later commericalized some of these looks as 'punk' style (Lydon 1993).

5. Lull (1987: 230) also notes how punks 'inscribe sentiments directly onto the surface of clothing with a marking pen'.

6. See Lull (1987: 227) on 'punkers': inauthentic punks who 'often buy expensive "punk-chic" clothing in fancy stores'.

7. As Gross puts it, 'they can don their metal oriented teeshirts that were bought at the mall, slip on some official metal oriented jewelry and toss on an AC/DC or Harley Davidson Cap and be ready to go. Is there a dollar to be made off the cult of heavy metal? You bet your Def Leppard T-shirt, there is' (1990: 127).

8. It might be said that the problem that punk posed in the late seventies for theorists of a left persuasion, such as Dancis (1978), Laing (1978) and Thompson (1979), was how to reconcile such an apparent contradiction. Tillman (1980) notes that by attempting this reconciliation these academics create 'pseudo-political movements . . . out of essentially apolitical forms' (1980: 173). For as Tillman argues, 'when punks invoke political symbols such as swastikas or songs about 'anarchy', they are not taking a political stance, but rather, are making a statement about the idea of politics: its irrelevance' (ibid.: 171).

9. Exactly the same attitude can be found in the bohemian counterculture. Miller remarks on the '"hippies' indifference or hostility towards politics . . . a common theme was simply suspicion of organized groups in general' (T. Miller 1991: 12). See also Polsky (1971: 159-60) and Buff (1970). We must be aware, however, of the distinction within the 1960s counterculture between the libertarian hippies and the overtly political 'New Left' radicals (see Keniston 1968; Berger 1970; Lipset 1971; Nelson 1989; T. Miller 1991).

10. Female subculturalists are also likely to be regarded in this way because of the equation of femininity with consumption. Hence, the references to Top Shop in extracts (C) and (D) of this chapter. See also Note 1 to Chapter 5.

8

Cultural Expression or Class Contradiction?

Friends, schools, communities, the media, the legal system, and the cultural belief system in the American middle class all generally promote the individualism of broad socialization. What results is a culture in which people feel they have license to express their inclinations to a large degree, whatever those inclinations might be. Such a culture is likely to be colorful, as this one is, and creative, as this one is, and constantly changing, as this one is. But if people are encouraged to express their inclinations, not everything they express is likely to be conducive to social order.

> Jeffrey Arnett: *Metalheads: Heavy Metal Music and Adolescent Alienation* (1996: 88)

When I returned to London in 1961, there I was with a little kid. I had hair an inch long when everyone else had a great big beehive, and everyone else's dress was two inches below the knee, and mine was two inches above. I got every remark you could think of, and Simon heard all this. I tried to inculcate into his psyche: 'You are you, you can do anything you like providing you don't hurt anybody else while doing it. You should be able to do what the fuck you like.' At four, five, six, that's gone in.

> Anne Beverley on sartorial unconventionality and libertarian childrearing practices. Her son is John Simon Ritchie, a.k.a Sid Vicious. Quoted in Jon Savage: *England's Dreaming: Sex Pistols and Punk Rock* (1992: 117)

Modern or Postmodern Subcultures?

The last four chapters have enabled us to assess our hypotheses against the views of our subcultural sample. We are now in a position to consider the extent to which contemporary subcultural sensibilities can be regarded as postmodern. In Chapter 4, we hypothesized that subcultural group identities would be fragmented rather than holistic and that boundaries would not be maintained with conventional style. We found that it was precisely through a comparison with a homogenized conventional 'Other' that subculturalists maintained their distinctive individuality and heterogeneity. The hypothesis in Chapter 5 was that subculturalists would be characterized by a part-time and transient affiliation as they regularly transgressed conventional and subcultural boundaries. In fact, too little and too much commitment – ephemerality *and* stasis – were regarded as equally indicative of the inauthentic and were imputed to a subcultural 'Other'. Informants alternatively saw their own style as an evolving expression of a gradually changing self. Our hypothesis in Chapter 6 was that mobility and change would prevent the formation of negative, oppositional relationships between different sub-cultures. We discovered that change was accomplished in a partial and fragmented manner, but was expressed through opposition with a stereo-typical and homogeneous subcultural 'Other'. In Chapter 7 we proposed that subculturalists would express positive sentiments towards fashion, commercialism and the media, and view their affiliation in apolitical terms. Although the first part of this hypothesis was not generally supported while the second was, it was not fashion, the media and politics in themselves that were viewed negatively, but their implications for homogeneity.

We can, I feel, grant a qualified acknowledgement of a postmodern sensibility. Subculturalists are postmodern in that they demonstrate a fragmented, heterogeneous and individualistic stylistic identification. This is a liminal sensibility that manifests itself as an expression of freedom from structure, control and restraint, ensuring that stasis is rejected in favour of movement and fluidity. Yet there is no evidence here of some of the more excessive postmodern claims. Informants did not rapidly discard a whole series of discrete styles. Nor did they regard themselves as an ironic parody, celebrating their own lack of authenticity and the superficiality of an image-saturated culture. On the contrary, attitudes were held to be more important than style, while appearance transformation was anchored in a gradually evolving sense of self. Subcultural sensibilities were, in other words, informed by a combination of a modernist depth model of reality and a postmodern emphasis on hybridity and diversity.

It is possible to summarize these findings by the following series of logically opposed traits.[1] Informants characterize themselves by reference to the left-hand column, while drawing upon the opposite set of traits to inauthenticate others:

authentic	inauthentic
alternative	mainstream
minority	mass
individualism	collectivism

heterogeneity	homogeneity
hybridity	holism
amalgamation	specificity
open-minded	narrow-minded
diversity	restriction
diffusion	cohesion
freedom	regulation
liberation	constraint
variation	predictability
liminality	structure
gradual change	rapid change
movement	stasis
attitude	appearance
innovation	copying
adaptation	adoption

Although many of the traits on the left-hand side have been labelled as postmodern, we can regard them as having their roots in aesthetic modernity and the Romantic countercultures of the nineteenth century. Indeed, I want to propose that the sensibilities of contemporary subculturalists have an 'elective affinity' with the two central 1960s countercultural values of licence and liberation (see also Chapter 3). Licence can be understood here as the *freedom to* express oneself. Liberation is the *freedom from* those social and cultural constraints that inhibit and prohibit this self-expression. Since the former rather depends upon the latter, both sentiments are usually found to be articulated simultaneously, as we see in the following three extracts.

(A)   LUCY

L: *I dress like I do because I like the way it looks and, you know, people are shocked, but I don't do it to particularly go against the system. I just don't want to be the same as everyone else because I think that's silly. I don't wanna be the same, you know, 'cos I feel more comfortable dressed like this than if I had nice long hair or just normal clothes all the time, because I wouldn't feel like I was being myself. It's more an expression of myself, I suppose.*

(B)   PETE AND ALISON

A: *It's just basically, this is me. I'm not offensive. I'm not out to offend people. It's just a total expression of the way I feel inside. Anyone else's opinion doesn't matter, because they're not me.*

P: *I'm not concerned about fitting in with any particular niche or group or anything. I'm not concerned about fitting in at all. The only thing I do, I do for me, because I like what it looks like. It's self-expression.*

A: *It's only if people try to mess with my head, if people try to interfere with the way I express myself, that's the only time I'm anti anything. Anti people interfering with me and my life. Anti people trying to tell me what to do.*

(C)   JIM, JANE AND SEAN

Ja: *We don't feel we have to go along with everything that says we have to do this or that.*

S: *Don't believe in authority figures*

Jim: *That's the way I was brought up with.*

S: *To always question authority.*

Ja: *Be free. Be free to do what you want. It's more anti being told what to do really. We know we don't have to do what we were told during life.*

It is important to stress again how this sense of individual freedom has a social origin. It is derived from the cultural belief system of Romanticism, in which emphasis is placed on giving full expression to the creative potential of the unique individual. In the view of Bellah and his colleagues, the outlet for this 'expressive individualism' in contemporary American culture is the 'therapeutic attitude' in which individuals are encouraged to find fulfilment and awareness through 'self-knowledge and self-realization' (Bellah *et al.* 1985: 98).[2] Martin makes a similar case for post-war Britain. Its culture, she argues, has become increasingly permeated by an 'expressive ethic' that prizes 'subjective experience and self-expression . . . exploration, feeling, self-discovery' (Martin 1985: 200, 208). In each case the quest is to *be* oneself, to *express* oneself and, above all, to *liberate* oneself from constraints and conventions (see also Hetherington 1998: Ch. 2; Wilson 1999). This is a culture in which young people are encouraged to, as Sean and Jane (extract C) put it, 'always question authority', to 'be free to do what you want'.

Historically it was the upper middle classes who were the carriers of this expressive ethic, and it was the youth of that class who, as we saw in Chapter 3, made up the majority of the 1960s counterculturalists. I want to claim, however, that over the last forty or so years there has been a cultural convergence between sections of the middle and working classes, as the new expressive professions and cultural industries have expanded. There appear to be two arguments here. First, that these emergent groups 'are having significant effects upon the wider society' (Urry 1990: 91), as they attempt to establish their tastes hegemonically. Second, that the absolute growth in middle-class occupations ensures that their personnel has also been drawn from the socially mobile youth of the skilled manual and routine white-collar classes, who have themselves taken advantage of the post-war expansion in higher education. As a result, an increasing number of subculturalists from what Martin (1985) terms 'this intermediate zone' between the privatized manual and higher professional classes can also be characterized as 'expressive individualists'.

Let us first assess the evidence for the contemporary situation. I pointed out in Chapter 2 that there are two issues here. The first is the extent to which there is a cross-class membership of a subculture. The second, the extent to which members from different class backgrounds articulate the same sentiments and values. It is actually quite difficult to come to firm conclusions about the first issue in my own study, for a number of reasons: (a) some individuals have been affiliated to a number of subcultures; (b) informants typically resist categorization or offer alternative ambiguous or hybrid identifications; (c) many individuals are, in any case, not easy to classify into subcultural types; (d) information on the backgrounds of some inform-ants is either not provided or not detailed enough; (e) the parents of some informants experienced intra-generational social mobility; and (f) the relatively small number of informants in each subcultural group makes this a statistically dubious exercise. The furthest I am willing to go here is to say that while my informants are drawn from both working- and middle-class backgrounds, the evidence does not suggest that punk, mod, goth and metal should be regarded as specifically *working-class* subcultures.[3] Evidence from other British, American and Canadian studies of the past fifteen years also suggests that certain subcultures straddle class boundaries.[4]

It is the second issue, however, that is the most important. And this is that subculturalists have in this study consistently expressed similar sentiments and values, particularly those concerning individual freedom and autonomy, irrespective of their different class backgrounds. With only one or two exceptions there was little evidence in any of my interviews of what the CCCS approach has led us to believe is typical of a working-class subcultural sensibility – a definite sense of group solidarity, a 'them and us' perception of society, a collectivist value system.[5] Indeed, we find these traits are typically regarded by subculturalists as indicative of the inauthentic. We need, however, to be careful here, for it is not working-class solidarity in itself that a subcultural sensibility opposes, but predictability, order, regulation, restriction, demarcation and structure – traits that are also to be found in both the lower and 'bourgeois' middle classes (Martin 1985). For the clash that appears here between individualism and collectivism is a symptom of the wider conflict between an expressive culture of freedom and a puritan culture of control.

In Chapter 7 we raised the question of what subcultures were resisting, and suggested that they could be seen quite as much as an expression of certain liberal premises as a reaction against these. We are now in a position to clarify this matter, for while contemporary subcultures can (like the 1960s counterculture) be interpreted as a challenge to the puritan values of order and control, they also display an 'elective affinity' with the Romantic values of individual freedom and self-expression. Given that both sets of values are bourgeois in origin, and that a postmodern culture is arguably predicated upon an intensification of the latter, it would appear that subculturalists are as much reproducing as resisting aspects of the dominant ideology.

Two Versions of Subcultural History

It would further appear that the CCCS distinction between working-class subcultures as 'clearly articulated, collective structures – often "near-" or "quasi-" gangs', and middle-class countercultures as 'diffuse, less group-centred, more individualised' (J. Clarke *et al.* 1986: 60) is not particularly appropriate to the contemporary cultural climate, and that its relevance to the past may also have been somewhat overstressed. When was the point at which this distinction began to lose its clarity? Here we can propose two views of subcultural history. Let us deal first with the orthodox version in which highly cohesive, group-centred, working-class subcultures – teds, mods, rockers, skins – unfolded in post-war modernist linear time. These groups were formed in direct homological opposition both to each other (hence the famous mods vs. rockers clashes) and to the middle-class hippies, as can be seen in Willis's (1978) ethnography of hippies and bikers, or in Brake's (1977) research on a group of hippies and a gang of skinheads. In neither of these studies does it appear remotely likely that any one member from either group could have ever affiliated to any other subculture, just as it would have seemed equally improbable to have suspected a mod of having previously been a rocker.

Then punk happened. After which, so the orthodox version goes, we entered postmodern subcultural time. Punk messed up the linear sequence by plundering and recycling all the previous styles; it straddled class boundaries by being both 'dole queue rock' (Marsh 1977) and the 'new bohemia' (Frith 1978). It was as much the sound of the suburbs as the authentic voice of the proletariat, and was seemingly more concerned with expressive individualism and libertarianism than with class solidarity.[6] After 1979, subcultural theory could never be quite the same again, overwhelmed as it was by evidence of a glut of ironic revivals, amorphous hybrids and individual *bricoleurs* refusing traditional identifications. As Polhemus is moved to comment:

> In researching the 'Streetstyle' exhibition ... I discovered that the nearer I got to the present day, the harder it was to find young people prepared to label themselves. I couldn't find a single person prepared to say, for example, 'I'm a Techno', 'I'm a Raggamuffin', 'I'm a Raver', 'I'm a Cyberpunk', 'I'm a Traveller', etc. Everyone, it seems, is 'an individual'. One suspects that on Brighton beach in 1964 things would have been different (Polhemus 1997: 149).

Here Polhemus is proposing a shift from group to individual identity. But has this really occurred? As we saw in chapter six, people are *always* likely to regard the past, but not their own present situation, in terms of stereotypical labels, suggesting that 1964 mods would also have resisted the imposition of a group label.[7] Moreover, it is still relatively easy to find contemporary situations exhibiting the collective effervescence and group formations that characterized the past – any well-attended heavy metal concert, for instance, or the annual gathering of the goths in Whitby, North Yorkshire. The point, however, as was demonstrated in Chapter 4, is that such subcultures are, paradoxically, a socially shared means of expressing an *individualistic* sensibility, and may always have been.

The major problem with the orthodox view of subcultural history to which Polhemus subscribes is its reliance on the CCCS 'modernist' theory as a benchmark against which to measure postmodern change. The artificially pure version of subcultures produced by the CCCS has obscured the disjunctions, confusions and complexities of a pre-punk era. As Redhead puts it, '"authentic" subcultures were produced by subcultural theories, not the other way around' (1991b: 25). 'Beginning initially with the teddy boy style ... in the early/mid-50s, working-class subcultures have been *retrospectively mapped back* onto British cultural history every few years by fashion and music journalists and entrepreneurs eager to perpetuate some enduring myths about some spectacular subcultures' (Redhead 1993: 2; my emphasis). Osgerby has recently put forward much the same argument:

> The tendency to celebrate a multiplicity of 'styletribes' during the nineties has exaggerated the degree to which stylistic choice was circumscribed in earlier periods. Indeed, throughout the post-war era British youngsters have always faced a relatively open and flexible range of stylistic options rather than a simple choice between being 'cool' or 'square' ... Rather than being perfectly formed cultural

entities, subcultures have always been fluid and fragmented 'hybrids' in which cultural allegiances have been mutable and transient. Instead of making a firm set of stylistic commitments most youngsters have instead cruised across a range of affiliations, constantly forming and reforming their identities according to social context. In this respect the open-ended, fragmented identities many theorists see as common to the late twentieth century were, perhaps, anticipated by tendencies already present within the youth cultural formations of the 1950s and 1960s (Osgerby 1998: 201, 203).

It is the failure to recognize this version of the past that has created much of our supposed postmodern present. Gottschalk, for example, emphasizes the stylistic ambiguity and individual creativity of his contemporary sample of 'freaks' in 'comparison to other counter- or subcultural styles such as the 19th century Bohemians, the Beats, the Hippies, the Punks, or the Rastafarians, who adopt(ed) a particular and recognizable dressing code' (1993: 367). But Gottschalk's descriptions of these codes (ibid.: 373) are simply lists of crude stereotypes, including the standard flower-power, bearded hippie and the mohawked, leather-jacketed punk.

The past never was, of course, as simple as either Polhemus and Gottschalk make out. I knew this much about punk from experience, but remember being surprised by a cursory look at a recording of the Monterey pop festival of 1967 that told me that many of the crowd did not conform to the standard hippy dress codes. I was further surprised by what I saw as the *internal diversity* of the mod and skinhead styles on show at the 'Streetstyle' exhibition,[8] for both subcultural theory and my own simplification of the past had led me to expect a stylistic homogeneity. It is this reading of the past as stereotypical that always informs our perceptions of the present. So I suspect that had Gottschalk conducted research at the time on 1960s hippies or 1970s punks he would also have found diversity and eclecticism in relation to some other past stereotype.

Hence, the second, alternative, version of subcultural history, in which, travelling back from the late 1970s, it is possible to attempt something of a postmodern re-reading of a supposedly modernist period, a re-evaluation in which 'pure' subcultural forms now become fragmented and diversified. Phil Cohen, for example, refers to the 'parkas or scooter boys . . . a transitional form between the mods and skinheads', and to those groups following the skinheads, 'variously known as crombies, casuals, suedes and so on' (1984: 83, 84). Going back a little further, Stan Cohen can be found claiming that 'by now, the beginning of the sixties, changes were diffusing rapidly, the youth culture was being opened up to new influences and it was difficult to sort out the types' (1973: 184). Indeed, he goes so far as to state that 'by 1964–5, the so-called Mod was hardly recognisable', its place taken by 'scooter boys', 'hard mods', and 'smooth mods' (ibid.: 187). These alternative readings should not surprise us, for if there has always been an aesthetic dimension to modernity then observers will have always been able to remark on the stylistic heterogeneity and fragmentation of their own era. Even a century ago Simmel (1896, 1978) was talking of 'the multitude of styles' and the 'bewildering plurality of styles' (cited in Frisby 1985b: 65).

What would this fragmentation and diversity have meant for the individual wearers of a style? Would we have discovered the same references to hybridity and mobility that we have seen in this study? We can certainly find Frith (1983) commenting in postmodern terms on the 'image changes', sartorial 'playfulness' and lack of subcultural commitment ('styles were usually a matter of convenience') of a group of high-school fifth-formers back in 1972. 'I'm in between a skinhead and a hippie ... I wear "mod" clothes but I listen to both kinds of music', claimed one of his informants (1983: 207). Other people apparently ahead of their time were the 'mids' and 'mockers' of the early 1960s.[9] Barnes recalls that both groups mixed together the styles of the mods and rockers, only the mockers 'did so intentionally' (1991: 123). The first recorded example of postmodern mix and match? This might sound implausible, given what we know about the social and cultural differences between these two subcultures; yet in the 'vox pop' of Hamblett and Deverson we nevertheless find someone claim, 'I've been everything under the sun – a Mod and a Rocker, just to be myself' (1964: 70). Here is a change of allegiance and a clear expression of individuality that runs completely counter to modernist subcultural theory.

This is not, however, to propose a flat-earth view of subcultural history, completely evacuating class distinctions and simply replacing collectivism with individualism. It is, for instance, difficult to contest the CCCS portrayal of the more 'lumpen' teds and skinheads as traditionally working-class, group-centred, and concerned with the marking of territorial boundaries. On the other hand, Martin's following assessment of the original mod subculture provides a sense of historical development and specificity that can be contrasted to Hebdige's description of 'the mod's solidarity' (1974: 11), and to the 'abstract essences' produced by the CCCS and generalized to all working-class subcultural styles:

The mods of the early to mid-1960s form an interesting bridge between the unmistakably tribal communitas of the lower working class and the detailed elaboration of anti-structure which the bohemian middle-class sub-cultures developed ... The mods were not organized into gangs like some of the lower-working class subcultures: they were loose and shifting agglomerations of individuals 'with a bit of style', drifting around to find the place where the action might be. They were the first real instalment of individualistic, grid-patterned competitiveness in the vocabulary of liminal anti-structure (Martin 1985: 146).

It is Martin's contention that as the expressive ethic of a specific middle-class fraction pervaded the cultural sphere as a whole, effecting 'a transformation in the assumptions and habitual practices which form the cultural bedrock of the daily lives of ordinary people' (1985: 1), post-war British working-class youth were increasingly subject to liminal tendencies from the 1950s onwards. While, for example, the teds were (in my opinion) undoubtedly motivated by a narcissistic attitude towards consumption, this anti-puritanical element was carefully framed, kept within limits, expressed within the traditional boundaries of class solidarity and masculinity.[10] The mods, on the other hand, took Romantic narcissism to extremes. As the progeny of the new 'affluent' and privatized working class, they were the first fully-fledged subcultural manifestation of expressive individualism. Frith also views the mods in this manner, 'the point was exclusivity . . . not solidarity; theirs was a self-conscious gesture against conformity of any sort . . . their position prefigured the hippies, was an aspect of bohemianism' (1983: 223).

I began this book by commenting on an approach to subcultural theory that understands working-class subcultures as reactions to their shared material conditions of existence, as solutions to class-based contradictions, yet that made no sense in terms of my own experience. According to Henry, punks 'were basically lower class white youths who were hit hard by England's economic situation' (1984: 31). Burr argues that punks 'were clearly a product of their times and a reaction to recession and unemployment' (1984: 932). Yet I completely fail to recognize my own past as a working-class teenager in these interpretations. Now, in a time of even worse youth unemployment during the 1980s and 1990s, these 'materialist' explanations continue to be pressed into service to account for the cross-class membership of subcultures. A particularly good example of this approach is that of Susan Willis, who explains the widespread appeal of American 'hardcore' style as a response to the shared economic problems facing middle-class and working-class teenagers. The youth of both classes are 'fundamentally united by the fact that they constitute a common employment pool . . . a labor *lumpenproletariat* (1993: 376–7; italics in original).

I stated in Chapter 2 that while this book provides a one-sided focus on cultural values, I would certainly agree that socioeconomic factors are also implicated in the development and formation of subcultures. This is not, however, to grant legitimacy to the neo-Marxist claim that subcultures are 'solutions' to 'class contradictions'. The problem with asserting, as Hebdige does, that punks were 'directly *responding*' to 'increased joblessness . . . the rediscovery of poverty . . . "Britain's decline"' (1979: 87; original emphasis), is that the link posited between structure and action is never demonstrated by a connecting sequence of motivations and values. Willis completely sidesteps this issue by insisting that subcultures are nonetheless responding to 'larger social and economic structures, many of which are not available to the subcultural practitioners in a conscious political way' (1993: 382). But here we are again faced with the problem of the analysts imposing their own conceptual reality (and political world-view) upon the subjects of the study. Despite the fact that over half my sample were either unemployed or in causal and part-time work at the time of interview,[11] only a small minority made any sort of references to economic conditions, and there were certainly no suggestions that their affiliation was a response to such factors. Faced with this evidence, I have to agree with Arnett that holding to the afore-mentioned neo-Marxist explanation requires 'quite a leap of interpretation' (1996: 172).

What did, however, appear consistently throughout the interviews, regard-less of the style and social backgrounds of the informants, were references to *freedom* – freedom from rules, structures, controls and from the predict-ability of conventional lifestyles. The subculturalists quoted in this book are what Frith terms 'the culturally adventurous of all classes. They provided the continuity of bohemian concern that runs from the beats to the punks' (1983: 224). And also, I would add, from the punks to contemporary mods, goths, metallers and other post-punk subcultural forms. I can therefore conclude this book by proposing one necessarily partial and limited explan-ation that does have the merit of being adequate at the levels of both meaning and causality – that subcultures are manifestations of self-expression, individual autonomy and cultural diversity, and that these traits have an elective affinity with bohemian values that have increasingly come to define the experiences of sections of post-war working-class and lower-middle-class youth. In this sense, the emergence of a postmodern (or liminal) working-class subcultural sensibility (and its convergence with middle-class values) can be traced back at least to the beginning of the 1960s.

Notes

1. It is interesting to compare this with a similar table in Thornton (1995: 115).
2. Bellah's thesis is consistent with findings from two contemporary American ethnographic studies of subcultures. Webb (1995, 1996), for example, claims that the 'freaks' (skater punks, ravers and grunge kids) in his study were 'expressive individualists'. It was only by breaking the social conventions of dress and behaviour

that Webb's respondents felt able to display, express and explore their individuality. 'I was told by many of these young people that they "go the extra mile" in being different' (1996: 3). Arnett's metalheads likewise placed a high value on individual self-expression (Arnett 1996: 100). In their 'especially large appetite for intensity and novelty of experience' (ibid.: 88), they display the Romantic characteristic of deriving emotional pleasure from strong sensations and feelings.

3. For example, the majority of the mods/scooterists were from lower- or upper-middle-class families. The 'goth–indie–metal' contingent came equally from manual and non-manual backgrounds. A number of punks or ex-punks were also of middle-class origin.

4. Of the American freaks studied by Gottschalk (1993) most were from upper-middle-class backgrounds; Webb (1996) also suggests that most of his 'freak' sample were of middle-class origins. The majority of metalheads in Arnett's (1996) study were from middle- to upper-middle-class families, although the author mentions other evidence that indicates a more even class divide within heavy metal fans. Evidence on the punk subculture from both America (Fox 1987; Roman 1988) and Canada (Baron 1989a, b) suggests that members are recruited evenly from both manual and non-manual backgrounds. Burr (1984) mentions that seven of his sample of nineteen British punks were 'upperclass' (middle-class?), but does not provide details on parental background. Willis states that American 'hardcore' style 'draws youth equally from middle- and working-class families' (1993: 375). Sixteen of the fifty hippies in Brake's (1977) British study were of working-class origin. Contemporary research on Canadian skinheads (Baron 1997; K. Young and Craig 1997) interestingly reports a substantial minority of members from middle-class homes.

5. The only clear-cut example of this was from Jeff, an ex-skinhead who defined the subculture in terms of a collective group-centred experience. 'A gang of lads walking down the road, and that used to give you the feeling of so much power. It made you feel good 'cos you were part of a big group. There was a nice feeling of a family group. You looked after each other.' Such descriptions recalled previous characterizations of the skinhead subculture as a 'gang' (Daniel and McGuire 1972). Lull also argues that 'the group context ... defines the skinhead lifestyle' (1987: 247). Further insights into the skinhead subculture can be found in J. Clarke (1973a, b), Brake (1974, 1977), Knight (1982), Martin (1985: Ch. 7), Marshall (1991) and Moore (1994).

6. In a comparison of the American hippy and punk press, Lamy and Levin (1985) discovered twice as much content relating to 'self-expression' in the punk publications as in the hippy sample. Barensten (1999) interprets punk's 'do-it-yourself ethic' as a manifestation of the Romantic impulse towards self-expression and creativity.

7. Barnes reports how 'Faces stopped calling themselves Mods towards the latter part of 1964 ... They called themselves "Individualists" or "Stylists". They wanted to differentiate themselves from the over-all uniformity they saw in the suburban and provincial Mod' (1991: 123).

8. Open at the Victoria and Albert Museum, London, from 16 November 1994 to 19 February 1995.

9. See Barnes (1991). According to Thorne, 'the less radical mods were known as "Mids", stragglers as "Tickets"'(1993: 160).

10. For accounts and analyses of the teddy boy subculture, see Fyvel (1963), Rock and Cohen (1970), Jefferson (1973) and Rushgrove (1994).

11. An issue that is equally relevant is the high degree of cultural creativity in the sample as a whole. Twenty had been, or were at the time of interview, students in further and higher education, particularly in arts, social science and humanities subjects. At least two had been to Art College, while a number of others were artists of various kinds. Others in the sample were either managers of (or employees in) second-hand clothes or record shops, were working in graphic design, printing and desk-top publishing, or were part-time and aspirant DJs and journalists, etc. As one might expect, many had an exceptional knowledge of youth (sub)cultural history, popular culture, music and fashion. These cultural literati were affiliated to all types of subcultures and came from skilled working-class and lower-middle-class as well as professional backgrounds.

Appendix: Fieldwork Details and Interview Schedule

There is nothing wrong with high level speculative theory, except if it becomes presented and legitimated as having surpassed, or succeeded in discrediting the need for, empirical research.

Mike Featherstone: *Consumer Culture and Postmodernism* (1992: ix)

Any account of an activity that ignores or marginalises the experiences of those directly engaged in it can hardly claim much accuracy or authenticity.

Batsleer *et al.*: *Rewriting English: Cultural Politics of Gender and Class* (1985: 146)

To collect my subcultural sample, I interviewed a total of fifty-seven different people (of whom fourteen were female), in thirty-eight separate interviews. The age range was sixteen to thirty-four; the average age was twenty-four. There were also four non-subcultural people (two females, two males) interviewed for the purpose of providing a 'conventional' control sample (these interviews are not used in this book). Subcultural informants were selected for this study on the basis of what I regarded as their unconventional appearance. All but three interviews (involving six subcultural informants) were conducted in Brighton, East Sussex, in six separate visits: (1) September 1993, (2) December 1993–January 1994, (3) April 1994, (4) July to September 1994, (5) January 1995, and (6) April 1995. The fifth session was to interview only the 'conventional' sample. The other three interviews were conducted in Preston, Lancashire, in February 1994. Interviews were conducted mainly in the pubs and clubs where the informants were approached.

The interviews can best be described as semi-structured, often conversational, and the order of the questions was not always strictly adhered to. Informants would sometimes initiate the discussion and provide a more promising line of inquiry to be followed, or they might pre-empt my intended order of questioning. Nor was the wording of the questions particularly important, for I treated them more as areas for discussion. After each fieldwork session the questions were slightly revised to take account of new themes and hypotheses generated inductively from the data (see Glaser and Strauss 1967). All interviews were taped and transcribed. The duration of the interviews varied considerably, from twenty minutes to one and a half hours, with the typical time taken being around forty minutes.

The Interview Schedule

How old are you?

What job (or otherwise) do you now do?

What different jobs, if any, have you done previously?

What jobs do (did) your parents do?

How would you describe yourself? Who are you?

Do you think of yourself as identifying with a particular sort of people because of the way you dress?

Would you say that you are a (whatever)?

How long have you been dressing like this?

What made you choose the way you look, your style?

What were the main influences for you? Where did you get your ideas about the style from?

Was it only because your friends were into (whatever) (this style)?

What was it about the image that you liked?

Where do you get your various items of clothing from?

Do you think about how to mix or match different items together?

Is there a degree of creativity in obtaining your look?

Do you take a lot of trouble or effort over it, or is it something that doesn't take much thinking about?

Do you ever make, dye or customize clothes?

Do you always dress in this way nowadays?

Are there any occasions when you dress differently?

Do you tend to change between a number of different styles, or is your look fairly consistent?

Do you ever consciously copy the styles of other people?

Is it important to you to feel that you have your own, unique, individual way of dressing?

What's being a (whatever) all about? / What's dressing in this style all about?

Are you trying to say anything by wearing this style? / Can you tell me what it means to you?

Do people who dress in this way tend to have anything in common apart from the style? (a particular way of life, attitudes or ideas, way of behaving, music?)

Is this true for you personally?

So what's the difference between people who dress like you and people who dress more conventionally?

Is it enough just to wear the style, or is there more to it than the way you look?

Do you ever feel ties or bonds with other (whatever) people who you see dressed in a similar style, even if you don't know them personally?

Do you dress this way to be different from the norm, or do you think the way you look is just another way of dressing, nothing special?

It's sometimes said that people who dress similarly to you are anti-conventional or anti-system. Is this true for you?

Is being a whatever / dressing in this style important to you?

Do you feel you have a commitment to (whatever) this (life)style? How seriously?

How long do you see yourself dressing in this way? Is this something you ever think about?

Do you think it possible or likely that you might be into a different style soon?

Nowadays, do you think its possible to identify groups of people according to their style? (Name them)

Do you ever compare yourself (whatever) to other groups, like punks, goths, skinheads, hippies, etc.?

In what ways do you think (whatever) you are similar to or different from other groups?

It's sometimes said that nowadays it's difficult to identify different style groups because everything is becoming too mixed together and complicated. What do you think?

What are your views on people who dress 'straight' or conventionally?

Do you ever compare yourself to them?

In what ways do you think you are similar to or different from conventionally dressed people?

Have you ever previously dressed in a different style?

Did you feel you were a (whatever)?

Why did you change?

Was it difficult to change?

Bibliography

Abercrombie, N., Lash, S. and Longhurst, B. (1992), 'Popular representation: recasting realism', in S. Lash and J. Friedman (eds), *Modernity and Identity*, Oxford: Blackwell.

Althusser, L. (1971), 'Ideology and ideological state apparatuses', in *Lenin and Philosophy and Other Essays*, London: New Left Books.

Andersen, M. (1985), Extract from various home made handouts given out in shows in Washington, DC.

Andes, L. (1998), 'Growing up punk: meaning and commitment careers in a contemporary youth subculture', in J. S. Epstein (ed.), *Youth Culture: Identity in a Postmodern World*, Oxford: Blackwell.

Arnett, J. (1991a), 'Adolescents and heavy metal music: from the mouths of metalheads', *Youth and Society*, 23 (1) (September): 76–98.

Arnett, J. (1991b), 'Heavy metal music and reckless behaviour among adolescents', *Journal of Youth and Adolescence*, 20 (6): 573–92.

Arnett, J. (1992), 'The soundtrack of recklessness: musical preferences and reckless behaviour amongst adolescents', *Journal of Adolescent Research*, 7 (3) (July): 313–31.

Arnett, J. (1993), 'Three profiles of heavy metal fans', *Qualitative Sociology*, 16 (4): 423–43.

Arnett, J. (1996), *Metalheads: Heavy Metal Music and Adolescent Alienation*, Oxford: Westview Press.

Back, K. W. (1985), 'Modernism and fashion: a social psychological interpretation', in M. R. Solomon (ed.), *The Psychology of Fashion*, Lexington, MA: Lexington Books.

Barensten, G. (1999), 'Where is the Anti-Nowhere League? English Romanticism and Punk Subculture', Unpublished MA thesis, Interdisciplinary Studies, York University, Toronto, Canada.

Barnard, M. (1996), *Fashion as Communication*, London: Routledge.

Barnes, R. (1991), *Mods!*, London: Plexus.

Baron, S. W. (1989a), 'The Canadian west coast punk subculture: a field study', *Canadian Journal of Sociology*, 14 (3): 289–316.

Baron, S. W. (1989b), 'Resistance and its consequences: the street culture of punks', *Youth and Society*, 21 (2) (December): 207–37.

Baron, S. W. (1997), 'Canadian male street skinheads: street gang or street terrorists?', *Canadian Review of Sociology and Anthropology*, 43 (2): 125–54.

Barthes, R. (1975), *S/Z*, London: Cape.

Batsleer, J., Davies, T., O'Rourke, R. and Weedon, C. (1985), *Rewriting English: Cultural Politics of Gender and Class*, London: Methuen.

Baudrillard, J. (1983a), *In the Shadow of the Silent Majorities*, New York: Semiotext.

Baudrillard, J. (1983b), *Simulations*, New York: Semiotext.

Baudrillard, J. (1993), *Symbolic Exchange and Death*, London: Sage.

Beattie, G. (1990), *England After Dark*, London: Weidenfeld and Nicolson.

Becker, H. (1963), *Outsiders: Studies in the Sociology of Deviance*, New York: Free Press.

Beezer, A. (1992), 'Dick Hebdige, *Subculture: The Meaning of Style*', in M. Barker and A. Beezer (eds), *Reading into Cultural Studies*, London: Routledge.

Bell, D. (1976), *The Cultural Contradictions of Capitalism*, London: Heinemann.

Bell, D., Binnie, J., Cream, J. and Valentine, G. (1994), 'All hyped up and no place to go', *Gender, Place and Culture: A Journal of Feminist Geography*, 1(1): 31–47.

Bell, Q. (1992), *On Human Finery*, London: Allison and Busby.

Bellah, R. N., Madsen, R., Sullivan, W. M., Swidler, A. and Tipton, S. M. (1985), *Habits of the Heart: Individualism and Commitment in American Life*, Berkeley, CA: University of California Press.

Benton, T. (1977), *The Philosophical Foundations of the Three Sociologies*, London: Routledge and Kegan Paul.

Berger, P. L. (1968), *Invitation to Sociology: A Humanist Perspective*, Harmondsworth: Penguin.

Berger, P. L. (1970), 'Between system and horde', in P. L. Berger and R. J. Heuhaus, *Movement and Revolution*, New York: Doubleday.

Berman, M. (1987), *All that is Solid Melts into Air*, London: Verso.

Bhaskar, R. (1978), *A Realist Theory of Science*, Hassocks: Harvester.

Billington, R., Hockey, J. and Strawbridge, S. (1998), *Exploring Self and Society*, London: Macmillan.

Blackman, S. (1995), *Youth: Positions and Oppositions – Style, Sexuality and Schooling*, Aldershot: Avebury.

Blair, M. E. (1993), 'Commercialisation of the rap music youth subculture', *Journal of Popular Culture*, 27 (3) (Winter): 21–33.

Blair, M. E. and Hatala, M. N. (1991), 'The use of rap music in children's advertising', in J. Sherry and B. Sternthal (eds), *Advances in Consumer Research*, 19: 719–24.

Blundell, V., Shepherd, J. and Taylor, I. (eds), (1993), *Relocating Cultural Studies*, London: Routledge.

Bocock, R. (1992), 'Consumption and lifestyles', in R. Bocock and K. Thompson (eds), *Social and Cultural Forms of Modernity*, Cambridge: Polity.

Bourdieu, P. (1984), *Distinction: A Social Critique of the Judgement of Taste*, London: Routledge and Kegan Paul.

Brake, M. (1974), 'The Skinheads: an English working class subculture', *Youth and Society*, 6 (2) (December): 179–200.

Brake, M. (1977), 'Hippies and Skinheads – Sociological Aspects of Subcultures', Unpublished Ph.D. thesis, London School of Economics.

Brake, M. (1980), *The Sociology of Youth Culture and Youth Subcultures*, London: Routledge and Kegan Paul.

Brake, M. (1985), *Comparative Youth Sub-Cultures*, London: Routledge and Kegan Paul.

Brown, B. B., Eicher, S. A. and Petrie, S. (1986), 'The importance of peer group ("crowd") affiliation in adolescence', *Journal of Adolescence*, 9: 73–95.

Brown, J. W. (1973), 'The values and norms of the expressive student subculture', *Youth and Society*, 4 (4) (June): 483–98.

Buff, S. (1970), 'Greasers, dupers and hippies: three responses to the adult world', in L. K. Howe (ed.), *The White Majority: Between Poverty and Affluence*, New York: Random House.

Burr, A. (1984), 'The ideologies of despair: a symbolic interpretation of punks' and skinheads' usage of barbiturates', *Journal of Social Science and Medicine*, 19 (9): 929–38.

Burrows, R. (1989), 'Some notes towards a realistic realism: the practical implications of realist philosophies of science for social research methods', *International Journal of Sociology and Social Policy*, 9 (4): 46–63.

Butler, J. (1990), *Gender Trouble: Feminism and the Subversion of Identity*, London, Routledge.

Butler, J. (1993), *Bodies That Matter: On the Discursive Limits of 'Sex'*, London, Routledge.

Cagle, V. M. (1995), *Reconstructing Pop/Subculture*, London: Sage.

Calluori, R. A. (1985), 'The kids are alright: new wave subcultural theory', *Social Text*, 4 (3): 43–53.

Campbell, B. (1985), *Wigan Pier Revisited*, London: Virago.

Campbell, C. (1980), 'Accounting for the counter culture', *Scottish Journal of Sociology*, 4 (1) (Jan.): 37–51.

Campbell, C. (1987), *The Romantic Ethic and the Spirit of Modern Consumerism*, Oxford: Blackwell.

Carter, A (1983), 'The recession style', *New Society*, 63 (1052), 13 January.

Cartledge, F. (1999), 'Distress to impress?: local punk fashion and commodity exchange', in R. Sabin (ed.), *Punk Rock: So What?*, London: Routledge.

Cashmore, E. E. (1984), *No Future: Youth and Society*, London: Heinemann.

Chambers, I. (1990), *Border Dialogues: Journeys in Postmodernity*, London: Routledge.

Chaney, D. (1996), *Lifestyles*, London: Routledge.

Clarke, D. (1980), 'The state of cultural theory: a review of past and present fashions', *Alternate Routes*, 4: 106–56.

Clarke, G. (1982), *Defending Ski-Jumpers: A Critique of Theories of Youth Sub-Cultures*, Occasional Paper 71, CCCS, University of Birmingham.

Clarke, J. (1973a), *Football Hooliganism and the Skinheads*, Stencilled Occasional Paper 42, CCCS, University of Birmingham.

Clarke, J. (1973b), *The Skinheads and the Study of Youth Culture*, Stencilled Occasional Paper 23, CCCS, University of Birmingham.

Clarke, J. (1986), 'Style', in S. Hall and T. Jefferson (eds), *Resistance Through Rituals: Youth Subcultures in Post-War Britain*, London: Hutchinson.

Clarke, J. (1991), *New Times and Old Enemies: Essays on Cultural Studies in America*, London: Harper Collins Academic.

Clarke, J. and Jefferson, T. (1978), 'Working class youth cultures', in G. Mungham and G. Pearson (eds), *Working-Class Youth Culture*, London: Routledge and Kegan Paul.

Clarke, J., Hall, S., Jefferson, T. and Roberts, B. (1986), 'Subcultures, cultures and class: a theoretical overview', in S. Hall and T. Jefferson (eds), *Resistance Through Rituals: Youth Subcultures in Post-War Britain*, London: Hutchinson.

Cohen, A. P. (1986), *Symbolising Boundaries: Identity and Diversity in British Cultures*, Manchester: Manchester University Press.

Cohen, P. (1984), 'Subcultural conflict and working-class community', in S. Hall, D. Hobson, A. Lowe and P. Willis (eds), *Culture, Media, Language*, London: Hutchinson.

Cohen, S. (1973), *Folk Devils and Moral Panics*, St Albans: Paladin.

Cohen, S. (1980), 'Symbols of trouble: introduction to the new edition', in *Folk Devils and Moral Panics*, Oxford: Martin Robertson.

Connor, S. (1991), *Postmodernist Culture*, Oxford: Blackwell.

Coon, C. (1982), *1988: The New Wave Punk Rock Explosion*, London: Omnibus.

Coupland, D. (1993), *Shampoo Planet*, London: Simon and Schuster.

Coupland, D. (1995), *Generation X: Tales for an Accelerated Culture*, London: Abacus.

Coward, R. and Ellis, J. (1977), *Language and Materialism*, London: Routledge.

Craik, J. (1994), *The Face of Fashion: Cultural Studies in Fashion*, London: Routledge.

Crook, S., Pakuliski, J. and Waters, M. (1992), *Postmodernization: Change in Advanced Society*, London: Sage.

da Costa, M. R. (1995), *A Political and Cultural Analysis of Punk and Skinhead Phenomenon, and Fanzines in Brazil*. Paper given at 'Youth 2000: International Conference', University of Teesside, Middlesbrough, 19–23 July.

Dancis, B. (1978), 'Safety pins and class struggle: punk rock and the left', *Socialist Review*, 8 (3): 58–83.

Daniel, S. and McGuire, P. (eds) (1972), *The Paint House: Words from an East End Gang*, Harmondsworth: Penguin.

Davies, J. (1996), 'The future of "no future": punk rock and postmodern theory', *Journal of Popular Culture*, 29 (4) (Spring): 3–25.

Donnelly, P. (1985), 'Sport subcultures', *Exercise and Sport Science Reviews*, 13: 539–78.

Dorn, N. and South, N. (1982), *Of Males and Markets: A Critical Review of 'Youth Culture' Theory*, Research Paper 1, Middlesex Polytechnic, Centre for Occupational and Community Research.

Downes, D. and Rock, P. (1988), *Understanding Deviance*, 2nd edn, Oxford: Clarendon Press.

Dworkin, D. (1997), *Cultural Marxism in Postwar Britain*, London: Duke University Press.

Ehrich, L. C. (1993), 'Youth subculture: does it exist in the real world?', *Youth Studies Australia*, 12 (3): 31–3.

Evans, C. (1997), 'Dreams that only money can buy . . . or, the shy tribe in flight from discourse', *Fashion Theory: The Journal of Dress, Body and Culture*, 1 (2) (June): 169–88.

Evans, C. and Thornton, M. (1989), *Women and Fashion: A New Look*, London: Quartet.

Ewen, S. and Ewen, E. (1982), *Channels of Desire*, New York: McGraw-Hill.

Faurschou, G. (1990), 'Obsolescence and desire: fashion and the commodity form', in H. J. Silverman (ed.), *Postmodernism – Philosophy and the Arts*, London: Routledge.

Featherstone, M. (1992), *Consumer Culture and Postmodernism*, London: Sage.

Fine, G. A. and Kleinman, S. (1979), 'Rethinking subculture: an interactionist analysis', *American Journal of Sociology*, 85 (1): 1–20.

Flügel, J. C. (1930), *The Psychology of Clothes*, London: Hogarth Press.

Fornäs, J. (1995), *Cultural Theory and Late Modernity*, London: Sage.

Fox, K. J. (1987), 'Real punks and pretenders: the social organisation of a counter-culture', *Journal of Contemporary Ethnography*, 16 (3) (October): 344–70.

Frank, T. (1998), *The Conquest of Cool: Business Culture, Counterculture, and the Rise of Hip Consumerism*, Chicago and London: University of Chicago Press.

Frisby, D. (1985a), *Fragments of Modernity*, Oxford: Polity.

Frisby, D. (1985b), 'Georg Simmel: first sociologist of modernity', *Theory, Culture and Society*, 2 (3): 49–67.

Frith, S. (1978), 'The punk bohemians', *New Society*, 805, 9 March.

Frith, S. (1983), *Sound Effects: Youth, Leisure and the Politics of Rock n Roll*, London: Constable.

Frith, S. and Horne, H. (1987), *Art into Pop*, London: Methuen.

Frith, S., Goodwin, A. and Grossberg, L. (eds) (1992), *Sound and Vision: The Music Video Reader*, London: Routledge.

Fyvel, T. R. (1963), *The Insecure Offenders: Rebellious Youth in the Welfare State*, Harmondsworth: Pelican.

Gaines, D. (1991), *Teenage Wasteland: Suburbia's Dead End Kids*, New York: Pantheon.

Gane, M. (1991), *Baudrillard's Bestiary: Baudrillard and Culture*, London: Routledge.

Gitlin, T. (1989), 'Postmodernism defined, at last!', *Utne Reader*, (July/August): 52–61.

Glaser, B. and Strauss, A. (1967), *The Discovery of Grounded Theory*, Chicago: Aldine.

Goffman, E. (1976), *The Presentation of Self in Everyday Life*, Harmondsworth: Penguin.

Gold, B. D. (1987), 'Self-image of punk rock and nonpunk rock juvenile delinquents', *Adolescence*, XXII (87) (Fall): 535–44.

Goldthorpe, J. (1992), 'Intoxicated culture: punk symbolism and punk protest', *Socialist Review*, 22 (2): 35–64.

Goldthorpe, J., Lockwood, J., Bechhofer, F. and Platt, J. (1969), *The Affluent Worker in the Class Structure*, Cambridge: Cambridge University Press.

Gottdiener, M. (1995), *Postmodern Semiotics: Material Culture and the Forms of Postmodern Life*, Oxford: Blackwell.

Gottschalk, S. (1993), 'Uncomfortably numb: countercultural impulses in the postmodern era', *Symbolic Interaction*, 16 (4): 351–78.

Gramsci, A. (1971), *Selections from the Prison Notebooks*, London: Lawrence and Wishart.

Gross, R. L. (1990), 'Heavy metal music: a new subculture in American society', *Journal of Popular Culture*, 24: 119–30.

Grossberg, L. (1992), *We Gotta Get Out of this Place: Popular Conservatism and Postmodern Culture*, London: Routledge.

Hall, S. (1981), 'Cultural studies: two paradigms', in T. Bennett, G. Martin, C. Mercer and J. Woollacott (eds), *Culture, Ideology and Social Process: A Reader*, London: Open University Press.

Hall, S. (1984), 'Cultural studies and the Centre: some problematics and problems', in S. Hall, D. Hobson, A. Lowe and P. Willis (eds), *Culture, Media, Language*, London: Hutchinson.

Hall, S. (1989), 'The meaning of new times', in S. Hall and M. Jacques (eds), *New Times: The Changing Face of Politics in the 1990s*, London: Lawrence and Wishart.

Hall, S. and Jefferson, T. (eds) (1986), *Resistance Through Rituals: Youth Subcultures in Post-War Britain*, London: Hutchinson.

Hamblett, C. and Deverson, J. (1964), *Generation X*, London: Tandem.

Hansen, C. H. and Hansen, R. D. (1991), 'Constructing personality and social reality through music: individual differences among fans of punk and heavy metal music', *Journal of Broadcasting and Electronic Media*, 35 (3) (Summer): 335–50.

Harvey, D. (1991), *The Condition of Postmodernity*, Oxford: Blackwell.

Hebdige, D. (1974), *The Style of the Mods*, Stencilled Occasional Paper 20, CCCS, University of Birmingham.

Hebdige, D. (1979), *Subculture: The Meaning of Style*, London: Methuen.

Hebdige, D. (1981), 'Subculture: image and noise', in R. Dale, G. Esland, R. Fergusson and M. MacDonald (eds), *Education and the State: Politics, Patriarchy and Practice*, Vol. 2, Lewes: Falmer Press.

Hebdige, D. (1988), *Hiding in the Light: On Images and Things*, London: Comedia.

Hebdige, D. (1989), 'After the masses', in S. Hall and M. Jacques (eds), *New Times: The Changing Face of Politics in the 1990s*, London: Lawrence and Wishart.

Hebdige, D. (1992), 'A report on the Western front: postmodernism and the "politics" of style', in F. Frascina and J. Harris (eds), *Art in Modern Culture*, London: Phaidon.

Heelas, P. (1996), *The New Age Movement*, Oxford, Blackwell.

Henry, T. (1984), 'Punk and avant-garde art', *Journal of Popular Culture*, 17 (4): 30–6.

Henry, T. (1989), *Break All Rules! Punk Rock and the Making of a Style*, London and Ann Arbor, MI: UMI Research Press.

Hetherington, K. (1998), *Expressions of Identity: Space, Performance, Politics*, London: Sage.

Himmelfarb, G. (1995), *The De-moralization of Society*, London: IEA.

Hindess, B. (1977), *Philosophy and Methodology in the Social Sciences*, Hassocks: Harvester.

Hirst, P. (1979), *On Law and Ideology*, London: Macmillan.

Hogan, J. V. (1983), 'Sociological Interpretations of Counter Cultural Movements', Unpublished M. Litt. thesis, Oxford University.

Holdsworth, A. (1989), *Out of the Doll's House: The Story of Women in the Twentieth Century*, London: BBC.

Home, S. (1996), *Cranked Up Really High: Genre Theory and Punk Rock*, Hove: Codex.

Hughes, J., Martin, P. and Sharrock, W. W. (1996), *Understanding Classical Sociology: Marx, Weber, Durkheim*, London: Sage.

Huyssen, A. (1986), *After the Great Divide: Modernism, Mass Culture, Postmodernism*, London: Macmillan.

Jackson, P. (1995), 'Towards a cultural politics of consumption', in J. Bird, B. Curtis, T. Putnam, G. Robertson and L. Tickner (eds), *Mapping the Futures: Local Cultures, Global Change*, London: Routledge.

Jameson, F. (1984), 'Postmodernism, or the cultural logic of late capitalism', *New Left Review*, 146 (July–August): 53–92.

Jameson, F. (1985), 'Postmodernism and consumer culture', in H. Foster (ed.), *Postmodern Culture*, London: Pluto.

Jameson, F. (1991), *Postmodernism, or the Cultural Logic of Late Capitalism*, London: Verso.

Jefferson, T. (1973), *The Teds: A Political Resurrection*, Stencilled Occasional Paper 22, CCCS, University of Birmingham.

Jenkins, R. (1996), *Social Identity*, London: Routledge.

Jenks, C. (1993), *Culture*, London: Routledge.

Johnston, L. (1993), 'Post-punk nostalgia', *Youth and Policy*, 40 (Spring): 70–4.

Kaiser, S. (1990), *The Social Psychology of Clothing: Symbolic Appearances in Context*, 2nd edn, New York: Macmillan.

Kaiser, S. B., Nagasawa, R. H. and Hutton, S. S. (1991), 'Fashion, postmodernity and personal appearance: a symbolic interactionist formulation', *Symbolic Interaction*, 14 (2): 165–85.

Keat, R. and Urry, J. (1982), *Social Theory as Science*, 2nd edn, London: Routledge and Kegan Paul.

Kellner, D. (1992), 'Popular culture and the construction of postmodern identities', in S. Lash and J. Friedman (eds), *Modernity and Identity*, Oxford: Blackwell.

Keniston, K. (1968), *Young Radicals: Notes on Committed Youth*, New York: Harcourt, Brace and World, Inc.

Keniston, K. (1971), *Youth and Dissent: The Rise of a New Opposition*, New York: Harcourt, Brace, Jovanovich.

Kinsey, B. (1982), 'Killum and eatum: identity consolidation in a middle-class polydrug abuse subculture', *Symbolic Interaction*, 5 (2): 311–24.

Kitwood, T. (1980), *Disclosures to a Stranger: Adolescent Values in an Advanced Industrial Society*, London: Routledge and Kegan Paul.

Knight, N. (1982), *Skinhead*, London: Omnibus Press.

König, R. (1973), *The Restless Image: A Sociology of Fashion*, London: George Allen and Unwin.

Kotarba, J. A. (1991), 'Postmodernism, ethnography and culture', in N. K. Denzin (ed.), *Studies in Symbolic Interactionism*, 12, London: JAI Press

Kotarba, J. A. and Wells, L. (1987), 'Styles of participation in an all-ages, rock 'n' roll nightclub: an ethnographic analysis', *Youth and Society*, 18 (4) (June): 398–417.

Kratz, C. and Reimer, B. (1998), 'Fashion in the face of postmodernity', in A. A. Berger (ed.), *The Postmodern Presence: Readings on Postmodernism in American Culture and Society*, London: AltaMira.

Kroker, A. and Cook, D. (1991), *The Postmodern Scene: Excremental Culture and Hyper-Aesthetics*, London: Macmillan Education.

Kroker, A., Kroker, M. and Cook, D. (1989), *Panic Encyclopaedia: The Definitive Guide to the Postmodern Scene*, London: Macmillan.

Laclau, E. and Mouffe, C. (1985), *Hegemony and Socialist Strategy: Towards a Radical Democratic Politics*, London: Verso.

Lahusen, C. (1993), 'The aesthetic of radicalism: the relationship between punk and the patriotic nationalist movement of the Basque country', *Popular Music*, 12 (3): 263–80.

Laing, D. (1978), 'Interpreting punk rock', *Marxism Today*, (April): 123–8.

Laing, D. (1985), *One Chord Wonders*, Milton Keynes: Open University Press.

Lamy, P. and Levin, J. (1985), 'Punk and middle-class values: a content analysis', *Youth and Society*, 17 (2) (December): 157–70.

Langman, L. (1992), 'Neon cages: shopping for subjectivity', in R. Shields (ed.), *Lifestyle Shopping*, London: Routledge.

Larrain, J. (1984), *Marxism and Ideology*, London: Macmillan.

Lash, S. (1990), *The Sociology of Postmodernism*, London: Routledge.

Lash, S. and Friedman, J. (1992), 'Introduction: subjectivity and modernity's other', in S. Lash and J. Friedman (eds), *Modernity and Identity*, Oxford: Blackwell.

Lash, S. and Urry, J. (1988), *The End of Organised Capitalism*, Cambridge: Polity.

Lash, S. and Urry, J. (1994), *Economies of Signs and Space*, London: Sage.

Lee, D. and Newby, H. (1985), *The Problem of Sociology*, London: Hutchinson.

Leech, K. (1973), *Youthquake: The Growth of a Counter-Culture Through Two Decades*, London: Sheldon Press.

Levin, J. and Spates, J. L. (1970), 'Hippie values: an analysis of the underground press', *Youth and Society*, 2 (September): 59–73.

Levine, H. G. and Stumpf, S. H. (1983), 'Statements of fear through cultural symbols: punk rock as a reflective subculture', *Youth and Society*, 14 (4) (June): 417–35.

Lipovetsky, G. (1994), *The Empire of Fashion: Dressing Modern Democracy*, Princeton, NJ: Princeton University Press.

Lipset, S. M. (1971), 'Youth and politics', in R. K. Merton and R. Nisbet (eds), *Contemporary Social Problems*, New York: Harcourt Brace Jovanovich.

Lloyd, M. (1999), 'Performativity, parody, politics', *Theory, Culture and Society*, 16 (2): 195–213.

Locher, D. A (1998), 'The industrial identity crisis: the failure of a newly forming subculture to identify itself', in J. S. Epstein (ed.), *Youth Culture: Identity in a Postmodern World*, Oxford: Blackwell.

Lockwood, D. (1966), 'Sources of variation in working class images of society', *Sociological Review*, 14 (3) (November): 249–67.

Lovatt, A. and Purkis, J. (1996), 'Shouting in the street: popular culture, values and the new ethnography', in J. O'Connor and D. Wynne (eds), *From the Margins to the Centre: Cultural Production and Consumption in the Post-Industrial City*, Aldershot: Arena.

Lull, J. (1987), 'Thrashing in the pit: an ethnography of San Francisco punk subculture', in T. R. Lindlof (ed.), *Natural Audiences: Qualitative Research of Media Uses and Effects*, Norwood, NJ: Ablex.

Lurie, A. (1992), *The Language of Clothes*, London: Bloomsbury.

Lury, C. (1996), *Consumer Culture*, Cambridge: Polity.

Lydon, J. (1994), *Rotten: No Irish, No Blacks, No Dogs*, London: Hodder and Stoughton.

Lyon, D. (1999), *Postmodernity*, 2nd edn, Buckingham: Open University Press.

Lyotard, J. F. (1984), *The Postmodern Condition: A Report on Knowledge*, Manchester: Manchester University Press.

MacCannell, D. (1992), *Empty Meeting Grounds: The Tourist Papers*, London: Routledge.

MacRae, D. G. (1982), *Weber*, London: Fontana/Collins.

Maffesoli, M. (1996), *The Times of the Tribes: The Decline of Individualism in Mass Society*, London: Sage.

Malbon, B. (1998), 'Clubbing: consumption, identity and the spatial practices of every-night life', in T. Skelton and G. Valentine (eds), *Cool Places: Geographies of Youth Cultures*, London: Routledge.

Malbon, B. (1999), *Clubbing: Dancing, Ecstasy and Vitality*, London: Routledge.

Marchak, M. M. (1975), *Ideological Perspectives on Canada*, Toronto: McGraw-Hill Ryerson Ltd.

Marcus, G. E. (1986), 'Contemporary problems of ethnography in the modern world system', in J. Clifford and G. E. Marcus (eds), *Writing Culture: The Poetics and Politics of Ethnography*, Berkeley, CA: University of California Press.

Marsh, P. (1977), 'Dole queue rock', *New Society*, 746, 20 January.

Marsh, P., Rosser, E. and Harre, R. (1978), *The Rules of Disorder*, London: Routledge and Kegan Paul.

Marshall, G. (1990), *In Praise of Sociology*, London: Unwin.

Marshall, G. (1991), *Spirit of '69: A Skinhead Bible*, Dunoon: ST Publishing.

Martin, B. (1985), *A Sociology of Contemporary Cultural Change*, Oxford: Blackwell.

Marx, K. (1973), *Grundrisse*, Harmondsworth: Penguin.

Marx, K. and Engels, F. (1979), *The Communist Manifesto*, Harmondsworth: Penguin.

Matlock, G., with Silverton, P. (1996), *I was a Teenage Sex Pistol*, London: Virgin.

McCracken, G. (1990), *Culture and Consumption*, Bloomington and Indianapolis, IN: Indiana University Press.

McDonald, J. R. (1987), 'Suicidal rage: an analysis of hardcore punk lyrics', *Popular Music and Society*, 11 (3): 91–102.

McGuigan, J. (1992), *Cultural Populism*, London: Routledge.

McRobbie, A. (1989), 'Second-hand dresses and the role of the rag market', in A. McRobbie (ed.), *Zoot-Suits and Second Hand Dresses: An Anthology of Fashion and Music*, London: Macmillan.

McRobbie, A. (1994), *Postmodernism and Popular Culture*, London: Routledge.

McRobbie, A. (ed.) (1997), *Back to Reality? Social Experience and Cultural Studies*, Manchester: Manchester University Press

McRobbie, A. and Garber, J. (1986), 'Girls and subcultures: an exploration', in S. Hall and T. Jefferson (eds), *Resistance Through Rituals: Youth Subcultures in Post-War Britain*, London: Hutchinson.

McVeigh, B. (1997), 'Wearing ideology: how uniforms discipline minds and bodies in Japan', *Fashion Theory: The Journal of Dress, Body and Culture*, 1 (2) (June): 189–214.

Medhurst, A. (1999), 'What did I get?: punk, memory and autobiography', in R. Sabin (ed.), *Punk Rock: So What?*, London: Routledge.

Mick, S. (1976), 'The Steve Mick column', *Sniffin' Glue*, 4 (October): 2.

Middleton, R. and Muncie, J. (1982), 'Pop culture, pop music and post-war youth: countercultures', in Open University, Block 5, Units 18 and 19/20, *Politics, Ideology and Popular Culture 1*, Milton Keynes: Open University Press.

Mignon, P. (1993), 'Drugs and popular music: the democratisation of bohemia', in S. Redhead (ed.), *Rave Off: Politics and Deviance in Contemporary Youth Culture*, Aldershot: Avebury.

Miles, C. (1993), *Spatial Politics: A Gendered Sense of Place*, Working Paper in Popular Cultural Studies, 4, Manchester Institute for Popular Culture, Manchester Metropolitan University.

Miles, C. (1997), 'Spatial politics: a gendered sense of place', in S. Redhead, D. Wynne and J. O'Connor (eds), *The Clubcultures Reader: Readings in Popular Cultural Studies*, Oxford: Blackwell.

Miles, S. (1995), *Pleasure or Pressure? Consumption and Youth Identity in the Contemporary British Shopping Centre*, Paper presented at BSA Annual Conference: 'Contested Cities', University of Leicester, 13–15 April.

Miles, S. (1998), *Consumerism – as a Way of Life*, London: Sage.

Miles, S., Cliff, D., Burr, V. (1998), '"Fitting in and sticking out": consumption, consumer meanings and the construction of young people's identities', *Journal of Youth Studies*, 1 (1): 81–120.

Miller, D. (1987), *Mass Consumption and Material Culture*, Oxford: Blackwell.

Miller, J. (1995), *Vox Pop: The New Generation X Speaks*, London: Virgin.

Miller, T. (1991), *The Hippies and American Values*, Knoxville, TN: University of Tennessee Press.

Mills, R. (1973), *Young Outsiders: A Study of Alternative Communities*, London: Routledge and Kegan Paul.

Mitchell, J. C. (1971), *The Kalela Dance*, Manchester: Manchester University Press.

Moore, D. (1994), *The Lads in Action: Social Process in an Urban Youth Subculture*, Aldershot: Arena.

Moorhouse, H. F. (1991), *Driving Ambitions: An Analysis of the American Hot Rod Enthusiasm*, Manchester: Manchester University Press.

Morrison, K. (1998), *Marx, Durkheim, Weber: Formations of Modern Social Thought*, London: Sage.

Mort, F. (1988), 'Boy's Own? Masculinity, style and popular culture', in R. Chapman and J. Rutherford (eds), *Male Order: Unwrapping Masculinity*, London: Lawrence and Wishart

Mort, F. (1989), 'The politics of consumption', in S. Hall and M. Jacques (eds), *New Times: The Changing Face of Politics in the 1990s*, London: Lawrence and Wishart.

Muggleton, D. (1995), *From Subculture to Neo-Tribe: Paradox and Postmodernism in Alternative Style*, Paper first presented at 'Youth 2000: International Conference', University of Teesside, Middlesbrough, 19–23 July.

Muggleton, D. (1997), 'The post-subculturalist', in S. Redhead, D. Wynne and J. O'Connor (eds), *The Clubcultures Reader: Readings in Popular Cultural Studies*, Oxford: Blackwell.

Muncie, J. (1982), 'Pop culture, pop music and post-war youth: subcultures', in Open University, Block 5, Units 18 and 19/20, *Politics, Ideology and Popular Culture 1*, Milton Keynes: Open University Press.

Muncie, J. (1984), *The Trouble with Kids Today: Youth and Crime in Post-War Britain*, London: Hutchinson.

Mungham, G. and Pearson, G. (eds), (1978), *Working-Class Youth Culture*, London: Routledge and Kegan Paul.

Murdock, G. and McCron, R. (1978), 'Youth and class: the career of a confusion', in G. Mungham and G. Pearson (eds), *Working-Class Youth Culture*, London: Routledge and Kegan Paul.

Murdock, G. and McCron, R. (1986), 'Consciousness of class and consciousness of generation', in S. Hall and T. Jefferson (eds), *Resistance Through Rituals: Youth Subcultures in Post-War Britain*, London: Hutchinson.

Murray, R. (1989), 'Fordism and post-fordism', in S. Hall and M. Jacques (eds), *New Times: The Changing Face of Politics in the 1990s*, London: Lawrence and Wishart.

Negrin, L. (1999), 'The self as image: a critical appraisal of postmodern theories of fashion', *Theory, Culture and Society*, 16 (3): 99–118.

Nehring, N. (1996), *Flowers in the Dustbin: Culture, Anarchy and Postwar England*, Ann Arbor, MI: University of Michigan Press.

Nelson, E. (1989), *The British Counter-Culture, 1966–73: A Study of the Underground Press*, London: Macmillan.

Neville, R. (1973), *Play Power*, St Albans: Paladin.

Nixon, S. (1992), 'Have you got the look?: masculinities and shopping spectacle', in R. Shields (ed.), *Lifestyle Shopping*, London: Routledge.

O'Hara, C. (1995), *The Philosophy of Punk: More than Noise!*, Edinburgh: AK Press.

Osgerby, B. (1998), *Youth in Britain since 1945*, Oxford: Blackwell.

Outhwaite, W. (1987), *New Philosophies of Social Science*, Basingstoke: Macmillan.

Parkin, F. (1982), *Max Weber*, Chichester: Ellis Horwood.

Parsons, T. (1951), *The Social System*, New York: Free Press.

Partington, A. (1992), 'Popular fashion and working-class affluence', in J. Ash and E. Wilson (eds), *Chic Thrills: A Fashion Reader*, London: Pandora.

Pearson, K. (1979), *Surfing Subcultures of Australia and New Zealand*, St Lucia: University of Queensland Press.

Pilkington, H. (1997), 'Putting back the "youth" in youth cultural studies', *Sociology Review*, 7 (1): 22–8.

Pini, M. (1997), 'Women and the early British rave scene', in A. McRobbie (ed.), *Back to Reality? Social Experience and Cultural Studies*, Manchester: Manchester University Press.

Polhemus, T. (1994), *Streetstyle*, London: Thames and Hudson.

Polhemus, T. (1996), *Style Surfing: What to Wear in the 3rd Millennium*, London: Thames and Hudson.

Polhemus, T. (1997), 'In the supermarket of style', in S. Redhead, D. Wynne and J. O'Connor (eds), *The Clubcultures Reader: Readings in Popular Cultural Studies*, Oxford: Blackwell.

Polsky, N. (1971), *Hustlers, Beats and Others*, Harmondsworth: Pelican.

Powell, R. and Clarke, J. (1986), 'A note on marginality', in S. Hall and T. Jefferson (eds), *Resistance Through Rituals: Youth Subcultures in Post-War Britain*, London: Hutchinson.

Price, P. (1977), *Heat* (October/November).

Redhead, S. (1990), *The End of the Century Party: Youth and Pop Towards 2000*, Manchester: Manchester University Press.

Redhead, S. (1991a), 'An era of the end, or the end of an era? football and youth culture in Britain', in J. Williams and S. Wagg (eds), *British Football and Social Change*, Leicester: Leicester University Press.

Redhead, S. (1991b), 'Rave off: youth subcultures and the law', *Social Studies Review*, January: 92–4.

Redhead, S. (1993), 'The end of the end-of-the-century-party', in S. Redhead (ed.), *Rave Off: Politics and Deviance in Contemporary Youth Culture*, Aldershot: Avebury.

Reimer, B. (1995), 'Youth and modern lifestyles', in J. Fornäs and G. Bolin (eds), *Youth Culture in Late Modernity*, London: Sage.

Rietveld, H. (1993), 'Living the dream', in S. Redhead (ed.), *Rave Off: Politics and Deviance in Contemporary Youth Culture*, Aldershot: Avebury.

Ritzer, G. (1981), *Towards an Integrated Sociological Paradigm*, Boston, MA: Allyn and Bacon.

Roberts, K. (1978), *Contemporary Society and the Growth of Leisure*, London: Longman.

Roberts, K. (1985), *Youth and Leisure*, London: Allen and Unwin.

Robins, D. and Cohen, P. (1978), *Knuckle Sandwich: Growing Up in the Working Class City*, Harmondsworth: Penguin.

Rock, P. and Cohen, S. (1970), 'The teddy boy', in V. Bogdanor and R. Skidelsky (eds), *The Age of Affluence 1951–1964*, London: Macmillan.

Rojek, C. (1995), *Decentring Leisure: Rethinking Leisure Theory*, London: Sage.

Roman, L. (1988), 'Intimacy, labor, and class: ideologies of feminine sexuality in the punk slam dance', in L. Roman and L. K. Christian-Smith (eds), *Becoming Feminine: The Politics of Popular Culture*, London: Falmer Press.

Rose, M. (1996), *The Post-Modern and the Post-Industrial*, Cambridge: Cambridge University Press.

Roszak, T. (1970), *The Making of a Counter Culture: Reflections on the Technocratic Society and Its Youthful Opposition*, London: Faber and Faber.

Rushgrove, B. (1994) *Teddy Boy*, London: B&B Publications.

Ryan, J. and Fitzpatrick, H. (1996), 'The space that difference makes: negotiation and urban identities through consumption practices', in J. O'Connor and D. Wynne (eds), *From the Margins to the Centre: Cultural Production and Consumption in the Post-Industrial City*, Aldershot: Arena.

Sabin, R. (1999a), 'Introduction', in R. Sabin (ed.), *Punk Rock: So What?*, London: Routledge.

Sabin, R. (1999b), '"I won't let that dago by": rethinking punk and racism', in R. Sabin (ed.), *Punk Rock: So What?*, London: Routledge.

Sanders, C. (1988), 'Marks of mischief: becoming and being tattooed', *Journal of Contemporary Ethnography*, 16 (4) (January): 395–432.

Sardiello, R. (1998), 'Identity and status stratification in the deadhead subculture', in J. S. Epstein (ed.), *Youth Culture: Identity in a Postmodern World*, Oxford: Blackwell.

Saunders, P. (1989), *Social Theory and the Urban Question*, 2nd edn, London: Unwin Hyman.

Savage, J. (1989), 'The age of plunder', in A. McRobbie (ed.), *Zoot-Suits and Second Hand Dresses: An Anthology of Fashion and Music*, London: Macmillan

Savage, J. (1992), *England's Dreaming: Sex Pistols and Punk Rock*, London: Faber and Faber.

Savage, M., Barlow, J., Dickens, P. and Fielding, T. (1992), *Property, Bureaucracy and Culture*, London: Routledge.

Sayer, A. (1984), *Method in Social Science: A Realist Approach*, London: Hutchinson.

Sayer, D. (1979), *Marx's Method: Ideology, Science and Critique in Capital*, Hassocks: Harvester.

Scheys, M. (1987), 'The power of life style', *Society and Leisure*, 10 (2) (Autumn): 249–66.

Schouten, J. W. and McAlexander, J. H. (1995), 'Subcultures of consumption: an ethnography of the new bikers', *Journal of Consumer Research*, 22: 43–61.

Schutz, A. (1963), 'Concept and theory formation in the social sciences', in M. Natanson (ed.), *Philosophy of the Social Sciences*, New York: Random House.

Schutz, A. (1980), *The Phenomenology of the Social World*, London: Heinemann.

Seago, A. (1995), *Burning the Box of Beautiful Things: The Development of a Postmodern Sensibility*, Oxford: Clarendon Press.

Sherwood, S. J., Smith, P. and Alexander, J. C. (1993), 'The British are coming . . . again!: the hidden agenda of "cultural studies"', *Contemporary Sociology*, 22 (3): 370–5.

Shields, R. (1992), 'Spaces for the subject of consumption', in R. Shields (ed.), *Lifestyle Shopping*, London: Routledge.

Simmel, G. (1896), 'Soziologische Aesthetik', *Die Zukunft*, 17: 204–16.

Simmel, G. (1978), *The Philosophy of Money*, London: Routledge.

Stahl, G. (1998), 'Troublin Below: Rethinking Subcultural Theory', Unpublished MA thesis, Graduate Programme in Communications, McGill University.

Steedman, C. (1986), *Landscape for a Good Woman*, London: Virago.

Steele, V. (1997), 'Anti-fashions: the 1970s', *Fashion Theory: The Journal of Dress, Body and Culture*, 1 (3) (September): 279–96.

Stephanson, A. (1987), 'Regarding postmodernism – a conversation with Fedric Jameson', *Social Text*, 17: 29–54.

Stone, G. P. (1981), 'Appearance and the self: a slightly revised version', in G. P. Stone and H. Farberman (eds), *Social Psychology through Symbolic Interaction*, 2nd edn, New York: John Wiley and Sons.

Strinati, D. (1995), *An Introduction to Theories of Popular Culture*, London: Routledge.

Stuart, J. (1987), *Rockers!*, London: Plexus.

Tanner, J. (1978), 'New directions for subcultural theory: an analysis of British working-class youth culture', *Youth and Society*, 9 (4) (June): 343–72.

Taylor, I. and Wall, D. (1978), 'Beyond the skinheads: comments on the emergence and significance of the glamrock cult', in G. Mungham and G. Pearson (eds), *Working-Class Youth Culture*, London: Routledge and Kegan Paul.

Thompson, P. (1979), 'Youth culture and youth politics in Britain', *Radical America*, 13 (2) (March–April): 53–65.

Thorne, T. (1993), *Fads, Fashions and Cults: From Acid House to Zoot Suit – via Existentialism and Political Correctness – the Definitive Guide to (Post-)Modern Culture*, London: Bloomsbury.

Thornton, S. (1994), 'Moral panic, the media and British rave culture', in A. Ross and T. Rose (eds), *Microphone Fiends: Youth Music and Youth Culture*, New York: Routledge.

Thornton, S. (1995), *Club Cultures: Music, Media and Subcultural Capital*, Cambridge: Polity.

Tillman, R. H. (1980), 'Punk rock and the construction of "pseudo-political" movements', *Popular Music and Society*, 7 (3): 165–75.

Tomlinson, L. (1998), '"This ain't no disco" . . . or is it?: youth culture and the rave phenomenon', in J. S. Epstein (ed.), *Youth Culture: Identity in a Postmodern World*, Oxford: Blackwell.

Trowler, P. and Riley, M. (1985), *Topics in Sociology*, Slough: University Tutorial Press.

Tseëlon, E. (1992a), 'Fashion and the signification of social order', *Semiotica*, 91: 1–14.

Tseëlon, E. (1992b), 'Is the presented self sincere? Goffman, impression management and the postmodern self', *Theory, Culture and Society*, 9: 115–28.

Tseëlon, E. (1992c), 'Self presentation through appearance: a manipulative vs. a dramaturgical approach', *Symbolic Interaction*, 15 (4): 501–13.

Tseëlon, E. (1995), *The Masque of Femininity*, London: Sage.

Tsoukas, H. (1989), 'The validity of idiographic research explanations', *Academy of Management Review*, 14 (4): 551–61.

Turner, G. (1992), *British Cultural Studies: An Introduction*, London: Routledge.

Tyrrell, A. V. (1986), *Changing Trends in Fashion: Patterns of the Twentieth Century 1900–1970*, London: Batsford.

Urry, J. (1990), *The Tourist Gaze: Leisure and Travel in Contemporary Societies*, London: Sage.

Veal, A. J. (1993), 'The concept of lifestyle: a review', *Leisure Studies*, 12: 233–52.

Venturi, R. (1977), *Complexity and Contradiction in Architecture*, 2nd edn, New York: Museum of Modern Art.

Wai-Teng Leong, L. (1992), 'Cultural resistance: the cultural terrorism of British male working-class youth', *Current Perspectives in Social Theory*, 12: 29–58.

Walker, J. A. (1994), *Art in the Age of Mass Media*, London: Pluto Press.

Waters, C. (1981), 'Badges of half-formed inarticulate radicalism: a critique of recent trends in the study of working-class culture', *International Journal of Labour and Working Class History*, 19 (Spring): 23–37.

Waugh, P. (1992), *Practising Postmodernism, Reading Modernism*, London: Edward Arnold.

Webb, J. M. (1995), *A Matter of Mischief and Rebellion: Skater Punks, Ravers, and Grunge*, Department of Sociology, University of Northern Iowa, USA, Paper given at April 1995 Annual Meetings of The Midwest Sociological Society, Chicago, Illinois.

Webb, J. M. (1996), 'Expressive Individualism in a Midwestern Situated Youth Subculture Group', Unpublished MA thesis, Department of Sociology, University of Northern Iowa.

Weber, M. (1949), *The Methodology of the Social Sciences*, New York: Free Press.

Weber, M. (1968), *Economy and Society – An Outline of Interpretative Sociology*, New York: Bedminster Press.

Weber, M. (1970), 'Class, status, party', in H. H. Gerth and C. W. Mills (eds), *From Max Weber: Essays in Sociology*, London: Routledge and Kegan Paul.

Weber, M. (1976), *The Protestant Ethic and the Spirit of Capitalism*, London: Allen and Unwin.

Weeks, J. (1990), 'The value of difference', in J. Rutherford (ed.), *Identity: Community, Culture, Difference*, London: Lawrence and Wishart.

Weinstein, D. (1991), *Heavy Metal: A Cultural Sociology*, New York: Lexington Books.

Wheaton, B. (1997), 'Consumption, Lifestyle and Gendered Identities in Post-Modern Sports: The Case of Windsurfing', Unpublished Ph.D. thesis, University of Brighton.

Widdicombe, S. (1993), 'Autobiography and change: rhetoric and authenticity of "gothic" style', in E. Burman and I. Parker (eds), *Discourse Analytical Research: Repertoires and Readings of Texts in Action*, London: Routledge.

Widdicombe, S. and Wooffitt, R. (1990), '"Being" versus "doing" punk: on achieving authenticity as a member', *Journal of Language and Social Psychology*, 9 (4): 257–77.

Widdicombe, S. and Wooffitt, R. (1995), *The Language of Youth Subcultures: Social Identity in Action*, Hemel Hempstead: Harvester Wheatsheaf.

Williamson, J. (1986), *Consuming Passions: The Dynamics of Popular Culture*, London: Marion Boyers.

Willis, P. (1978), *Profane Culture*, London: Routledge and Kegan Paul.

Willis, P. (1984), 'On method', in S. Hall, D. Hobson, A. Lowe and P. Willis (eds), *Culture, Media, Language*, London: Hutchinson.

Willis, P. (1986), 'The cultural meaning of drug use', in S. Hall and T. Jefferson (eds), *Resistance Through Rituals: Youth Subcultures in Post-War Britain*, London: Hutchinson.

Willis, P. (1990), *Common Culture*, Milton Keynes: Open University Press.

Willis, S. (1993), 'Hardcore: subculture American style', *Critical Inquiry*, 19 (Winter): 365–83.

Willmott, P. (1969), *Adolescent Boys of East London*, Harmondsworth: Penguin.

Wilson, E. (1985), *Adorned in Dreams: Fashion and Modernity*, London: Virago.

Wilson, E. (1990), 'These new components of the spectacle: fashion and postmodernism', in R. Boyne and A. Rattansi (eds), *Postmodernism and Society*, London: Macmillan.

Wilson, E. (1998), 'Bohemian dress and the heroism of everyday life', *Fashion Theory: The Journal of Dress, Body and Culture*, 2 (3) (September): 225–44.

Wilson, E. (1999), 'The bohemianization of mass culture', *International Journal of Cultural Studies*, 2 (1): 11–32.

Wilson, E. and Taylor, L. (1989), *Through the Looking Glass*, London: BBC Books.

Wilson, J. (1983), *Social Theory*, Englewood Cliffs, NJ: Prentice-Hall.

Wirth, L. (1938), 'Urbanism as a way of life', *American Journal of Sociology*, XLIV (1): 1–24.

Wollen, P. (1987), 'Fashion/Orientalism/The Body', *New Formations*, 1: 5–33.

Woods, P. (1977), *Youth, Generations and Social Class*, Open University, E202 Schooling and Society, Block V, Culture and Class, Units 27–28, Milton Keynes: Open University Press.

York, P. (1980), *Style Wars*, London: Sidgwick and Jackson.

Young, J. (1971), 'The role of the police as amplifiers of deviancy', in S. Cohen (ed.), *Images of Deviance*, Harmondsworth: Penguin.

Young, K. and Craig, L. (1997), 'Beyond white pride: identity, meaning and contradiction in the Canadian skinhead subculture', *Canadian Review of Sociology and Anthropology*, 34 (2): 175–206.

Young, M. and Willmott, P. (1980), *Family and Kinship in East London*, Harmondsworth: Penguin.

Subject Index

Author Index